COLONIALISM AND CHRISTIANITY IN MANDATE PALESTINE

JAMAL AND RANIA DANIEL SERIES
*in Contemporary History, Politics,
Culture, and Religion of the Levant*

COLONIALISM *and* CHRISTIANITY *in* MANDATE PALESTINE

LAURA ROBSON

UNIVERSITY OF TEXAS PRESS

Austin

Requests for permission to reproduce material from this work should be sent to:

Permissions

University of Texas Press

P.O. Box 7819

Austin, TX 78713–7819

utpress.utexas.edu/about/book-permissions

♾ The paper used in this book meets the minimum requirements of
ANSI/NISO Z39.48–1992 (R1997) (Permanence of Paper).

LIBRARY OF CONGRESS CATALOGING-IN-PUBLICATION DATA

Robson, Laura.

Colonialism and Christianity in Mandate Palestine / Laura Robson. — 1st ed.

p.   cm. — (Jamal and Rania Daniel series in contemporary history,
politics, culture, and religion of the Levant)

Includes bibliographical references (p.   ) and index.

ISBN 978-0-292-74765-4

1. Christianity and politics—Palestine—History—20th century.   2. Palestine—
Church history—20th century.   3. Palestinian Arabs—Religion.
4. Mandates—Palestine.   I. Title.

BR1110.R63   2011

322′.109569409041—dc22

2011011983

To I.E.R., A.E.R., and T.J.R.
with love

CONTENTS

NOTE *on* TRANSLITERATION

In this work I have generally followed the *International Journal of Middle East Studies* system of transliteration from Arabic to English. For the sake of clarity, I have chosen to leave place names in their most common forms. When individuals have expressed a preference for the transliteration of their names, I have used their own spellings; in a few cases when a name appears only in English in the archival sources, I have maintained the sources' spelling. Where an anglicized spelling appears in a source, I have included the *IJMES* transliteration in brackets.

ACKNOWLEDGMENTS

It is a pleasure to acknowledge the assistance I received from so many during the course of researching and writing this book.

At Yale University, where this book had its beginnings, I benefited hugely from the help and support of my advisers Abbas Amanat, Paul Kennedy, and Lamin Sanneh. I owe a special thanks to Laila Parsons, whose advice and insights throughout the course of my research and writing strengthened the work immeasurably. My fellow students were constant sources of inspiration and new ideas; I especially thank the members of my writing group in New Haven, Sarah Cameron, Lisa Pinley Covert, Catherine Dunlop, and Yedida Kanfer, all of whom put considerable time and effort into commenting on parts of this work.

Other scholars generously assisted with every aspect of this project. I would like to thank Ted Bromund, Geraldine Chatelard, James Grehan, Tarif Khalidi, Issam Nassar, Christine Philliou, Ken Ruoff, Thomas Ricks, Heather Sharkey, Salim Tamari, and Linda Walton for their help and suggestions at various points in the process. My attendance at the 2008 International Seminar on Decolonization in the Twentieth Century, held by the National History Center in Washington, D.C., provided a terrific forum for the testing of new ideas; I owe thanks especially to its leaders, William Roger Louis, Dane Kennedy, Philippa Levine, Pillarisetti Sudhir, and Jason Parker, as well as to my fellow seminarians, who offered valuable feedback and sparked new ideas. Since 2009, Portland State University has provided a wonderful intellectual home for me, and I thank the Department of History and the Middle East Studies Center for their support.

The archivists and scholars I met in Palestine/Israel and the United Kingdom during the course of the research for this book were invariably helpful and accommodating. I would like to extend a special thanks to the scholars and experts who generously met with me during my time abroad and provided invaluable suggestions and assistance in my research: Uri Bialer, Raymond Cohen, Ruth Kark, Hosan Naoum, Anthony O'Mahony, David Neuhaus, Andrew Porter, Ron Pundak, Bernard Sabella, and Robert Tobin. I also thank the many archivists who facilitated my work in various collections and research centers in Palestine/Israel and the United Kingdom.

This project has received invaluable assistance from a number of granting bodies. I am grateful to the Andrew Mellon Foundation, the American Council of Learned Societies, the Mrs. Giles Whiting Foundation, the MacMillan Center for International and Area Studies at Yale University, and the Smith Richardson Foundation for their financial support of my research and writing. I would like to acknowledge the assistance of the federal Foreign Language and Area Studies grant program, which made possible some of my language training during the course of my graduate studies.

Jim Burr and Sebastian Langdell at the University of Texas Press have been superb guides throughout the editing and publication process, and I would like to thank them for their terrific work. I am also grateful for the thoughtful and perspicacious suggestions of the two anonymous readers for the press.

Finally, I thank my family and friends, whose love and support made this project seem not only possible but worthwhile. Thanks to my parents, Ione and Andrew Robson, who have been unfailingly encouraging not just during this project but in all my endeavors. And most of all, thanks to my husband, Tam Rankin, without whose patience, good humor, and incisive critiques this book would never have been completed.

INTRODUCTION

To contemporary global audiences, Palestine often seems an ancient bastion of violent sectarianism. Frequently described as a "crossroads" of Christianity, Islam, and Judaism, it is understood as a place where religious identifications trump all other loyalties, where ancient communal hostilities can flare up at any moment, and where a primitive, tribal religiosity has always held sway. Jerusalem, in particular, has become the modern era's most recognized symbol of sectarian strife—a status made visible in tourist maps of its Old City that depict a walled enclosure strictly divided by religion. The Muslim, Christian, and Jewish quarters appear on such literature as fixed and unchanging entities, representative of centuries-old, perpetually hostile divisions in the "Holy Land."

The idea that a violent sectarianism has characterized Palestine since time immemorial is widespread, powerful—and fundamentally mistaken. In fact, sectarianism did not emerge as a primary aspect of Palestinian politics until the third decade of the twentieth century when Palestine officially became part of the British Empire. Palestine's new colonial rulers permanently transformed the nature of its politics by introducing an inflexible sectarianism as a major organizing principle of the new state; they also propagated the idea that it was an ancient and inevitable aspect of political life in the "Holy Land," a notion that continues to reverberate in the affairs of the region to the present day.

In this book I am concerned with two main themes. First, I seek to discover how sectarianism came to be a major feature of the political landscape in twentieth-century Palestine, under the aegis of the new British colonial state. Second, I endeavor to understand one of the most significant consequences of this shift toward sectarianism: the nearly total marginalization of the region's Arab Christian communities as a politics of Muslim versus Jew took hold in interwar Palestine.

In the first decades of the twentieth century, Arab Christians represented

I

more than 10 percent of Palestine's population. Prominent in every profession and present at every level of politics, Arab Christian leaders did not view themselves as a part of a disenfranchised or threatened community; they considered themselves central actors in Palestine's emergence as a modern Arab nation. But during the period of British colonial rule, from 1917 to 1948, Palestinian Christians saw their political fortunes erode drastically and suddenly. From a prominent and influential place in a multi-religious, middle-class, nationalist discourse in the early years of the twentieth century, they fell to a position of almost total exclusion from Muslim-dominated national politics by the late 1930s.

In the context of British imperial rule and the anticolonial resistance it engendered, "Muslim" and "Christian" became oppositional political categories for the first time, with ruinous consequences for Palestine's Arab Christians. The British colonial state provided the backdrop for the transformation of Palestinian Christians into a legally defined "religious minority" and the development of politically meaningful Muslim and Christian communal identifications. This making of sectarianism in Palestine—and the subsequent erasure of the Arab Christian communities from the country's political history—is essentially a modern colonial story.

In Ottoman Palestine, prior to the British takeover, communal identifications often had a bearing on citizens' occupations, economic status, and social milieu but did not absolutely define their political affiliations or the nature of their representation vis-à-vis the state. By contrast, the British colonial administration made the early decision to promote communally organized legal and political structures on the model of imperial policy in India and elsewhere. This move allowed for the easy incorporation of a new, relatively autonomous European Jewish settler community into Palestine; it also deliberately encouraged the emergence of much more rigid forms of sectarian identification among Palestinian Arabs. In response to these policies, Arab Christian leaders began to reinvent their religious communities as political entities in the hopes of taking a leading role in a communally organized political system.

This politicization of Christianity, which both reflected and furthered the construction of an increasingly sectarian political landscape, failed to reverse the colonial ghettoization of the Christian communities. In the late 1930s some of Palestine's Muslim leaders began to use the new sectarian political structures of the mandate state to garner support for a nationalist movement increasingly deploying Islamist rhetoric and organization. "Muslim" and "Christian" were now something more than communal designations; they were competing political categories. By the time the British abandoned their imperial project in Palestine in 1948, their colonial policies had helped to sideline the Arab Christian communities by redefining Christians as a political entity separate from the Muslim and Jewish populations.

The emergence of a rigid sectarianism in British-ruled Palestine connects it with a global colonial history, including South Asia and Africa, of the modern construction of supposedly "traditional" categories of religion and ethnicity. As in other parts of the British Empire, the colonial making of sectarianism permanently transformed local, national, and regional politics. It cast Palestine as a place where religious affiliation inevitably equaled political identity, and it diminished Palestine's Arab Christian communities, previously central to Arab politics, to the point of near-invisibility. Further, the promotion of sectarian organization served to advance a colonial vision of Britain as a necessary mediator between inveterate religious enemies in Palestine and in the Middle East more broadly, thereby legitimating its continued presence there—an idea that continues to influence Anglo-American approaches to the Middle East to the present day.[1]

The making of sectarianism in Palestine, with its ensuing marginalization of the Palestinian Arab Christian communities, constituted one of the most significant transformations wrought by imperial rule in the modern Middle East. The international community's contemporary interventions into what it understands as the sectarian affairs of the "Holy Land" continually demonstrate that the consequences of this colonial history are still with us.

PALESTINIAN ARAB CHRISTIANS: AN INTRODUCTION

During the late nineteenth century, Palestine was part of the Ottoman Empire, run from Istanbul. Its most important city, Jerusalem (al-Quds), had a population of about fifty thousand, 45 percent of whom were Christian. Jerusalem constituted an autonomous district that reported directly to Istanbul; Palestine's other two districts, Nablus and Acre, were administratively linked with Beirut.[2] Already in 1900 the trickle of Zionist Jews from Europe proclaiming the revival of a Jewish homeland in Palestine was beginning to worry Palestinian Arabs, but the number of European immigrants was as yet very small. In 1914, at the end of the Ottoman period and just before World War I began, Arab Christians constituted about 10 percent of the population.[3]

Three-quarters of Palestine's Christians lived in cities, with particular concentrations in the Jerusalem district but present in all the region's major urban centers. The Greek Orthodox Church (a major branch of Eastern Orthodox Christianity, headed by the Greek Orthodox Patriarchate in Jerusalem) represented the largest denomination of Palestinian Arabs, making up nearly half of the Christian population. The patriarchate owned huge tracts

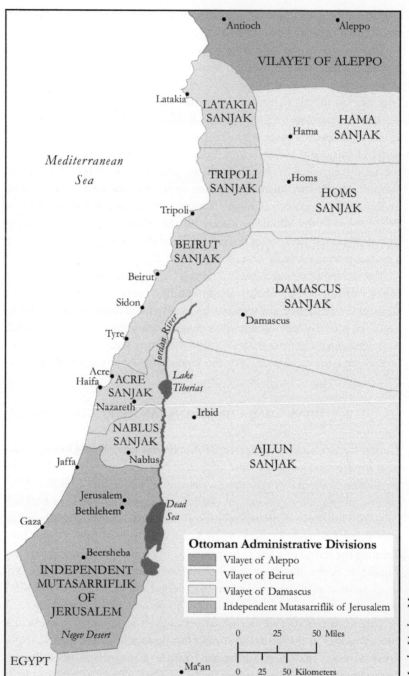

Antioch
Aleppo

VILAYET OF ALEPPO

Latakia

LATAKIA
SANJAK

Hama

HAMA
SANJAK

*Mediterranean
Sea*

TRIPOLI
SANJAK

Homs

HOMS
SANJAK

Tripoli

BEIRUT
SANJAK

Beirut

DAMASCUS
SANJAK

Sidon

Damascus

Tyre

Jordan River

Acre
Haifa
ACRE
SANJAK

*Lake
Tiberias*

Nazareth

NABLUS
SANJAK

Irbid

AJLUN
SANJAK

Jaffa
Nablus

Jerusalem
Bethlehem

*Dead
Sea*

Gaza

Beersheba

INDEPENDENT
MUTASARRIFLIK
OF
JERUSALEM

Ottoman Administrative Divisions
Vilayet of Aleppo
Vilayet of Beirut
Vilayet of Damascus
Independent Mutasarriflik of Jerusalem

Negev Desert

EGYPT

Maᶜan

| 0 | 25 | 50 Miles |
| 0 | 25 | 50 Kilometers |

Map by Lindsay Mayer

Late Ottoman Palestine and Syria

of land in and around Jerusalem, including some of the city's most important Christian sites; today, it is still the largest nonstate landowner in Israel. The patriarchate and the brotherhood of monks who headed the church were, by ecclesiastical law, ethnically and nationally Greek, while the whole of the laity and most of the lower clergy were Palestinian Arab—a situation that caused considerable tension within the church.

The second-largest community was Greek Catholic, which followed the Byzantine Catholic rite; its members were clustered in the Galilee and the northern parts of the country. There were smaller communities of Latin Catholics (headed by the Latin Patriarchate in Jerusalem and under the jurisdiction of the Vatican), Maronites, Armenian Orthodox, Syrian Orthodox, Syrian Catholics, and Copts. The small but influential Protestant community consisted primarily of Arab Episcopalians, mainly converted from Greek Orthodox Christianity by British missionaries during the second half of the nineteenth century.

During the nineteenth century, the Ottoman millet system helped to define the social, political, and economic meanings of these communal labels. This system involved the recognition of Christians and Jews as *ahl al-kitab*, "people of the book," who were entitled to the protection of the state and a certain degree of communal autonomy in return for a number of restrictions on their participation in civil society and public worship as well as special tax requirements.[4] They were organized into semi-autonomous communities known as millets. The Ottoman government recognized six millets: the Greek Orthodox, the Armenian Orthodox, and the Jews, and the more recent additions of the Syrian, Armenian, and Chaldean Catholics. The Latin Catholic community, although substantial, did not officially constitute a millet because it was considered a non-indigenous group despite the predominance of Arabs within the church.[5] The newly established Arab Protestant community received a kind of partial recognition in 1850.[6]

The Ottoman millet system underwent substantial changes during the mid-nineteenth-century period of empire-wide reforms and reorganization known as the *tanzimat*, the goal of which was the defensive modernization of the Ottoman Empire against internal and external military and economic challenges.[7] The tanzimat reforms lifted a number of the restrictions on non-Muslim communities, allowing greater leeway in religious worship, permitting non-Muslims to serve in governmental administration, and consenting to the construction of some churches. Furthermore, *dhimmis* ("protected peoples," members of recognized non-Muslim religious communities) would now be subject to conscription for the first time. These changes transformed the status and visibility of Christian communities throughout the Arab provinces, and the upheaval contributed to a wave of popular sectarian violence in Damascus, Mount Lebanon, and Nablus during the mid-nineteenth century—an early example of the ways in which increasingly interventionist imperial policies could contribute to the emergence of new kinds of communalism.[8]

Under the influence of the shifting millet system, Christian and Jewish communities began to dominate certain social and economic spheres, particularly the commercial and merchant classes. By the beginning of World War I, Christians had become an important part of an emerging middle class in Palestine that stood between Palestine's peasantry and impoverished city dwellers on one hand and the "urban notables" who had long dominated the Palestinian political landscape on the other.[9] These new, primarily urban middle-class elites (which included Muslims as well as Christians) understood themselves as a potential ruling force and viewed themselves as the intellectual vanguard of Palestine and as contributors to a broader Arab and Ottoman political discourse.[10] Members of this rising middle class did not define themselves politically in terms of their religious affiliation but in terms of their status as elites and, especially, their commitment to new forms of Arab modernity. Their interest in modernity—which Carol Gluck has usefully summed up as characterized by "industrialization, the nation-state, expanded political participation, forms of middle-class or mass society, and inescapable integration in the world"[11]—had counterparts all over the world during this period; these Christian and Muslim Arab middle classes were part of a global trend of non-Western elites engaged in exploring how to remake their societies in "modern" but not necessarily Western terms.

In 1917, during the later stages of World War I, the British occupied Jerusalem under the leadership of General Edmund Allenby. The European powers already had begun to divide up the Middle East among themselves, and Britain's de facto possession of Palestine helped to assure that the "Holy Land" would become part of the British Empire. In the postwar peace agreements, France took the newly defined territories of Syria and Lebanon, and Britain claimed Iraq and Palestine, carving out the new region of Transjordan soon thereafter. All of these were technically "mandates" rather than "colonies" and were supposed to be under the supervision of the League of Nations with an eye toward eventual independence. In reality, though, the European imperial powers made no essential distinction between their new Middle Eastern "mandated" possessions and their directly held colonies elsewhere.[12]

Britain appointed its first high commissioner for Palestine in 1920 and began the reorganization of the colonial state; the League of Nations finalized Britain's possession of the mandate for Palestine three years later. By this time, Britain's support for the Zionist movement—which proposed the

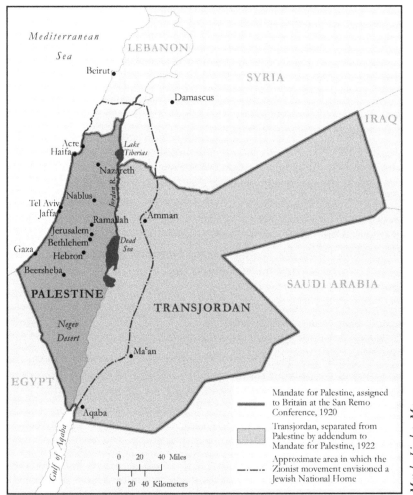

Map by Lindsay Mayer

Legend:
Mandate for Palestine, assigned to Britain at the San Remo Conference, 1920

Transjordan, separated from Palestine by addendum to Mandate for Palestine, 1922

Approximate area in which the Zionist movement envisioned a Jewish National Home

0   20   40 Miles

0   20   40 Kilometers

Palestine and Transjordan under the British Mandate

construction of a "Jewish National Home" in Palestine as a response to European anti-Semitism—had crystallized. The famous Balfour Declaration of 1917, a letter from British Foreign Secretary Arthur Balfour to the Zionist leader Walter Rothschild, gave the Zionist movement formal notice that "His Majesty's Government view with favour the establishment in Palestine of a national home for the Jewish people, and will use their best endeavours to facilitate the achievement of this object."[13] This promise was now formalized in the text of the league's mandate despite having already caused intense hostility, resentment, and rebellion among Palestinian Arabs. The new European Zionist presence in Palestine would shape the nature of British rule there and have a major impact on the construction of new kinds of sectarian identities for Palestine's Arab Christian communities between 1917 and 1948.

The Palestinian Christian communities' eighteenth- and nineteenth-century history as sites of European intervention in Ottoman affairs would also influence British mandate policy toward Arab Christians. During the last two centuries of Ottoman rule, a number of European powers—beginning with Russia and France and later including Greece, Italy, and Britain—had laid claims to "protectorates" over the Christian communities of the empire, claiming that they needed to be shielded from the depredations of Muslim Ottoman rule. Although the British themselves had engaged in this practice during the nineteenth century, they now worried that this legacy of association between indigenous Arab Christians and the other European powers might lead to unwelcome French, Russian, or Italian interventions in Palestine through the Arab Christian communities. This suspicion, combined with considerable domestic British Protestant support for the Zionist project (evident in popular literary works like George Eliot's *Daniel Deronda*, first published in 1876), served to distance mandate officials from Palestinian Christian leaders. The British would not view Arab Christians in Palestine as natural allies of the colonial state.[14]

Above all, British rule over Palestine and policy toward its Arab Christians drew on models of imperial administration elsewhere, especially in India. The structures of the mandate state were nearly identical to those of direct colonial rule throughout the British Empire, a parallel that also held between the French-controlled mandate territories of Syria and Lebanon and France's directly held colonial possessions elsewhere. More important, colonial methods originally designed to maintain British suzerainty over large Indian and African subject populations were vital to the battery of tactics British officials deployed in their new Middle Eastern possessions after World War I. These included violence, intimidation, public humiliation, and collective punishment, as well as subtler methods of co-opting local elites, establishing new economic hierarchies, making use of educational and health networks to support the colonial enterprise, and creating and maintaining ethnic and religious divides.

To produce and enforce these religious and ethnic divisions, the British engaged in extensive legal, political, and administrative classifications of their colonial subjects. These methods—which Benedict Anderson has summed up as "census, map, and museum"—became central to how mandate officials understood and enforced the meaning of religious identity and the place of Arab Christians in Palestinian Arab society. As Anderson has written, "The effect of this [classificatory] grid was always to be able to say of anything that it was this, not that; it belonged here, not there. . . . This is why the colonial state imagined a Chinese series before any Chinese, and a nationalist series before the appearance of any nationalists."[15] The British colonial state in Palestine could not imagine a web of interlocking identities in which religion might not have absolute political meaning; it needed to define and then enforce both Islam and Christianity as irreducible political entities under a state-designed rubric.

In Palestine, as in India and Africa, the British claimed to adhere to a "status quo" policy, by which they meant that as few changes would be made to the extant legal, political, and social structures of the new colonial possession as possible—a strategy intended to promote easy relations with the subject population, reduce imperial operating costs, and forestall anticolonial rebellion. In practice, colonial officials tended to claim imperial adherence to previously existing institutions while in fact continually altering and modifying them to suit the demands of the British colonial state. This paradigm provided the basis for the British approach to the Ottoman millet system in Palestine. While declaring their commitment to maintaining the millet system, the British actually substantially reworked and extended it, emphasizing communal representation as a basic political principle of the mandate government and classifying their new Arab subjects into rigidly defined sectarian blocs. Armed with a specifically colonial understanding of the meaning of religious identity in Palestinian society and the means to enforce British views, the mandate government now began both to assume and to enforce a radical legal and political separation between Muslims and Christians, enshrining a new kind of sectarian politics in Palestine.

CONCEPTS OF SECTARIANISM

The word "sectarian" has a particular set of connotations in Middle Eastern history. Western scholarship about the Middle East has a long history of understanding sectarianism as an essential and permanent aspect of Islamic societies.[16] This idea, which continues to influence both scholarly and popular portrayals of the Middle East, has had a powerful ally in the "clash of civilizations" literature that reached its apogee in the work of historian Bernard Lewis and political scientist Samuel Huntington and found a mass audience in the United States and Europe following the attacks of September 11, 2001.[17] This approach rests on the assumption that Islam constitutes the primary intellectual and political loyalty of all Muslims and that Islam is at its core an antimodern, feudal, fanatical force operating in direct opposition to the Western commitment to progress, democracy, and modernity.

The "clash of civilizations" thesis has helped to reinforce popular perceptions of a "primitive" sectarianism driving all political activity in the Middle East. It understands sectarianism in the Middle East as a natural result of an inherent fanaticism, characteristic of the Islamic world and absent from the West. Further, it offers a Western explanation—and self-exoneration—for the "failure" of the Middle East to construct viable nation-states; the region's ongoing political turmoil and the difficulties of nation-building can be attributed to unalterable confessional loyalties rather than to a history of destructive Western political and military intervention.[18] This vision of the meaning of sectarianism in the Middle East, then, says a great deal more about the self-representation of the West as liberal, rational, and beneficent than it does about the social and political roles of religion in the Middle East.[19]

In fact, sectarianism cannot be understood as a primitive, atavistic clinging to religious identity. Rather, following Ussama Makdisi's definition, it is a modern historical process through which religious affiliations take on specific political meanings.[20] Such a definition makes it possible to trace exactly how sectarian identities emerged in particular historical circumstances in the modern Middle East instead of merely assuming their ancient, unchanging existence.[21]

In late-nineteenth- and early twentieth-century Palestine, communal affiliations coexisted with local, ethnic, familial, and regional identities without contradiction, all contributing to the texture of Arab social and political life.[22] Communal tensions did arise during this period, most notably in mid-nineteenth-century Nablus, where the implementation of major Ottoman reforms concerning the rights of religious minorities in the empire combined with growing panic about Christian-Muslim violence in Mount Lebanon to produce a brief outbreak of intercommunal conflict. But Muslims and Christians also had a long history of cultural and social accommodation; sources from nineteenth-century Palestine record a daily existence in which the various religious communities engaged in a wide variety of social interactions, shared holy sites and spaces, and celebrated one another's religious holidays and festivals. Communal boundaries helped to define the shape of social, familial, and geographic relations but were generally flexible and porous.

The European powers saw little of this complexity. They had a long history of conceiving of Palestine as the "Holy Land" and were coming off a century of intense involvement in the disputes between Palestine's many (largely foreign-dominated) churches and the Ottoman government. Bitter conflicts among Palestine's European-run churches had sometimes even provided a *casus belli* for the European powers, as when a dispute over control of Bethlehem's Church of the Nativity contributed to the outbreak of the British-French-Russian Crimean War in 1854. As a consequence of this fraught involvement, the European powers tended to view Palestine—especially its Christian populations—as irretrievably torn by sectarian impulses. Religious difference did carry social, economic, and political meaning in Ottoman Palestine, but the intense disputes among Palestine's churches, mainly over control of property, were not an expression of local sectarian politics but of foreign powers exerting their might in a kind of proxy struggle against other European nations. Local Arab Christians and Muslims experienced and practiced their religious affiliations in less exclusively political (and, usually, less contentious) ways, as one among many identities.

With the British assumption of power in Palestine in 1917, the landscape changed dramatically. Now, a European state with a long history of commitment to nationalist power politics among Palestine's church institutions wielded direct control over its indigenous Arab Muslim and Christian communities. The British, and to some degree the other European powers involved in the church politics of the "Holy Land," could now apply their vision of a sectarian Palestine not only to its foreign-dominated churches but also to its local Christian communities on the ground. Almost immediately they began to shape a much more rigidly sectarian political system for Palestine in which access to government and representation was possible only through state-sponsored communal institutions. This restructuring coincided with conversations throughout the Arab world about the role of Islam in a post-Ottoman political order and a rising awareness of the potential relevance of religious identities for molding modern nations. Arab Christians in all the Ottoman successor states were facing the question of how to shape their participation in new political structures that often explicitly recognized Islam as central to ethnic, regional, and national identities.[23]

As the British began to construct a colonial administration that assumed the political centrality of communal identifications, Arab Christians—responding to the new colonial system, pressures within their foreign-dominated church institutions, and broader currents in the Arab world—gradually started to re-imagine their religious communities as modern political entities. They began to model their religious institutions after secular systems, to define communal movements in nationalist political terms, and to inscribe their communal histories at the center of nationalist political mythologies. These actions, designed to respond to British policies and carve out a space for Christian political participation, ultimately helped to advance the sectarian political system being built under mandate authority.

ARGUMENT AND SOURCES

This study begins with the last years of Ottoman rule and the first years of the British occupation of Palestine, when the meaning of religious affiliation was undergoing a major reexamination. In chapter 1 I examine the ways in which the European presence in Palestine from the late nineteenth century on encouraged new forms of communal identification among Palestinian Arabs while simultaneously assisting the emergence of a new kind of multi-religious public space for urban elites. During this period, as both Muslim and Christian elites worked to imagine their post-Ottoman political future, the meanings of their communal affiliations were especially fluid.

In chapter 2 I argue that during the first years of the British presence, the mandate government—under pressure to incorporate an autonomous European Jewish settler community into the Palestinian mandate state—began to lay the legal and political groundwork for an essentially sectarian political system in Palestine, expanding the Ottoman millet system into a much more comprehensive communally organized state structure. This new imperial approach reified sectarian affiliation as a primary marker of Palestinian Arab political identity and helped to marginalize Palestinian Christians as a minority religious community rather than an integral part of a Palestinian Arab citizenry.

Palestinian Christian leaders responded with a number of efforts to build and promote a specifically Christian polity in Palestine. In chapter 3 I examine the movement for the Arabization of the Greek Orthodox Church, focusing on how Orthodox leaders billed this effort as part of the broader crusade against the foreign appropriation of Palestinian Arab land, resources, and cultural institutions. In chapter 4 I investigate an attempt to build a pan-Christian voting bloc for the purposes of legislative representation—the first effort to define all Palestinian Christians, regardless of denomination, as a single political entity. Chapter 5 is concerned with the small but highly influential Arab Episcopalian population, which concentrated its efforts on defining itself as a legitimate and authentically Arab community as well as promoting intellectual work that inscribed Arab Christian history at the center of Palestinian national identity. These narratives of the Palestinian Arab Christian experience under mandate show how both Muslims and Christians helped to produce sectarian identifications as they responded to the new conditions of the mandate state.

In this book I draw on a wide variety of Arab and British sources in examining the making of Christian and Muslim sectarian identities in mandate Palestine. Although a dearth of Arab sources and an overabundance of British colonial narratives is a perpetual problem for historians of Palestine, this project's focus on elites—many of whom were not only consumers but also producers of the written word—has made it possible to consult the Palestinian voice in a real way.[24]

The Arab press—especially the Christian-run journals *Filastin* (Jaffa), *al-Karmil* (Haifa), and *Mir'at al-sharq* (Jerusalem), all national newspapers that nevertheless often concerned themselves with issues bearing especially on the Christian communities—can usefully serve, at least in part, as a representation of the elite Palestinian Christian voice. These newspapers are particularly valuable for examining the construction of communal identifications in the context of the developing nationalist movement and the fractures and fissures along economic, political, class, and familial lines. Their editors saw themselves as promoting a national cause and viewed their papers as public venues in which to protest the Zionist incursion and British colonial injustices. Throughout the mandate period these editors wove their Christian identifications into this discourse of nationalism and anti-imperialism, in the process revealing a great deal about the often self-conscious development of a political significance for Christianity and how communal and political identities began to intertwine in new ways under the influence of colonial policy.

I have also made use of a rich set of memoirs, published diaries, books, and articles—many overtly political—written by various intellectuals who self-identified as members of the Christian communities of Palestine. These range from the deeply personal diaries of Khalil al-Sakakini through the rather programmatic and didactic memoirs of Imil Ghori, the political tracts of ʿIzzat Tannus and Matiel Mughannam, and the scholarly monographs produced by Asʿad Mansur and Ilyas Marmura. All of these give a variety of answers to the question of what it meant to be a Palestinian Christian during the mandate period, and many deal quite explicitly with the ways in which their communal affiliations began during this time to have newly specific political implications. These writings give a sense of the implications of a developing sectarian political landscape not just for Palestinian civic and political society but also for personal narratives of identity and belonging.

The extensive British colonial records relating to the mandate period are likewise valuable. This material, which includes Colonial Office and Foreign Office files, Government of Palestine correspondence, police records, and private correspondence of British officials, remains useful for historians of Palestine for its detailed record of the workings of colonial administration, the interactions between British officials and colonial subjects, and the attitudes and activities of the colonial state toward Palestinians. This material has been especially important for exploring topics about which there was extensive correspondence between Palestinian Arabs and the mandate government—in particular, the Greek Orthodox controversy (chapter 3) and the discussions about legislative council representation (chapter 4). In the absence of an official Palestinian national archive, the British records of correspondence sent from various Palestinian Arab nationalist organizations, parties, clubs, and societies as well as individuals to the mandate government remain a useful point of reference for historians.

Another British source has not yet received much attention from scholars of mandate Palestine: the records of missionary institutions. Particularly for the discussion of the Arab Protestant communities in chapter 5, the archives of the Church Missionary Society (CMS), the Jerusalem and East Mission (JEM), and Lambeth Palace (the seat of the Archbishop of Canterbury in London) reveal an alternative British perspective often in opposition to that of the mandate state—itself, of course, not monolithic but often internally contradictory. The CMS archives also contain extremely valuable records of the meetings of the all-Arab Palestine Native Church Council as well as extensive correspondence between "native" church leaders and European mission representatives in Palestine and London. These records of discussions of global Christianity and the development of a specifically Palestinian Arab Protestant church depict a new kind of sectarian consciousness worked out between Palestinian Arabs and British missionaries, whose relationship referenced the imperial subject-ruler relationship but did not necessarily reproduce it.

In this study I draw principally on Arab and British sources. One of my goals is to move Palestinian historiography away from a focus on the genesis of the Arab-Israeli conflict and the concomitant conception that the modern history of Palestine is *sui generis* in every way because of the Zionist presence. While in no way denying the importance of the narrative of the Jewish homeland and the Zionist movement or the relevance of Hebrew primary sources for the history of Palestine and the particular development of its national movement, Arabic and British materials represent the most appropriate sources for a project that deals primarily with the colonial relationship between Palestine's Arab Christian communities and the British imperial presence.

Further, with its focus on the construction of sectarian identities in a colonial context and the shift from elite multi-religious nationalism to a sectarian political landscape, this narrative has obvious resonances with Lebanese, Syrian, and Iraqi stories that have yet to be fully explored. By focusing on Arabic rather than Hebrew sources, I hope to begin to make these parallels evident and encourage other scholars to re-imagine Palestine's history as deeply relevant to the broader Arab world as well as considering its own idiosyncratic narrative.

This study, then, places Palestine in the context of a global colonial history including much of the Middle East and looking beyond to India and Africa. As in other parts of the world under European imperial rule, the changes and dislocations the British wrought in Palestine continued to shape local, regional, and national politics long after their departure. By the time the British finally relinquished the mandate in 1948, their colonial policies—in conjunction with the responses of Palestinian Muslim and Christian leaders themselves as well as the interventions of other European powers—had enshrined a specifically modern sectarianism as a major organizing principle of the Palestinian Arab political landscape. They had defined Arab Christians as a political entity in opposition to the Muslim population, permanently diminishing their role in a broader Palestinian Arab body politic. In the years after 1948, this marginalization would become ever more evident with the disproportionate emigration of Arab Christians out of Palestine/Israel.[25]

The fact that this historical trajectory has now brought about the radical diminution of the Palestinian Christian community in its homeland is not a reflection of any innate sectarianism in the Middle East. Rather, it is a commentary on the continuing reverberations of Palestine's colonial history.

CHAPTER I

PALESTINIAN CHRISTIAN ELITES
from the LATE OTTOMAN ERA
to the BRITISH MANDATE

*[We lived together] during centuries of peace and love, and we want
to continue this life together, striving against conspiracies that are being
concocted against our country . . . from the days of ʿUmar ibn al-Khattab
we have worked together as brothers and we do not want anything
to change this, or an evil year to separate us, or schemes by our
waiting enemies to come between us.*

BISHOP GRIGORIOS HAJJAR, LEADER OF THE GREEK CATHOLIC
COMMUNITY, HAIFA, C. 1920

In the late nineteenth and early twentieth centuries, increasing European
penetration and major Ottoman reform efforts began to transform the political meaning of religious affiliation in the eastern Mediterranean and especially in Palestine. A sudden and dramatic increase in the presence of European institutions, combined with major empire-wide reforms from Istanbul,
created new kinds of separations between Palestine's Muslims and Christians.
As Palestinian Arab Christians became more closely associated with foreign
powers and institutions and their position within the empire became an issue
of ever more interest to Europe, their communal identity took on a political
aspect it had never before possessed. But simultaneously, this internationalization of Palestine's affairs sparked an interest among Palestine's urban elites
in constructing a modern, middle-class political and social space including
both Muslims and Christians. In late Ottoman Palestine, the same forces that
produced new forms of communal identifications also assisted the emergence
of a middle class that rejected sectarian confines in favor of a modern, multi-
religious civil society.

These changes were particularly evident in the geography of Palestine's
cities, where the burgeoning presence of European Christian organizations
encouraged the emergence of sectarian urban organization but also assisted

the development of upwardly mobile, religiously mixed middle-class neighborhoods. Similarly, the founding of European-style mission schools mainly serving Arab Christian populations created divides between Muslims and Christians and led to explicitly nonsectarian "national" schools that became foundational spaces for Palestine's emerging multi-religious, modern middle class. This new demographic soon began to develop an urban civil society engaging with major contemporary debates about Arabism and Ottomanism as well as more local concerns about the growth of European Zionist immigration into Palestine. In the context of this discourse, Palestinian Christian elites did not see themselves as a disadvantaged minority vis-à-vis a Muslim majority. Instead, many saw themselves—along with their elite Muslim compatriots—as avatars of a multi-religious Arab identity that could serve as the basis for a new kind of modern nationhood.

In the first years of British rule, political clubs and societies like the Muslim-Christian Associations emerged as important players in Palestinian Arab politics. Christian leaders displayed a wide range of political opinions in these fora; they did not organize along sectarian lines or develop a specifically Christian political platform. Instead, the Muslim-Christian Associations deployed an explicitly multi-religious rhetoric, responding to the possibility of emerging sectarian divides in Palestine by encouraging a vision for an Arab politics including both Muslims and Christians and hoping to use their Palestinian Christian members' religious heritage to appeal to British Christians for support against Zionism.

The international presence in Palestine in the late nineteenth and early twentieth centuries coincided with new intellectual currents in the Arab world, as elites from Egypt to Syria and Palestine debated the political implications of Arab identity and the possibilities for a post-Ottoman Middle Eastern political order. These developments helped to foster forms of communal awareness among Palestine's Arab Christian communities, but they also encouraged the emergence of a kind of urban, modern, multi-religious, middle-class society to which many Christian elites became deeply committed.[1]

CHRISTIANS AND MUSLIMS IN LATE OTTOMAN PALESTINE

In 1831 the ruler of Egypt, Muhammed 'Ali, sent forces that conquered Jerusalem and inaugurated a new era in Palestine's history during which the legal and political positions of the Palestinian Christian communities would undergo radical changes. His son Ibrahim Pasha, the commander of the Egyptian army, initiated a number of reforms in Palestine, reintroducing and enforcing Muslim conscription, terminating many of the political prerogatives of the Muslim religious leadership, and opening the region to European influence in the form of consulates, trade centers, and a European Christian mission. He encouraged Christian pilgrimage by lifting some of the tolls and fees levied on visitors to the Church of the Holy Sepulcher and allowed the repair and construction of some churches and synagogues. A contemporary observer reported that Ibrahim paid a visit to the Holy Sepulcher on his second day in Jerusalem and attended the Easter service of the Holy Fire in 1834.[2] All these actions represented a significant upheaval in the mode of governance in Palestine and the place of its religious minorities in civil and political society. By 1834 these changes had disturbed some Muslims so greatly that a revolt broke out against the Egyptian government; the fighting destroyed a number of villages around Jerusalem and caused substantial damage in the city itself.

Nevertheless, the radical redefinition of the place of religious minorities in the Ottoman Empire continued. In 1839 the Ottoman sultan Abdulmecid issued the *Hatt-i sherif* (Noble Rescript) of Gülhane, which set out a number of principles for reforming and modernizing the Ottoman Empire. This edict expanded responsibility for paying taxes and for military conscription, requiring Muslims to register with the state alongside their non-Muslim compatriots for the first time. Although the edict claimed that this was merely a return to earlier patterns of governance as part of a reinvigoration of the empire, it actually represented a major change of attitude toward the underlying social structure of the empire, and many Muslims reacted with alarm and anger. These transformations were part of the broader set of reforms known as the tanzimat, designed to reorganize, modernize, and strengthen the empire against European encroachment and internal revolt.

In 1841 British pressure forced Muhammed 'Ali and Ibrahim Pasha out of Palestine and Syria, and the Ottomans resumed control of the region. The *sanjaks* (districts) of Jerusalem, Acre, and Nablus were taken over by *mutasarrifs* (district governors) who reported to the governor of Sidon or Beirut. As more European consuls and representatives of various sorts streamed into Palestine, the regions—and especially the city of Jerusalem—became more important to the Ottoman government, which sought to control the administration of Palestine much more closely than it had before the intervention of Muhammed 'Ali. The strictures of the tanzimat reforms, especially those dealing with the long-standing system of "capitulations" (privileges for foreigners, most notably immunity from Ottoman civil and criminal law) had special relevance for Palestine's unprecedented number of foreign residents and its new status as a destination for European Christian travel and pilgrimage. The Ottomans also established commercial courts for settling intercommunal disputes, requiring non-Muslim representatives to participate in their boards. The model of introducing a quota of non-Muslims as the political representatives of a religious community had already been discussed with regard to the provincial councils in Damascus in 1844; the Ottoman decision in 1850 to establish intercommunal commercial courts firmly established the principle.[3] For the first time, Christians were given what Ottoman historian Bruce Masters calls "an officially sanctioned, political voice in a non-sectarian government body."[4]

In 1856 the *Hatt-i humayun*, a new *firman* (decree) that explicitly established the principle of religious equality, signaled a much more radical reworking of the relationship between the empire's Muslims and Christians. It lifted restrictions on religious worship and allowed some construction of churches; mixed tribunals now took the place of *shari'a* (Islamic law) courts in the event of intercommunal court cases; non-Muslims were to be allowed to serve in governmental administration; and dhimmis would now be subject to conscription, although payment for substitutes or exemption would be possible. The firman declared that communal autonomy for non-Muslims would be achieved through the expansion of the millet system, which itself would be subject to periodic reviews by the state and was supposed to be moving in the general direction of democratization.[5]

All this upheaval meant a heightened awareness of communal divisions and an expansion of their political meaning. In the Palestinian context, the tanzimat reforms were met with considerable resistance from Muslims who regarded them as a European attack on Arab social norms but also from Christians who were alarmed that they might now be vulnerable to conscription.[6] Palestinians resisted the edict so strongly that it had to be put in place very slowly, over a number of years, and spurts of intercommunal violence often followed its implementation. British consul James Finn reported to London that he was witnessing an increased level of Muslim-Christian hostility in Palestine, citing a number of incidents in which Muslims and Christians clashed over conversion and the European presence.[7] In 1855 an English missionary shot and killed a beggar in Nablus; when the governor refused to hand the missionary over to a furious mob, rioting wreaked havoc on a number of prominent Christian sites in the city. The protesters targeted the Greek church, British and French consular dwellings, a Protestant school, and a Protestant missionary's house—although, as Alexander Scholch notes, in the aftermath of the riots "great qualms immediately arose. . . loot was secretly returned, and the city authorities and notables begged the French consular agent to put on the tricolor again."[8] In 1858 a group of Muslims wrecked the gate of the Greek Orthodox monastery in Gaza, protesting Greek Orthodox construction and renovation there. The much more dramatic riots in Damascus and Lebanon in 1860 in which Christians were targeted and massacred contributed substantially to a growing Christian anxiety in Palestine. Nevertheless, despite these outbursts, there was generally a high level not just of religious tolerance but also of syncretism. Muslim and Christian communities often shared holy sites, worshipped at the same saints' shrines, and celebrated one another's holidays; Muslims occasionally baptized their children in Christian churches, and Christians sometimes attended services at mosques.[9] In many cases the hostile behavior of foreign representatives of the Christian churches, not actions taken by local residents, helped to spark angry encounters between Palestine's Muslim and Christian communities.[10]

Beyond these encounters, the nineteenth-century disputes over the guardianship of what were broadly grouped as the "Holy Places," especially the Church of the Holy Sepulcher in Jerusalem, attracted much attention from Europe and were often deployed as evidence for a long-standing and particularly aggressive brand of sectarianism in Ottoman Palestine. Certainly, the debates over the ownership, maintenance, and control of these sites were long, complicated, and highly antagonistic. A series of Ottoman decisions in the second half of the eighteenth century established Greek Orthodox primacy in the ownership and maintenance of Jerusalem's Christian sites. During the nineteenth century, Russian pressure succeeded in convincing the Ottoman government to reconfirm Greek Orthodox control over the "Holy Places," defeating French efforts to secure these sites for Catholicism. The apparently constant arguments between the Greek and Latin churches over these shrines and their persistent appeals to the Ottoman sultanate over the minutest details of church upkeep made a strong impression on Western observers, often leading them to comment on the bitterness of these intercommunal disputes.

But the ongoing debates over access and control of the sites were primarily matters of competition among the so-called Great Powers, not local sectarian animosity. The Greek Orthodox patriarchate, which owned the Holy Sepulcher and acted as a major player in these highly publicized disputes, did not allow Arab membership in the brotherhood in charge of church affairs and thought of itself as representing Greek and Russian interests. Likewise, the Latin patriarchate made its claims over the "Holy Places" in the name of the Vatican, not Palestine's local indigenous Catholic communities. The increases in numbers of European church personnel in all of Palestine's churches during the nineteenth century gave rise to increasingly bitter disputes over the disposition of Christian sites, arguments that carried overtones of nationalist discord among the European powers. The centrality of intra-European politics to the question of the "Holy Places" became especially evident in 1878, when the stricture "No alterations can be made in the status quo in the Holy Places" found its way into the Treaty of Berlin.[11]

Through the second half of the nineteenth century, then, Palestinian Arab Christians were gaining a reputation for sectarian infighting that in reality owed a great deal more to European "Great Power" politics than to the state of relations among the various indigenous Arab Christian communities. Nevertheless, this European perception would continue to influence the relationship between religion and politics in Palestine throughout the mandate period and beyond.

PALESTINE'S URBAN GEOGRAPHY

During the nineteenth century, Palestine became the focus of a great deal of European diplomatic and religious attention. European consuls, backed by strong foreign governments, were now able to buy land in the Ottoman Empire and offer protection to European citizens living and working there. A number of German, French, American, and British mission societies set up branches in Palestine during the mid-nineteenth century; the first Protestant bishopric was founded in Jerusalem in 1841. Around the same time, both the Greek Orthodox and the Latin patriarchates set up permanent residences in Jerusalem and began to buy up land in the city.

Although many of these European missions had arrived in Palestine with the intention of proselytizing to the Jews, their lack of success among the small Palestinian Jewish communities and the Ottoman legal strictures against converting Muslims (a crime theoretically punishable by death, although infrequently enforced with that degree of severity) soon led them to focus their attention on Palestine's indigenous Christians. They made relatively few converts but developed strong ties to the Arab Christian communities through schools, charities, hospitals, and other institutions. By the late nineteenth century, Palestinian Christian populations were involved with the European powers in an unprecedented way. The links between Palestinian Christians and this European religious presence assisted the emergence of a sectarian urban geography, as Palestinian Christians took advantages of land, housing, and jobs available to them from these new European institutions. At the same time, though, the foreign-driven expansion of Palestine's cities also assisted the emergence of multi-religious, middle-class neighborhoods and public spaces.

In Jerusalem, members of religious communities often took advantage of the opportunities to work or live on institutionally owned land. Quite often, churches allowed the members of their congregations to live for free on church property, and these opportunities expanded with the rapid growth of European Christian mission institutions in the second half of the nineteenth century. This pattern continued through the mandate period and even beyond; the writer Jamil Toubbeh, for instance, recalled that the house in the Old City into which his Orthodox family moved after they fled the Qatamon neighborhood in 1948 was "leased to us at no cost by the Greek Orthodox Convent."[12]

Muslim and Jewish organizations followed similar patterns, further encouraging sectarian urban development. The Jewish community in Jerusalem appointed a chief rabbi with official powers of representation, and Jewish organizations began to receive large donations from Jewish communities abroad to support construction of Jewish houses and institutions in Palestine. Similarly, Muslim as well as Greek Orthodox *awqaf* (charitable institutions, which played an important role in Palestinian social and economic life) often allowed members of their communities to build and live on their land at little or no cost. These developments gave Jerusalem's urban development a distinctly sectarian appearance.

But gradually, foreign institutions began to offer financial and logistical support for construction projects outside Jerusalem's city walls, and these new neighborhoods soon became the site of an upwardly mobile, religiously mixed Arab middle class. On a map from 1864, the area of the "New City" (outside the city walls) contained the Russian Compound, the Anglican Bishop Gobat School, the Protestant Schneller Orphanage (also known as the Syrian Orphanage), the British consul's summer retreat, and a "Greek settlement" in Talbiyya, as well as cafés, shops, and a Turkish guardhouse.[13] The opportunities the New City provided to escape the crowded conditions of the Old City quarters and to construct new buildings appealed especially to Arabs of means, both Muslim and Christian. It offered more spacious conditions and greater possibilities for innovative, self-consciously "modern" architecture indicating upward mobility.[14] Although the Arab Christian presence in the New City was proportionately larger than the Muslim, due both to the greater wealth of the Christian communities and to the opportunities to build on church property outside the walls, the new neighborhoods of Baqʿa, Talbiyya, and Qatamon had mixed populations. These wealthy Arab neighborhoods were the preferred residences of many of the Arab Christian leaders who would emerge during the mandate period, and their bourgeois ethos did much to shape elite Christian political perceptions.

Social life in these new spaces was not only multi-religious but also multi-ethnic. Wasif Jawhariyya, a musician at the social center of this new middle class, gave a vivid portrait in his diary of a social life that included foreigners resident in Jerusalem as well as Palestinian Muslims, Christians, and Jews. He described both Christian and Muslim feast days as involving whole neigh-

borhoods regardless of the denominations of individual families, and he recorded close friendships between Muslim and Christian youth who jointly
frequented cafés and held boisterous gatherings.[15] Coffee shops in both the
Old City and the new neighborhoods became sites of this emerging multi-
religious, middle-class, internationalizing discourse. One café in the Old
City that the Arab nationalist educational leader and prolific diarist Khalil
al-Sakakini would later christen the Vagabond Café often hosted pilgrims
from eastern Europe and Russia to the Holy Sepulcher. The café owner's son
later recalled that "it was a sort of meeting locus for some of Jerusalem's most
renowned intellectuals and humorists. . . . Their discourse, over puffs on nar-
ghilehs and sips of Lebanon's renowned firewater at al-Mahal, still rings in
my ears. The environment of the café also tolerated occasional blasphemous
language away from the cultural revolution that was changing the character
of both Jerusalem and Palestine."[16]

This mix of sectarian and multi-religious urban geography emerged in
other Palestinian cities as well. In the late nineteenth century, Christians
made up about 45 percent of the population of the northern coastal city of
Haifa.[17] The Christian population in Haifa was more varied than in Jerusalem; as well as the Greek Orthodox community, Haifa had a substantial
number of Greek Catholics and smaller groups of Maronite, Latin Catholic,
and Protestant Arabs. This diversity had the effect of encouraging other small
denominations to settle in the city, and by the early twentieth century Haifa
boasted small numbers of Armenian Christians, Baha'is, and Druze, some of
whom lived in the city's new middle-class mixed neighborhoods and participated in public discussions of city politics.[18]

In Jaffa the Christian population, especially the Greek Orthodox community, grew rapidly and dramatically during the nineteenth century. As in Jerusalem and Haifa, the practice of using church land to house members led to
a clustering of Christian neighborhoods around each community's religious
buildings.[19] Unlike their counterparts in Haifa, the Christian communities of
Jaffa remained almost entirely separate, with very little ecumenical identification.[20] Perhaps as a consequence, even late into the tanzimat period there was
little Christian activity in urban politics in Jaffa. During the early twentieth
century, however, Jaffa's Christians emerged as a major force in the increasingly middle-class trade of journalism. In 1911 the Arab Orthodox cousins
'Isa and Yusef al-'Isa founded the newspaper *Filastin* in Jaffa; it would run
almost continuously until 1967 and play a central role in Palestinian intellectual and political life throughout the mandate period.

Jaffa's middle-class café culture was occasionally considered somewhat dis-
reputable, as in a description of a coffee shop called Café Baghdadi:

All hours of the day it is crowded with very shady characters, who sit and gamble, playing all manner of card games and dominoes. Here too, the 'chalk and slate' system of scoring is favoured, although on a few occasions players have been apprehended in flagrante delicto passing money. Many women, undoubtedly prostitutes, gather in this café, and hang about, passing from table to table.[21]

These cafés were not just for music, games, and gambling; they were also public spaces for reading and discussing the new media proliferating in cities like Jerusalem, Haifa, and Jaffa, and after 1914 they emerged as an important venue for disseminating information about the war. This aspect of café life was so prevalent that the British took note of it for their own use upon occupying Palestine in 1917, placing propaganda reports in cafés alongside the newspapers and journals available to patrons.[22]

During the late nineteenth and early twentieth centuries, the mass influx of European Christians into Palestine and their attempts to reinvent the local Arab Christian populations as their protégées caused communal identifications to manifest in novel ways in Palestine's urban geographies. But Palestine's international population and its cities' rapid growth also encouraged the emergence of urban areas where middle- and upper-class Muslims and Christians lived interspersed, expressing their participation in the project of modernity and progress through construction, architecture, sports, music, writing, and publishing. The same forces that produced new forms of sectarian identifications also produced multi-religious neighborhoods and public spaces for Palestine's emerging middle class.

THE ROLE OF EDUCATIONAL INSTITUTIONS

During the late Ottoman and early mandate periods, private institutions dominated Palestinian education. Many of these schools were outgrowths of the European missionary presence and affiliated with European churches and organizations; others were private Muslim schools that offered a different kind of education and outlook. During the late nineteenth century, these schools helped form new kinds of Muslim and Christian communal consciousness. At the same time, the European educational presence began to inspire the emergence of explicitly nonsectarian "national" schools that would become central to the self-definition of Palestine's multi-religious middle class.

For most of Palestine's Ottoman history, education had been a strictly private affair. In 1869 the Ottoman government passed a law requiring that primary schools be established in every community and that government-sponsored secondary education be made available in all the empire's large cities; but although there were ninety-five government schools in Palestine by 1914, they accommodated only about one-tenth of the country's children between the ages of seven and eleven.[23] In rural Palestine, Muslim elementary schools known as *kuttabs* often constituted the only educational options in places with no state schools. Their Christian counterparts were usually run by foreign churches or missions; A. L. Tibawi notes that "the bewildering diversity of the foreign schools [was] due to the diversity of the nations and the religious denominations involved."[24] Secondary educational institutions took several forms, including the *madrasa*, which mixed Islamic theological training with instruction in Arabic grammar, philology, and rhetoric. The many new secondary schools run by Christian missions, including German, Russian, French, American, and British institutions, diverged widely in their offerings but tended to have a rather Europeanized curriculum and often included some vocational training as well as academic coursework. There were no institutes of higher education anywhere in Palestine during the Ottoman or mandate periods. Students wishing to continue their education past the secondary level had to travel, most frequently to al-Azhar in Cairo or the American University of Beirut (AUB) — radically different options that represented another example of the increasingly sectarian choices on offer to Muslim and Christian Palestinians during this period.

The sudden proliferation of European Christian mission schools in Palestine during the second half of the nineteenth century complicated the question of Palestinian Christian identity, for they provided a kind of education for Arab Christian children to which the majority of Muslim children did not have access. The presence of these schools raised literacy and education rates for Christians considerably higher than those of their Muslim compatriots.[25] Christians began to enjoy greater access to business and professional opportunities requiring familiarity with Western languages. To some degree, then, mission schools contributed to a consciousness of sectarian divides in Palestine.

But in the last years of the Ottoman period these educational trends inspired the foundation of a number of national schools run by Muslim and Christian elites, promoting a curriculum based around concepts of Arabism and a kind of local Palestinian patriotism. These schools catered to both Christian and Muslim students; they were self-consciously secular and Western-facing, making use of European curricula and techniques of instruction.[26] Schools like these now began to constitute an important educational framework for the emerging multi-religious middle class; most of the people initially involved in such enterprises were Christian, like the educational theorist Khalil al-Sakakini and the journalist Yusef al-ʿIsa, but during the last decade of Ottoman rule this elite began to include a number of Muslims, among them nationalists like Muhammed al-Mughrabi, ʿAli al-Rimawi, and Isʾaf al-Nashashibi. Some of the earliest of these schools were Rawdat al-Maʿarif in Jerusalem, opened around 1908 by a group of prominent Muslim notables; Dusturiyya, opened in Jerusalem by Khalil al-Sakakini in 1909; and Najah in Nablus, founded by a local committee in 1918.

As a mark of their modernity, these institutions offered extracurricular activities modeled on those of English and French schools, reflecting the bourgeois orientation of Palestine's urban middle class. During al-Sakakini's brief tenure as director of the Men's Teacher Training College (later the Arab College) in Jerusalem, he suggested reforms of the curriculum to the British representative from the Department of Education: "I suggested to Legge that we add music and singing to the school program . . . In addition, I provided him with a long list of the various sports equipment we need."[27] Al-Sakakini's daughter Hala remembered her father's enthusiasm for the newly popular sport of roller-skating during her childhood.[28] Mousa Kaleel, recounting his childhood growing up in a Christian family in Ramallah, remembered playing a game of captives and prisoners called "Germany." He also recalled that "some of the modern games, such as football, [were] played as they are played in England, and the boys of Palestine, who posses a very keen sense of rivalry, are becoming proficient players even at these foreign games."[29] Sports and other extracurricular activities marked these students as participants in Palestine's bourgeoisie, a multi-religious elite including both Muslims and Christians.

CHRISTIANS IN THE NEW MIDDLE CLASS

Prominent Palestinian Christians coming out of these neighborhoods and schools shared a globally connected anti-imperial sensibility, an interest in the reinvigoration of Arab identity and "nationhood," and a strong anti-Zionist bent.[30] Rather than identifying as members of a disadvantaged minority struggling against a dominant Muslim majority, as the British mandate government and many subsequent historians would portray them, they viewed themselves as part of a new Arab intellectual elite, participating in European-style civil society but using it as a platform for a politics of anti-imperialism and emerging models of Arab nationalism.

Najib ʿAzuri, Khalil al-Sakakini, ʿIsa al-ʿIsa, Najib Nassar, and Bishop Grigorios Hajjar were all recognizable as members of a Christian elite that had emerged in Palestine as a result of the shifting position of the Christian communities during the late nineteenth century. Although their prominence, prolific writings, level of political involvement, and commitment to concepts of modernity necessarily make them all exceptional to some degree as individuals, together they serve to demonstrate the wide variety of political opinions and approaches within the Palestinian Christian communities during this period.[31] Well-known thinkers like ʿAzuri and al-ʿIsa, both of whom reached prominence in Palestine's political arena, provide an instructive comparison with less well-known figures like Hajjar, who worked primarily within church circles. The following brief examinations of the lives, productions, and activities of these people offer a lens into the social, intellectual, and political milieu in which many elite Palestinian Christians moved and the sorts of shared practices that were emerging among Christians of the new middle class during this period.

NAJIB ʿAZURI

Most of the details of Najib ʿAzuri's early life are unclear. He was a Maronite Christian born in either Jaffa or the southern Lebanese village of ʿAzur around 1870.[32] His brother Yusef was a priest and teacher at the Catholic ʿAyn Tura College, run by the French Lazarist brotherhood. Najib ʿAzuri attended the Mulkiye in Istanbul and then moved on to the École des hautes études in Paris; he was appointed assistant to the Ottoman governor of Jerusalem in 1898. According to his own writings, he left Palestine and went to Egypt in 1904 after coming into personal and political conflict with Kazim Bey and his dragoman, Bishara Habib, who also happened to be ʿAzuri's brother-in-law.[33] After a brief stint in Egypt, ʿAzuri moved on to Paris at the end of 1904. The next year he published the book for which he is still known today, *Le reveil de la nation arabe*, in which he called for an uprising against the Ottoman sultan, the formation of an independent Arab nation, and the restoration of the caliphate to an Arab.[34]

In this book he posited a clash between the rising Arab nation and the growing Zionist movement, which by this stage had set up numerous small settlements along Palestine's coast and in its valleys and had already caused some protest.[35] "Two important phenomena, similar and yet opposed," he wrote, "which have not yet received attention, are becoming evident today in Asiatic Turkey: the awakening of the Arab nation, and the latent effort of the Jews to restore on a very large scale the ancient kingdom of Israel."[36] Working with a French colleague in Paris, Eugene Jung, he founded an organization called La Ligue de la patrie arabe (The League of the Arab Nation) to promote his ideas.[37] Under the auspices of this organization ʿAzuri and Jung published a series of manifestos titled *L'independance arabe*, calling on Arabs to rise up against the Ottoman sultan and declare an independent Arab state. The positions 'Azuri set out in his book and expressed in his political activities indicate the globalizing, modernizing Ottoman context in which he was considering both the idea of Arab nationhood and the ramifications of his own Arab Christian identity.

In *Le reveil de la nation arabe* 'Azuri condemned participants in all levels of the Ottoman imperial bureaucracy as brutal oppressors of Arabs and especially of Palestinians. Arguing that the Ottomans were hated not only by the Arabs but by all the non-Turks in the empire (including Albanians, Armenians, Serbs, Greeks, and Bulgarians), he called for a revolt of the Arabs against the Ottomans and the formation of an Arab empire comprised of Syria, Palestine, Mesopotamia, and the Arabian Peninsula under the tutelage and protection of a European country, preferably France. 'Azuri's vision of this new Arab nation explicitly excluded Egypt, which he argued was separated from the Levant not only by a natural border but also by racial and linguistic differences.[38] He envisioned this new nation as a constitutional monarchy with a caliph based in the Hijaz who would have spiritual—but not temporal—authority over the whole of the Islamic world.[39] This interest from a Christian writer in the idea of an Arab Muslim caliphate demonstrates the degree of 'Azuri's (and his Palestinian Christian peers') cultural integration in the Islamic world.

'Azuri condemned the disputes among Christians over the control and use of the various "Holy Places" in Jerusalem and Bethlehem, suggesting that the Ottoman government was responsible for this state of constant conflict and that Christians in Palestine should reject the Ottomans' divisive tactics and come together as a unified entity. He also suggested that intercommunal disagreements over rites and church ownership were largely a production of foreign clergy representing external national interests, not lay Arab Christians representing their local communities who, he wrote, "do not attach any importance to these distinctions of ritual."[40] In 'Azuri's view, local communal identifications were being reworked into hostile sectarian conflicts at an international level. Prefiguring a number of later suggestions, 'Azuri declared that the way to unity was to create a national Arabic church in which only Arabic would be permitted as a liturgical language and whose rituals and practices would be wholly Arabic. The proposed church should have its own Arab patriarchate and should be encouraged and accepted by the pope.[41] He seems to have planned to expand his ideas on this topic into a book to be titled *Les puissances étrangeres et la question des sanctuaires chretiens de la Terre-Sainte* (Foreign Powers and the Question of the Christian Sites of the Holy Land).

This concept of a "national church"—meaningless except in the context of

European nation-state nationalism—had already begun to take hold in other parts of the Ottoman Empire, most notably the Balkans, by the late nineteenth century. In places like Albania and Bulgaria, protests against foreign languages, liturgies, and hierarchies in the churches added fuel to and overlapped with new anti-Ottoman local nationalisms.[42] 'Azuri's suggestion of a national Arabic church in Palestine, which would later be repeated by others in the context of the mandate, indicated a nascent vision of a sectarian landscape in which a defined religious affiliation would be necessary for political participation. His writings and political activities placed him firmly within a global, modern, Arab elite interested in emerging concepts of Arab nationhood but also aware of changing implications for the category of "Christian" in the Arab world.

KHALIL AL-SAKAKINI

Khalil al-Sakakini was born into a Greek Orthodox family in Jerusalem in 1878. His father, a well-regarded carpenter, was also the *mukhtar* (community head) of the Greek Orthodox community in Jerusalem.[43] Al-Sakakini attended school at the local Greek Orthodox church institution, then went on to the Anglican Bishop Blyth School in Jerusalem; he completed his education with a course in literature at the Zion English College. This Western-style education imbued in him an interest in secular humanism and in the study of language that he would bring to all his educational and political endeavors.

Like many other Palestinian Christians, the Sakakini family had members who were expatriates in the United States.[44] In 1907 al-Sakakini left Palestine for the United States to join his brother Yusef, a traveling salesman in Philadelphia. He had accumulated some debt in Palestine and undertook the journey in the hope of earning enough money to pay off his obligations and set up a house for himself and his fiancée, a young Arab Orthodox woman named Sultana 'Abdu. He planned to follow Yusef's example by making a living in trade and sales, but when he arrived he found Yusef in desperate financial straits and the economic situation for recent immigrants dire. Al-Sakakini settled in an unnamed, Arab-dominated (he called it "Syrian") neighborhood in Brooklyn and tried to scrape together a living teaching Arabic to American university students at Columbia, instructing Arab women in reading, and doing some translation work for an Orientalist scholar at Columbia named Richard Gottheil.

Al-Sakakini had a number of contacts with Arab intellectuals based in the United States including Farah Anton, a Lebanese Christian journalist and writer who had published a pan-Ottoman journal in Alexandria for several years and moved to New York in 1907. Anton continued to publish his journal from New York under the name *al-Jami'a*, and he recruited al-Sakakini to write and edit articles for the publications as well as to proofread and provide editorial support. Al-Sakakini had other contacts in New York including his cousin Hanna Farraj, and during his time in New York he remained almost entirely within an Arab social sphere, rarely emerging from Arab neighborhoods and confining his social interactions exclusively to Arab circles.[45] Financial desperation finally led al-Sakakini to leave New York for Maine, where he worked briefly in a paper mill. He returned to Jerusalem not quite a year after he had left it, having failed to conquer America in the way he had imagined.

But upon his return to Jerusalem, al-Sakakini founded a school he called the Dusturiyya (Constitutional) school, which became an experimental ground for his progressive educational theories. The school used Arabic rather than Turkish as its primary language of instruction; al-Sakakini was especially interested in methods of teaching Arabic grammatical principles, and he developed a number of important models for linguistic study.[46] The Dusturiyya school abolished grades, punishments, and prizes, focusing instead on an integrated secular curriculum that included athletics and music. Al-Sakakini's innovative approach to language teaching represented a radical departure from the educational norms of the day. Issa Boullata, himself later a prominent scholar and writer, recalled his encounter with al-Sakakini as a young student:

> He spoke in classical Arabic and I was asked by Sitt Wasila to read a text to him. I read it aloud, trying to conceal my nervousness and slight intimidation. When I finished, he asked for the meaning of the word *fawran* that I had read in the text. No one in the class knew, so he used it in a sentence and asked again for its meaning. I raised my hand with a few other students but he did not call on any of us. He used the word *fawran* in another sentence and asked for its meaning again. More students now raised their hands to answer. But he did not call on any of them until he gave a third sentence using the same word again. At that moment, almost all the students raised their hands eager to answer, and those asked said— correctly—it meant "immediately."[47]

Al-Sakakini's curricula and methods were intended to break radically with the rote learning of the day and establish a new kind of intelligentsia in Palestine, educated according to principles of modern pedagogical practice.[48]

Suspicious of his political activities, the Ottoman government briefly imprisoned al-Sakakini in Damascus during the final stages of World War I.

Upon returning to Palestine, he once again took up his educational work, and in 1919 both he and his wife, Sultana, were appointed to positions with the Educational Authority of Palestine in Jerusalem, where he eventually became educational inspector. During the mandate period he founded two more schools to carry out his educational principles, the Wataniyya (National) School and the Nahda (Revival) College in Jerusalem. Although he had expressed antipathy to the public role of women in the United States, his views on gender roles were progressive within the Palestinian context, perhaps formed by the liberal outlook of his wife's family.[49] His daughters attended a German school in Jerusalem and went on to study at the American University of Beirut.[50]

As one of the most recognizable figures of the new Muslim-Christian elite, al-Sakakini represented Arab modernity and intellectual accomplishment to many, but he also parodied middle-class practices. When he began what he called the Vagabonds Society in Jerusalem, he produced an ironic manifesto declaring the celebration of idleness in all its forms: "Idleness is the motto of our party. The working day is made up of two hours. Every holiday, including the memory of obscure saints, is a legitimate occasion for taking time from work in order to indulge in eating, drinking and merriment . . . Our party sees black as black, and white as white — there is no left or right, and we do not recognize people as elevated or demoted."[51] This kind of satirical commentary mocked the preoccupations of bourgeois society and suggests some of the humor that certainly arose around these emerging practices.[52]

Although he identified himself as a member of the Arab Orthodox community, al-Sakakini, probably like many of his contemporaries, was personally not religious. During the months of his imprisonment in Damascus he wrote of conversations with a German missionary who tried to arouse his interest in Christianity:

> We are both preachers. He preaches Christianity, and I preach my method.
> He asked me: Do you pray? And I said, "No." Don't you beg God's forgiveness for your sins? "No." "Don't you thank God for his goodness to you?" "No." "Don't you depend on Him?" "No." He received this with astonishment, and perhaps he pities me that it is my fate to be in hell.[53]

He once suggested that a pre-Islamic pagan poem replace the Lord's Prayer in the Christian liturgy.[54] This lack of belief and anticlericalism developed into a talking point for al-Sakakini; even his daughter Hala, who in her edited version of her father's diary extirpated many of his more radical comments, noted that he was not religious.[55] Eventually, al-Sakakini's secular outlook would combine with disgust for the communalism that emerged as a major force in mandate Palestine, leading al-Sakakini (under an assumed name) to produce a tract calling for all Christians to convert to Islam, though he himself did not follow this advice.[56]

Like 'Azuri, al-Sakakini developed an early and strong opposition to Zionism and to the European Jewish presence in Palestine. His position on Zionist immigration developed out of his interest in the idea of Palestine's independence as a part of a broader Arab state. In 1914 he gave an interview with the Egyptian newspaper *al-Iqdam* (edited by the expatriate Palestinian Muhammed al-Shanti), saying the Zionists "want to break the chain and divide the Arab Nation (*al-umma al-'arabiyya*) into two sections to prevent its unification and solidarity. The people should be conscious that it possesses a territory and a tongue, and if you want to kill a nation cut her tongue and occupy her territory and this is what the Zionists intend to do with the Arab nation."[57] Al-Sakakini's opposition to Zionism informed his opposition to the British assumption of the mandate;[58] the Balfour Declaration dismayed him, but he was no less suspicious of the decision to put Palestine under British control for what he called "training for independence."[59] For al-Sakakini, both Zionism and European imperial oversight were obstacles to Palestine's emergence as part of a successful, modern Arab nation.

NAJIB NASSAR

Najib Nassar, an Orthodox-turned-Protestant journalist, writer, and literary figure, was born in Lebanon in 1865,[60] but he moved to Tiberias to become a pharmacist at a mission hospital attached to the Free Church of Scotland.[61] In 1908 he founded the newspaper *al-Karmil* in Haifa that would quickly become one of the most influential journals in the region. His interest in literature led him to form a literary society whose members were equally devoted to the promotion of Arab literature and literary culture and to the "struggle against immorality and corruption."[62] Many of his pieces in *al-Karmil* dealt with issues of modernization; Nassar deplored Palestinian village standards of building, education, and hygiene, especially in comparison to the European Jewish settlements springing up in the Galilee and along the coast. Nassar's friendship and collaboration with the Jordanian poet Mustafa Wahbi al-Tall, known as 'Arar, led to a public meeting in Nazareth in 1922 in which the two men called for Palestinian Arabs to be on guard against Zionism but also against intercommunal strife.[63]

Unlike al-Sakakini and 'Azuri, Nassar remained committed for some time to the idea of a multi-ethnic, multi-religious Ottoman Empire. This theme of Ottomanism occupied him often in the early years of *al-Karmil*, in which he spoke out against Christian sectarian support for various European powers.

In 1911, when accusations were circling that some of Haifa's Christians supported the Italian occupation of Tripoli, he urged them to think of themselves as Ottomans and reject any thoughts of supporting their Italian co-religionists: "Christians, Jews and Muslims, you are all brothers . . . Unite to protect the homeland and Ottoman honor!"[64] Nassar interpreted divisions between Muslims and Christians not as an essential part of the Palestinian landscape but as arising from the recent and problematic loyalties some of the Christian communities harbored toward their European sponsors.

In *al-Karmil* Nassar focused heavily on the question of Zionism and the responsibility of the European nations involved in the post–World War I negotiations to preserve Palestine as an Arab nation. In 1911 he broke publicly with the Ottoman government over its policies regarding Zionism; that same year he published the first book in Arabic to detail the history, mission, and progression of the Zionist movement. *Al-Sahyuniyya: Tarikhuha, gharaduha, ahmiyyatuha* (Zionism: Its History, Aims, and Importance) focused on the organization of the Zionist movement, presenting it as a set of independent, quasi-military institutions, and on such aspects as its flag and the physical training Zionist societies provided to their members. In *al-Sahiyyunna* Nassar called for Arabs to campaign and work actively against Zionism without depending on the Ottoman government to take action. Almost simultaneously he followed his own advice by publishing a manifesto in *al-Karmil* calling on all like-minded newspaper editors in the Arab world to present a united front against the Zionist threat.[65] Nassar directed much of his anti-Zionist rhetoric at Britain, convinced that the British could be made to support the Arab point of view.[66]

Like ʿAzuri and al-Sakakini, Nassar viewed himself as part of a new international intellectual elite. As well as his political writings he produced several novels, an art form firmly associated with Western modernity.[67] These were infused with didactic political messages; Qustandi Shomali has noted, "The novel was intended to distract, amuse, educate, lecture, or make a didactic point."[68] In Nassar's novel *Mufleh al-Ghassani*, set during World War I, the hero is an Arab intellectual facing down a variety of threats to his life and welfare in Nazareth due to his impassioned support for Arab and Ottoman solidarity in the face of external dangers. In *Fi dhimmat al-ʿarab*, Nassar's second novel, similar themes emerge; he calls on events from pre-Islamic history, most notably the Arab-Persian battle of Dhi Qar in 609, to demonstrate his conviction of Arab nationhood. The strategy of locating Arab nationality in the region's pre-Islamic history meant that Arab Christians could be easily included in a heroic narrative of Arab nationhood; it also meant that Nassar was free to place the modern Western virtues of equality, justice, and patriotism at the center of his depiction of an Arab nation.[69]

Nassar viewed himself as a representative of Arab modernity and considered carefully what the basis of a new kind of Arab nationhood might be—first supporting a modernized Ottomanism (supporting a reformed Ottoman Empire as a viable modern political entity) and later moving toward pan-Arabism based on a shared pre-Islamic history that could include all religious communities. Nassar's careful consideration of the meaning of his Christian identity was evident in his warnings against communalism and his explicit inclusion of Christians in his categorizations of patriotic Arab leaders.

ʿISA AL-ʿISA

ʿIsa al-ʿIsa represented an altogether different, although equally prominent, kind of Palestinian Christian voice. He was born in Jaffa in 1878 to a Greek Orthodox family heavily involved in journalism; his uncle, Hanna al-ʿIsa, founded al-Asmai in Jerusalem in 1908. Al-ʿIsa was educated at Jaffa's École des frères, a Greek Orthodox school in northern Lebanon, and the American University of Beirut. His early employment included jobs with the Iranian consulate in Jerusalem and at a Coptic monastery as well as journalistic work in Egypt. In 1911, with his cousin Yusef al-ʿIsa (later the founder of the Damascus newspaper Alif ba), he founded the biweekly newspaper Filastin, which would become the most influential publication in Palestine during the years of the British mandate.[70] He was friendly with al-Sakakini and for a time was part of his group of "vagabonds" who assembled in Issa al-Tubbeh's coffee shop in the Old City.[71]

From its inception Filastin was dedicated to opposing the Zionist presence in Palestine. Like Nassar, ʿAzuri, and al-Sakakini, the ʿIsa cousins viewed Zionism as a major economic, political, and cultural threat to Palestine. Filastin was shut down numerous times in its first few years for its anti-Zionism and its criticisms of the Ottoman government. During the war years al-ʿIsa and his cousin were exiled to Damascus; ʿIsa became Faysal's private secretary there in 1918. His Arab nationalist convictions led him to join al-Fidaʾiyya (the Self-Sacrificers), an underground organization begun in Jaffa in 1919. Al-Fidaʾiyya, which eventually developed branches in Jerusalem, Nablus, Gaza, Ramleh, Hebron, and Tul Karm, promoted the idea of Palestine's incorporation into an independent Greater Syrian state.[72]

Unlike al-Karmil and ʿAzuri's work, Filastin quite often dealt explicitly with issues relating to Muslim-Christian relations and the problems of Christian communities in Ottoman Palestine. The ʿIsas wrote extensively about the conflicts within the Greek Orthodox Church, relating the contentious relationship between the Greek hierarchy and the Arab laity to the quest for an Arab nationalist identity in the Palestinian context.[73] In a speech he gave much later in his life al-'Isa told an audience in Jerusalem that he had originally been drawn to journalism as a way to fight for the Arab Orthodox cause against the Greek clergy.[74] For 'Isa al-'Isa, issues of Palestinian nationalism were closely related to questions of Palestinian Orthodox Christian identity.

GRIGORIOS HAJJAR

Our final case study, Grigorios Hajjar, was born in southern Lebanon in 1875 into an old and deeply rooted Catholic family.[75] In 1884 he entered the school at a monastery called Dayr al-Mukhlas, near Sidon. After a brief stint at school in Jerusalem he returned to the monastery, only to leave again for travels in Egypt. In 1899 he came back to Palestine to serve as deputy patriarch of the church at Acre. After some years presiding over the church there and consolidating his authority through a trip to Rome and a meeting with the pope, Hajjar eventually moved his church to Haifa, citing its preferable location and larger population.[76] At the beginning of the war his travels in France and his known pro-French views led to Ottoman accusations that he had recruited young Palestinian Catholics into the French army. An Ottoman court tried him on this charge in absentia and sentenced him to death.[77]

Hajjar returned to his diocese in 1919 and threw himself back into the life of the Catholic communities in Haifa, establishing a school named after himself. The early years of the mandate saw him emerge as a political figure, a pro-Arab nationalist, and a fervent opponent of Zionism. As an official representative of the church, he thought carefully about what it meant to be a minority in an Islamic context and concluded that it had no political ramifications except when external forces—the European powers and the Zionists—conspired to divide Palestinian society by sect. In one speech Hajjar invoked the name of a caliph—"since the days of 'Umar ibn al-Khattab we have worked together as brothers"[78]—who seems to have been a touchstone for Palestinian conceptions of Muslim-Christian cooperation; another Palestinian Christian, the artist Daoud Zalatimo, is thought to have produced a painting described as "the bloodless entry of Caliph 'Umar ibn al-Khattab to Jerusalem in 637 CE and his amiable encounter with Sophronius, the Arab Byzantine patriarch who personally guided him through the city."[79] Hajjar, then, was conscious of the possibilities for sectarian identifications to emerge in Palestine but thought of them as external rather than internal threats that could be prevented by rejecting divisive European influences in favor of Arab national solidarity.

What can we conclude from this brief investigation of the lives of these people who self-identified as elite members of the Palestinian Arab Christian communities? A number of scholars have identified in the relatively consistent Christian opposition to Zionism a kind of nascent Christian political philosophy, even going so far as to suggest, "The very fact that the bearers of the anti-Zionist standard in the press were then Christians (Najib Nassar and the two al-'Isa brothers [actually cousins]) undoubtedly limited the effect of their propaganda."[80] But anti-Zionism existed across communal and class divisions among the Arab population in the late Ottoman period, and while the examples discussed above certainly all shared the sense of alarm about Zionism that was nearly universal in elite circles in Palestine during the first decades of the twentieth century, there were no other issues on which they agreed so completely. Christians did not represent a political bloc in Palestinian society during this period.

Rather, the last decades of the Ottoman period witnessed the emergence of an urban Christian elite in Palestine beginning to consider the political implications of membership in a new kind of religious minority but much more centrally committed to participation in an emerging multi-religious, modern, Arab civil society. While all these elites had been heavily influenced by European political, social, and intellectual examples to the extent of self-consciously modeling their schools after European techniques, explicitly engaging with European ideas in their writings, and even producing books in European languages, they used this civil discourse to reject European imperialism and its protégée in the form of the Zionist movement.[81] The internationalization of their intellectual world extended not just to Europe but also to the anti-imperial and nationalist movements brewing in other parts of the colonized world.

In late Ottoman Palestine, then, membership in an Arab Christian community could indicate certain social, economic, and political ties but did not dictate political positions or a particular relationship to the state; it was only one among a number of identities that shaped the nature of these elites' political and social engagement. These men did not conceive of their religious community as a political entity. Rather, they understood themselves as participating in the shared practices of an emerging middle-class, multi-religious elite committed to developing new and modern political forms in Palestine.

CIVIL SOCIETY AND ELITE CHRISTIAN POLITICAL PARTICIPATION IN THE EARLY MANDATE

During the first years of the mandate, Palestine's elite Christian leaders continued to feel a primary loyalty to the civic and political culture of an emerging multi-religious middle class rather than to their coreligionists. The patterns of their political participation did not indicate a Christian political platform or approach; they exhibited a wide range of ideas and loyalties in the associations and societies that constituted such a major aspect of Palestinian Arab political life during the first years of the mandate.

Many of these political activities revolved not around communal affiliations or institutions but around the debates that surrounded the "Southern Syria" movement. In the immediate aftermath of World War I and the context of the ongoing peace negotiations, political discussion among Palestine's elites began to feature the idea of attaching Palestine to an independent Southern Syrian state under Faysal, Sharif Husayn's son who had come to prominence in the Arab Revolt of 1916–1918 and was now emerging as the most visible Arab leader of the postwar era.[82] The Southern Syria movement represented an addition to the multiple political loyalties and identities Arabs in Palestine professed during the late Ottoman period. It arose as part of a contemporary discourse on Arabism, taking on a particular urgency in the context of the peace negotiations and the evident European contest for control of the Middle East. While Arab elites in Palestine discussed the possibility of inclusion in the proposed Greater Syrian state, they also pondered the likelihood of being put under some form of British or American mandate rule or of emerging as an independent Palestinian Arab nation. This conversation reflected contemporary dialogues throughout the Arab world about the nature of a post-Ottoman political order, and it included the more specifically Palestinian concern of the phenomenon of Zionist immigration, already viewed as a potentially serious threat by the area's elite Christians and Muslims. The question of Southern Syria thus involved consideration of the nature of Palestinian identity as well as broader loyalties to Bilad al-Sham (Greater Syria) and the Arab world.[83]

The British occupied Jerusalem in December 1917, one month after the Balfour Declaration expressed British support for the idea of a Jewish National Home in Palestine. General Edmund Allenby's new military government (known as OETA, the Occupied Enemy Territories Administration) took over the task of administering the region, and politically aware Palestinian Arabs began jockeying for position. Muslim-Christian Associations, populated by an admixture of urban notables and members of the new urban middle class, quickly began to dominate the political landscape in Palestine's cities. These associations focused on promoting a joint Muslim-Christian, nationalist (encompassing both Southern Syrian sentiment and local Palestinian patriotism), and, especially, anti-Zionist message.[84] The very name indicated the nature and concerns of the explicitly multi-religious middle class that made up much of the associations' membership.

The first Muslim-Christian Association (MCA) was formed in Jaffa in

1918, with another branch emerging in Jerusalem a few weeks later. The Jerusalem association's statutes declared, "The purpose of this society is to elevate the interests of the country (Palestine) connected with agriculture, technics, economics and commerce, the revival of science and the education of the national youth and the protection of natural rights, morally and materially."[85] The main administrative committee was divided into four subcommittees that dealt with educational, technical and agricultural, commercial, and "general" matters. In the society's actual operation, this "general" committee — charged with "the civilization, political and moral matters which reflect the good of the country and the harmonious concurrence among the population"[86] — was by far the most important. In practice it concerned itself primarily with public expressions of opposition to Zionism.

The British government initially did not oppose the MCAs' formation and may even have provided some assistance to the organization in its earliest days.[87] The chief administrator of Palestine, Major General H. D. Watson, expressed the general opinion among the members of the British administration: "The Society has up to the present always been moderate in its action and I am inclined to think should be of assistance to the Administration rather than the reverse, and that when they know the extent of the Zionist policy to be adopted will tend to moderate public opinion rather than excite it."[88] In Jerusalem, Musa Kazim al-Husayni and ʿArif Hikmat al-Nashashibi headed the MCA in its initial stages but were forced out when Ronald Storrs, the governor of Jerusalem, declared that they could not continue to hold their governmental positions (as mayor of Jerusalem and general administrator of the awqaf, respectively) if they took up positions of political activism.[89] In January 1919 ʿArif al-Dajani replaced al-Husayni as president of the Jerusalem MCA. At this stage the various MCAs around the country had decided to form a loose network with its headquarters in Jerusalem. In drawing up its statutes the MCA's leaders declared their new organization to be representative of the whole of Palestinian Arab opinion; to that end they invited representatives from other Palestinian urban centers to join in their first congress, with the hope that they would be encouraged to start new branches in other parts of the country.

Two clubs, al-Muntada al-Adabi (the Literary Society) and al-Nadi al-ʿArabi (the Arab Club), offered a potential challenge to the centrality of the Muslim-Christian Associations. Al-Muntada al-Adabi had its origins in Istanbul, where Jamal al-Husayni of Jerusalem, Asim Bsaysu of Gaza, and Rashidi al-Salif Milhis of Nablus participated in a club intended to be an intellectual and social base for Arabs in the Ottoman capital. In 1918 this society emerged as a political organization in Palestine led by Jamal al-Husayni and members of the Nashashibi family. The organization was essentially pan-Arab in outlook and focused on exploring the political implications of Arab cultural and literary ties.

The idea of a Greater Syrian state received a major boost with Faysal's entrance into Damascus in 1918. At the peace negotiations he lobbied for European support for an independent Arab state with Damascus as its capital, citing earlier British promises of Arab independence in return for wartime military assistance in the form of the Arab Revolt. During the period 1918–1920 the members of al-Muntada al-Adabi became passionately committed to the idea of Palestine's inclusion in Faysal's proposed kingdom. Using a political rhetoric honed in Istanbul and Damascus, they fused concepts of pan-Arabism and anti-Zionism to support Faysal's bid for authority over a new Greater Syrian nation—vigorously opposing the idea of putting Palestine and Syria under a British and French "mandate," which they viewed (accurately) as a euphemism for colonial control. In May 1919 this activity had reached a level that prompted the British government to prohibit any further meetings, speeches, or public activities by the club.[90] These orders did not, however, prevent al-Muntada al-Adabi from spearheading an anti-Zionist demonstration in Damascus in the summer of 1919.[91]

Al-Nadi al-ʿArabi had similar origins. Like al-Muntada al-Adabi, it was founded as a society for expatriates—in this case, for Palestinian Arabs in Damascus associated with the mainly Syrian Arabist society al-Fatat. Most of al-Nadi al-ʿArabi's first members were Arab nationalists from Nablus, where the branch was headed by Dr. Hafiz Kanaʿan. Members of the Husayni family dominated the Jerusalem branch, with Muhammed Amin al-Husayni serving as president; Muhammad Muslih suggests that although the club essentially shared the political philosophy of al-Muntada al-Adabi, the nascent rivalry between the Husayni and Nashashibi families prevented the merging of the two organizations.[92] Al-Nadi al-ʿArabi had an extensive outreach program that included mobilizing mosque leaders to promote its vision of Arab nationalism, publishing a newspaper called *Suriyya al-janubiyya* (Southern Syria), and spearheading demonstrations in favor of the joint causes of anti-Zionism and Palestinian-Syrian unity. Like al-Muntada al-Adabi, it was committed to the Southern Syria cause and to supporting Faysal as the leader of a new Arab Syrian/Palestinian state.

Some historians have suggested that during these early years of the MCAs and their rival clubs, elite Christians constituted a communal political bloc, affiliating themselves with a relatively conservative and pro-British MCA rather than the other two clubs, which represented a more radical pan-Arab viewpoint. In his account of the origins of Palestinian nationalism, Muhammed Muslih categorizes the MCA as the "Older Politicians," noting that the average age of the leaders was older than that of the leaders of organizations like al-Nadi al-ʿArabi and al-Muntada al-Adabi, which he casts as competing organizations with different political visions. Muslih notes two primary feature of the MCAs: the dominance of traditional "urban notables" who had occupied prominent positions during the last years of Ottoman rule and the proportional overrepresentation of Christians in the organization, which he attributes to "the fact that commerce and education, and hence politics, attracted a disproportionate number of the relatively urbanized and educated Arab Christian community." For Muslih, the Arab Christian presence in the MCA was synonymous with an "old guard" of conservative outlook and patriarchal mentality, while the pan-Arabism of al-Muntada al-Adabi and al-Nadi al-ʿArabi represented a younger Muslim demographic that tended to be more radical.[93]

But in fact, Christian opinion varied enormously, and leaders of the Christian communities participated in the two clubs as well as in the MCAs. Moreover, the MCAs themselves did not represent any one particular political view except an opposition to Zionism that was as fierce among Muslims as it was among Christians. Members quite often had difficulty coming to agreement on the issues facing Palestine under the new British occupation. In 1919, when the MCAs held their first congress in Jerusalem, many of the delegates who attended were also members of al-Nadi al-ʿArabi or al-Muntada al-Adabi. Of the thirty-eight representatives in the Jerusalem MCA, ten were Christian—five from the Greek Orthodox community and five Latin Catholics.[94] Of the twenty-seven representatives from the whole of Palestine who attended the congress, six were Christian. The British intelligence report for the congress suggested that three of these were "pro-British," one "pro-French," one "pro-Arab," and one whose allegiances were unknown.[95] No Christian political bloc emerged in these negotiations.

The congress had four primary goals: to discuss the political future of Palestine, to address the question of Zionism, to elect a Palestinian Arab delegation to represent the country at the Paris peace negotiations, and to discuss domestic issues of concern to the Arab population. Its first action was to pass a resolution condemning Zionism, for presentation at the peace conference; all but four of the delegates signed it, with one of the abstainers being the Arab Orthodox leader Yaʿqub Farraj.[96] During the next few days the congress deliberated over a memorandum that declared support for the Southern Syria "unity" idea. With pressure from the representatives who were also members of al-Muntada al-Adabi and al-Nadi al-ʿArabi, the members passed the resolution after two days of intensive discussion. In its final form it read, "We consider Palestine as part of Arab Syria as it has never been separated from it at any time. We are connected with it by national, religious, linguistic, natural, economic and geographical bonds . . . In view of the above we desire that our district Southern Syria of Palestine should not be separated from the Independent Arab Syrian Government and be free from all foreign influence and protection."[97] The resolution also called for open relations with the British and a rejection of the idea of a French protectorate over any part of Syria: "The declaration made by M. Pichon, Minister for Foreign Affairs for France, that France has rights in our country based on the desires and aspirations of the inhabitants has no foundation . . . The Government of the country will apply for help to its friend Great Britain in case of need for improvement and development of the country provided that this will not affect its independence."[98]

Leaders of the Christian communities had a wide range of reactions to this resolution. Farraj once again declined to sign, along with the Muslim president of the Jerusalem MCA, ʿArif al-Dajani. Immediately after the resolution was passed, Farraj and al-Dajani wrote to the military governor of Jerusalem protesting the resolution and declaring invalid the votes of two members of the Jerusalem delegates (ʿAbd al-Hamid Abu Ghosh and the Latin Catholic representative Shukhri al-Karmi, both of whom had pro-French sympathies) on the grounds that they had "agreed to a division which is contrary to the purpose for which they were delegated," adding that "it was therefore decided in the Central Society to refuse them from the Society."[99] Iskandar Manassa, a Greek Orthodox delegate from Haifa, likewise renounced his support for the Syrian unity plan and declared that his signatures were only intended to support the anti-French aspects of the resolutions. The other Christians who had signed the resolution — Yusef al-ʿIsa of Jaffa, Ilyas Kaʿwar of Tiberias, and Jubran Iskandar Kazma of Nazareth — all maintained their pro-Syrian votes,[100] and the Jerusalem Catholics Society posted a public notice declaring that "considering the actual political circumstances . . . [we have decided] to ask for the annexation of Palestine to Syria."[101] Opinion on the resolutions, clearly, did not fall along sectarian lines.

These Christian defections from the Southern Syria resolution led the British to believe that the Christian communities generally were opposed to the unification idea, even while a political report from Haifa noted that there was "a tendency among some Christians in Haifa to entertain and discuss the idea of the fusion of Palestine with Syria."[102] In actuality there was a wide range of opinions and ideas crossing religious lines. This state of affairs continued into 1919 as the MCAs, al-Muntada al-Adabi, and al-Nadi al-ʿArabi pressed their different positions on the representatives of the American King-Crane Commission, an official government delegation sent to the region to determine local preferences for postwar rule, during its members' visit to Palestine. Even among the MCAs there was considerable disagreement; the Nablus MCA, in contrast to the Jerusalem and Jaffa organizations, was passionately pro-Syrian and continued to press for the inclusion of Palestine in a Southern Syrian state for some time after the other MCAs had moved in a more specifically Palestinian nationalist direction.

During the first years of the mandate, Christian leaders participated enthusiastically in the Muslim-Christian Associations and the other emerging political societies. But they saw themselves primarily as representatives of the new middle class, dedicated to some form of Arab independence and to anti-Zionism, not as representatives of a minority religious group. There was no identifiably Christian pattern of political opinion or participation in the early activities of the MCA or its rival associations.

DEPLOYING CHRISTIANITY IN INTERNATIONAL POLITICS

The French deposed Faysal in a violent invasion of Damascus in 1920, ending Arab hopes for an independent Greater Syria after just a few months of government. In Palestine, after Faysal's fall from power, the MCA ascended over al-Nadi al-'Arabi and al-Muntada al-Adabi to become the predominant organization representing elite Palestinian Arab political opinion. It now took on an explicitly multi-religious nature, with its members issuing manifestos in both mosques and churches about Muslim-Christian interdependence and conscripting religious heads of both communities to address themes of religious unity with their followers.[103] This development indicated both a wariness of potential sectarian divides and an interest in deploying the MCAs' Christian members to appeal for international Christian support against Zionism.

During the third Palestinian Arab Congress, in 1920, representatives were appointed to attend from Jam'iyyat al-Shabiba al-Masihiyya (Society of Christian Youth) and Jam'iyyat al-Shabiba al-Islamiyya (Society of Muslim Youth) as well as from all the cities, the MCA, al-Nadi al-'Arabi, and al-Muntada al-Adabi.[104] Some of this new Christian-inclusive rhetoric was clearly designed to appeal to a British Christian audience, as in the case of an English-language public announcement posted by the Jaffa MCA that pleaded, "From over the Mount of Olives Christ gave salvation, life and peace to the World and all the World owes its life to this sacred source. Will therefore the British Nation, known to history as the protector of weak nations and the holder of the flag of peace, allow a Government to give free hand to the Zionists so that they may pour death and vengeance from over that holy sacred place on both the Moslems and Christians of Palestine?"[105] Similarly, the third Palestinian Arab Congress' address to the high commissioner leaned heavily on Palestine's status as a holy site for Christians as well as Muslims in the hope of attracting the attention of British Christians.[106]

Numerous declarations in the press, Muslim- and Christian-run alike, that nationalist unity required that Muslim and Christian Arabs come together in defense of Palestine and in opposition to Zionism suggested that elites of both religious communities recognized the possibility that communal identifications could come to have divisive political implications. Upon the formation of an MCA branch in Gaza an article in *Suriyya al-janubiyya* rejoiced that "old sensitivities and frictions had been removed from spirits and hearts," allowing for the strengthening of Palestinian and broader Arab nationalist spirit.[107] When Herbert Samuel, the new high commissioner, visited Beisan in April 1921 the Christian MCA member Jubran Kazma gave a speech protesting Zionist immigration, and supporters staged a demonstration in the streets in which they carried signs declaring that "Muslims and Christians are brothers."[108] In Haifa an MCA demonstration in June 1921 against the Zionist presence proclaimed intercommunal solidarity by having a Greek Orthodox priest give a sermon in a mosque while the imam spoke at the cathedral.[109] Early fears of sectarian tensions led the MCAs to publicize themselves as explicitly multi-religious organizations. Their leaders also hoped that the deployment of Christian-inclusive language would bring support for the anti-Zionist cause from Christians in Europe.

Although an engagement with nationalist politics characterized most if not all of the Palestinian Christian middle classes, no specifically Christian political consciousness emerged during this period. In late Ottoman Palestine and in the first years of the mandate, religious affiliations could indicate a number of social, economic, and political affiliations, but they did not in themselves constitute political categories; elite Arab Christians expressed a wide range of opinions and attached themselves to a variety of political organizations. At this stage, most leading Palestinian Christians would have deliberately rejected the kind of specifically sectarian political consciousness that their new British rulers would systematize over the course of the next decade.

REINVENTING *the* MILLET SYSTEM: BRITISH IMPERIAL POLICY *and the* MAKING *of* COMMUNAL POLITICS

Whether Jerusalem be regarded as indeed a city of living faith or, in the words of a well known modern writer, as merely the swarming of sects about the corpse of religion, each member of a particular community regards it as his duty, perhaps not unnaturally, to bear witness for that community with all his might. Unfortunately, his conception of his role is determined by the secular tradition of the place, a tradition of incessant struggle on the part of each sect or religious body to maintain its footing against its rivals.

HARRY CHARLES LUKE, CHIEF SECRETARY
FOR PALESTINE, 1927

For most of the nineteenth century, Britain had shaped the Ottoman Empire's policy toward its non-Muslim communities by casting itself as an external "protector" of the sultan's Christian subjects, particularly those living among the contested sites of the "Holy Land." With the assumption of the mandate for Palestine, the British had the opportunity to remake the system entirely. During the early years of the British presence the mandate government decided not only to maintain the millet system but actually to extend its scope by redefining the Muslim community as a "millet" and inventing various communal institutions that would function as the basic structures of Palestinian political participation.[1] This decision permanently changed Palestine's political landscape, reifying sectarianism as a primary marker of Palestinian Arab political identity and labeling Christians as a religious "minority."

The production of these kinds of communal political identities was inspired partly by a model of imperial governance developed in India and used throughout the empire, involving the colonial preservation of a supposedly pre-existent legal and political "status quo."[2] British imperial philosophy tended to assume that cultural difference was an innate quality; consequently, ideal colonial policy would not try to force Western political or social structures on its African, Indian, or Middle Eastern subjects but rather would ensure the preservation of "native" forms of social, political, and cultural organization. But colonial governments throughout the British Empire tended to view these relations among their subjects through a distinctly Western lens, seeing political implications in ethnic, religious, and cultural divides that rarely corresponded to how individuals and communities actually experienced those identities in their own local contexts. As Adamantia Pollis has put it with reference to colonial India, "Differences were given a meaning within a modern political framework, a framework relevant to the British structuring of social reality, but initially of no particular relevance to Hindus [in this case, Christians] or Muslims."[3]

In the African context the British viewed ethnicity as the primary category of social and political division among their colonial subjects. Colonial policy there often assumed absolute and politically significant divisions among ethnic groups, thereby hardening and codifying ethnic identities that had been much more fluid and less rigidly defined in the pre-imperial period (and often laying the groundwork for new forms of ethnic conflict in the colonial and postcolonial periods).[4] Similarly, British officials in India helped construct a new version of the caste system, assigning social and political meanings to caste and then enshrining these meanings in colonial legal and political structures.[5] India also saw the colonial development of a communal politics that explicitly and deliberately pitted Hindus against Muslims; new systems of communal representation gave religion a central political significance.[6]

Much as colonial officials in Africa understood ethnicity to be all-important and caste seemed central in India, the British government viewed its Middle Eastern possessions—and especially Palestine—as essentially divided by religion and sect. As in these other colonial contexts, the assumption of unalterable fissures among the "natives" served the purposes of imperial rule. Officials in Jerusalem and London judged that the colonial promotion of Muslim communal identity in Palestine would appease Muslim opinion throughout the British Empire, particularly in India, and prevent the emergence of a global pan-Islamic rebellion against British suzerainty. Even more centrally, the first mandate government under Herbert Samuel hoped that the introduction of Muslim communal institutions as the primary mode of Palestinian Arab political participation would confine Palestinian Muslim political expression to religious issues, preempting a potentially dangerous challenge to British colonial rule from a multi-religious Palestinian Arab nationalist movement. The assumption of irreducible religious divides among its colonial subjects in Palestine emerged from a specifically British perception of social reality but also was designed to serve the broader interests of continued imperial domination.

Justifying an emphasis on communal political organization as merely a continuation of Ottoman policy and hoping this approach would serve a broader imperial aim, the mandate government in Palestine made the decision to expand the millet system to include the Muslim community and to invent new Muslim political institutions. This approach followed the strategy, a generation earlier, of Lord Cromer (formerly viceroy of India), who had promoted religious affiliation as a political category in the colonial context of Egypt.[7] Of course, this approach had some unexpected consequences as local populations reacted to the new system in unforeseen ways. Hajj Amin al-Husayni, for instance, used this British support for Muslim communal organization to his own political advantage, constructing a new kind of modern Islamist political rhetoric and organization that was eventually used to oppose the mandate in ways wholly unanticipated by the British administration.

The Christian communities were treated very differently under the British millet system. The long history of European intervention in the Ottoman Empire to "protect" minority religious communities, in which the British had enthusiastically participated during the nineteenth century, now led to British suspicion that Arab Christian Palestinians were to various degrees in league with potentially hostile European powers. In their writings, both official and personal, mandate officials portrayed Arab Christians as fundamentally distinct from their Muslim compatriots and as hopelessly divided by primitive theological and denominational disputes. These views contributed to the mandate government's decision to intervene as little as possible in Arab Christian communal organizations, a policy in sharp contrast to its constant monitoring and encouragement of Muslim communal institutions. As a consequence of this sectarian approach, the secular nationalist political expressions in which Christians had played such a major part during the first years of the British occupation quickly dwindled. With British encouragement, they were replaced with specifically Muslim organizations like the Supreme Muslim Council that were dominated by an Islamic rhetoric in which Christians could not participate. The British reinvention of sectarianism in Palestinian public life during the early years of the mandate would eventually force Arab Christians to move away from the multi-religious language of the previous few years and toward a search for new types of communal identity that might be viable in a sectarian colonial political system.

The millet system of the Ottoman Empire formed the backbone of the legal system the British inherited upon Allenby's entrance into Jerusalem in 1917. It entitled the Ottoman Christian and Jewish communities to the protection of the state and a certain level of communal autonomy in return for a number of restrictions on their participation in civil society and public worship as well as special tax requirements.[8] In many parts of the empire, as we have seen, these restrictions led to a Christian and Jewish domination of certain social and economic spaces and to a degree of segregation of religious communities.

The history of the Ottoman millet system remains disputed in Ottoman historiography, with some scholars arguing that the millet system was essentially constructed through European intervention; that there was no history of systematic, government-imposed religious legal differentiation prior to the late eighteenth century; and that the word "millet" itself had a very different meaning in an earlier Ottoman context.[9] At any rate, it is certain that the economic and cultural divides associated with the millet system were substantially deepened during the nineteenth century as a result of European involvement with Christian communities in the Arab provinces of the Ottoman Empire. This was particularly true in Palestine, which increasingly became a place of interest to European Christians with the nineteenth-century rise of biblical archaeology and historical geography.

Worried about the fate of its extensive economic interests in the Ottoman regions in the event of Ottoman imperial failure, the British government began as early as the 1830s to press for political reforms from the Ottomans. Among these demands were requests to lift the legal restrictions on Ottoman Christian and Jewish subjects that, the British claimed, were tantamount to religious persecution. British pressure for Ottoman reform was intended to lengthen the life of what the European powers habitually referred to as "the sick man of Europe" and thereby postpone a potential intra-European conflict over the remains of the Ottoman Empire. It also represented an effort to increase British influence in the region; the rival powers of France and Russia were claiming jurisdiction over, respectively, Catholic and Greek Orthodox subjects of the sultan in a similar play for influence. Concern over the rights of the Christian and Jewish minorities in the Ottoman Empire was likewise a pretext that played well to domestic audiences in Europe and particularly in Britain, where evangelical movements were heightening interest in the plight of Christian populations under "heathen" domination.[10]

These pressures from Europe as well as ongoing worries about Ottoman military, political, and economic decline vis-à-vis the West led to substantial changes in the Ottoman millet system in the nineteenth century during the period of empire-wide reforms and reorganization from 1839 to 1876 known as the tanzimat. The reforms lifted many of the restrictions on non-Muslim communities and redefined the meaning and structures of the millet system with the intention of expanding the rights of the non-Muslim communities and their participation in the state. Such reforms were driven by Ottoman concern about the empire's declining place in the international order and by the specifics of European demands regarding religious freedoms but also—perhaps more centrally—by the nineteenth-century tendency on the part of the Balkan Christian churches, particularly in Serbia and Albania, to cast themselves as venues for various kinds of anti-Ottoman nationalisms.[11]

In the Arab provinces, many Christians and Muslims alike perceived the reforms as a threat to the established order. The reforms were radically destabilizing and contributed to a wave of intercommunal violence in the Arab provinces in the mid-nineteenth century—just as Britain, France, and Russia were stepping up their claims to be protecting the various Christian subjects of the sultan in the Holy Land. By the time the British came into possession of the mandate, then, the millet system had been in transition for some time, and Arab Christian communities in Palestine had been involved in communal renegotiations of their status with both the Ottoman government and their various European "protectors" for more than a half-century.

PRESERVING THE MILLET SYSTEM: INDIA, PALESTINE, AND THE IMPERIAL MODEL OF THE "STATUS QUO"

The new British administration in Palestine made an early decision to maintain the millet system it had already helped to mold, legally enshrining religious difference through the establishment of communal legislative and judicial structures. This approach was consistent with the broader imperial strategy of preserving a presumed religious, legal, and political "status quo" to preempt comment, complaint, or rebellion from the newly colonized peoples.[12] In Palestine—as in colonial India, Egypt, and Africa—the implementation of this policy, far from preserving unaltered precolonial legal and political structures, actually involved the imperial invention of "native" tradition and the construction of "customary" ethnic, cultural, and especially religious categorizations.

Judicial structures offered the first opportunity for the colonial state to enshrine religious affiliation as a legal status. In India the British publicly justified their decision to maintain communal courts as a continuation of the policies of the previous rulers. British legal expert Sir George Rankin wrote in 1939 that the Mughal administration from which the British took over, "though exceedingly corrupt and inefficient, had the merit of leaving questions between Hindus to be decided according to their own Shastras," and he noted that Muslim criminal courts continued their operations until 1790.[13] Warren Hastings, the first governor general of India, ordered in 1772 that the religious laws of Muslims and Hindus continue to be applied to each group in matters of personal law.[14] Robert Travers describes Hastings' approach as partially "animated by a Montesquieuan sense of legal geography, in which different 'esprits des lois' attached to different people."[15] But it was also driven by pressing political concerns, as can be seen in a letter from Sir William Jones to the governor general in 1788:

> Nothing could . . . be wiser than by a legislative Act, to assure the Hindu and Mussulman subjects of Great Britain that the private laws, which they severally hold sacred, and violation of which they would have thought the most grievous oppression, should not be suppressed by a new system, of which they could have no knowledge, and which they must have considered as imposed on them by a spirit of rigour and intolerance.[16]

In reality, then, the British colonial state continually altered and modified interpretations of Muslim and Hindu communal law in India to suit its own demands; the very idea of a pre-existing Mughal constitution was primarily a product of the East India Company's attempt to tease order from what it viewed as the legal chaos of India.[17]

This paradigm of claiming imperial adherence to previously existing communal religious law for the sake of the stability of the colonial state provided the basis for the British approach to the Ottoman millet system in Palestine. The first high commissioner of Palestine, Sir Herbert Samuel, demonstrated his official commitment to this principle in his report to London on the administration from 1920 to 1925, in which he noted that "it has been the policy of the government not to change laws which closely touched the lives of the people and to which they were accustomed, except in cases of clear necessity."[18] His attorney general Norman Bentwich repeated this idea again and again in his writings about British legislation in Palestine: "The Ottoman Law, indeed, has remained the basis of the legal system of Palestine . . . In accordance with the established traditions of British Administration, the law and custom of the country have not been violently disturbed."[19] They viewed the millet system, like India's communal courts, as a potentially stabilizing element in the upheaval of colonial occupation.

The British presented their decision to maintain the millet system as a necessary concession to the political immaturity of the Palestinian Arabs. In contrast to the occupation of eighteenth-century India, the British took over their Middle Eastern mandates at a time of unprecedented international criticism of empire, when a Wilsonian rhetoric of self-determination and national rights had begun to dominate international diplomacy.[20] British officials in the Middle East were keenly aware of the shift. Mark Sykes, the co-author of the infamous Sykes-Picot Agreement of 1916 (a backstage treaty that divided the Middle East between Britain and France) wrote during the 1919 peace conference, "Imperialism, annexation, military triumph, prestige, White man's burdens, have been expunged from the popular political vocabulary, consequently Protectorates, spheres of interest or influence, annexations, bases etc., have to be consigned to the Diplomatic lumber-room."[21] Responding to this changed climate, the British developed a rationale for their "status quo" policy in the mandate states of Palestine and Iraq, claiming that it was intended to ease the difficult transition to self-determination and democracy.[22] The Palestinian Arabs, as yet "unready" for the duties and responsibilities of Western-style secular citizenship, would be better off under a "traditional" system of communal administration and personal law governed by religious texts.

The British further hoped that the maintenance of the millet system in Palestine would forestall protest from members of Christian communities in England and Europe who had committed considerable energy and resources to defending and promoting the political position of the Christian communities of the Ottoman Empire and especially of Palestine during the last century of Ottoman rule.[23] These groups were anxious to preserve the rights of foreign residents of Palestine (particularly those associated with mission institutions) gained through the "capitulations" of the Ottoman period.[24] Under the terms of the capitulations, foreign residents of Palestine were subject to consular courts, so that in matters of personal status they did not come under the jurisdiction of the Ottoman judiciary.[25] This precedent was important for the British, who were continually engaged in a refusal to allow French and Italian Catholic bodies, including the Vatican, to intervene in Palestine on behalf of their mission institutions or their citizens engaged in work in the Holy Land. The new British mandate government hoped that maintaining these Ottoman agreements regarding the status of foreigners would reduce friction with other European nations.

RECONCEPTUALIZING OTTOMAN LAW:
HERBERT SAMUEL AND NORMAN BENTWICH

Having decided to recognize and maintain the millet system as part of the imperial "status quo," the mandate government now turned its attention to determining the nature of the Ottoman millet system and deciding the specifics of the new British version. The officials initially responsible for rethinking the millet system—Sir Herbert Samuel, the first high commissioner, and Norman Bentwich, the first attorney general—constructed a concept of the previously existing legal and political systems that relied much more heavily on Orientalist conceptions of Ottoman despotism and Islamic fanaticism than on empirical knowledge of the conditions of the Ottoman state.[26] On one hand, they argued that the Ottoman legal code was backward, corrupt, despotic, and a major cause of the region's economic ills, concluding that Britain bore responsibility for bringing progress and modernity to Palestine's legal structures. On the other hand, they believed that Ottoman code had been corrupted by European influences and needed to be retraditionalized to reflect a pre-European, fundamentally Islamic past. Both these ideas contributed to Samuel's and Bentwich's decision not just to preserve the millet system but to extend it.

In some ways, Bentwich's and Samuel's backgrounds were rather similar. Samuel, born in Liverpool, had served in Parliament and in Asquith's cabinet, eventually becoming home secretary. Although he renounced organized religion while a student at Oxford, he remained in some respects a practicing Jew and was interested in the "Jewish question," participating in the discussions surrounding the Balfour Declaration in 1917.[27] Bentwich grew up in London in a wealthy Anglo-Jewish family interested in Palestine; their country estate outside London was named Carmel Court.[28] His sister Nina and her husband settled in Palestine in 1913, joining a Romanian Jewish colony on Mount Carmel. From 1912 to 1915 Bentwich served in the Ministry of Justice in Cairo, where he was also a professor in the Egyptian government law school, and he became a major in charge of transport during World War I. In 1918 he became the legal adviser to the British military government in Palestine and was officially appointed attorney general in 1922. In addition to taking charge of the legal system, he enshrined his changes and innovations by setting up a law school (known as "Law Classes") in Jerusalem to train a class of Anglo-Palestinian attorneys who would act as intermediaries between the British government and the Palestinian Arab and Jewish populations with regard to legal issues. He handpicked the English comparative law expert Frederic Goadby, who had taught at Leeds University in England and the government law school in Cairo, to direct the Jerusalem school and to write a textbook on Palestinian law.[29] Bentwich and Samuel represented schools of imperial thought developed in the metropole in the context of a domestic conversation about Zionism.

Neither of these men nor any of their staff was able to acquire more than the most rudimentary sense of how Ottoman law had functioned before 1917. Since there was no definitive version of the Ottoman land codes in English (or, for that matter, Arabic or Hebrew), British mandate officials worked from a French translation made in 1905 that was characterized as "not guaranteed."[30] Many Ottoman tracts were never translated at all or were translated only on a contract basis when a relevant case came up in the courts.[31] The Palestine mandate government had few legal experts; most staff members of the legal department were initially recruited from the pool of soldiers who happened to be in Jerusalem under Allenby's command after the British takeover. Bentwich himself had little of the requisite experience for a colonial attorney general and was appointed to the post based primarily on his presence in Palestine as part of the Egyptian Expeditionary Force's camel transport corps as well as his few years of legal work in Cairo before and during the war.[32]

Bentwich's and Samuel's sense that Palestine needed major legal reforms and that the Ottoman legal system was desperately inadequate, then, stemmed not from systematic study of the Ottoman code but from widespread Orientalist thought about the corruption, despotism, and oppressive nature of Ottoman rule. In 1918 the American legal scholar Philip Marshall Brown described this view in vivid terms, saying, "No longer will the people be in the attitude of humble suppliants for justice from distant officials more concerned with 'backsheesh' than with mercy. . . . British officials of special ability will watch vigilantly that the old wrongs and abuses shall not return, and that public law and order shall be vindicated."[33] Samuel thought that the Ottomans had fostered poverty and backwardness in Palestine; he described the Ottoman regime as having promulgated "primitive systems of land tenure and of taxation [that] discouraged good agriculture." (This referred to the traditional system of *musha'*, the prevailing pattern of communal land ownership in Palestine, which British officials viewed as an impediment to the modernization of agricultural techniques.)[34] In Samuel's view, the British had an obligation to rescue Palestine from its long economic and political oppression and bring it into a new era of prosperity. "We had to build, from the very beginning," he wrote, "a modern state."[35] Bentwich likewise criticized Ottoman law as "unscientific" and as "curious and medieval."[36]

But Bentwich simultaneously held the seemingly contradictory idea that some of the Ottoman code had been "corrupted" by French influence during the nineteenth century and needed to be purged of unsuitable European interpolations. In an article on legislative reforms in the early years of the mandate he noted that Ottoman law had "to a certain extent the form of modern scientific legislation" and that the codes of commercial, criminal, and maritime law had been "borrowed from France with uncritical admiration . . . [They] followed, all too closely, the Napoleonic archetypes."[37] These "Gallic" influences in the civil code were, Bentwich believed, "complicated and elaborate, and unsuited to the conditions of an Oriental country."[38] Some of the legal structures the British were inheriting would therefore require a kind of retraditionalizing, particularly along Muslim religious lines.

This idea overlapped with Samuel's romantic notions about the biblical "Holy Land" and his desire to return Palestine to a prelapsarian state. One of Samuel's first ordinances, for instance, banned outdoor advertisements throughout the country, a beautifying project he considered especially important in a region rich in historically significant sites.[39] He founded a Department of Antiquities to be "active in revealing or preserving the precious relics of earlier epochs," and he launched a campaign to bring back ancient names that had been "corrupted."[40] The desire to rework Ottoman law to reflect a romanticized British view of a pre-Ottoman (and even pre-Roman) Palestine constituted a major part of Samuel's reaction to the Ottoman legacy, although it contradicted his simultaneous desire for Palestine's modernization and development.

Applying these contradictory ideas to the millet system, Samuel and Bentwich decided to maintain the legal separation of religious communities— a decision that had the added benefit of making the political incorporation of the new European Zionist communities much easier.[41] But, they decided, the system also had to be "modernized" to guarantee greater autonomy for religious minorities and their freedom from Muslim domination.[42] Samuel would later describe this approach to the House of Lords as "continuing and developing" the millet system:

> The Turks, who with centuries of experience had developed a certain amount of wisdom in these matters . . . dealt with communities as such under the system known as millets . . . Consequently I continued and developed it, and I made it my duty to organise and legalise these communal entities . . . Education, religious endowments, marriage laws and other matters were dealt with, not in geographical areas, but by communities. The political system of that country should, in my judgment, be based mainly on these lines.[43]

This approach effectively defined all difference in Palestine as religious rather than political, positioning the mandate government as an impartial mediator among fundamentally divided religious communities. Samuel set out this goal in a report on his administration, saying Jerusalem

> has been notorious among the nations for the bitterness, and sometimes the violence, of its ecclesiastical disputes, creed contending against creed, and sect against sect . . . The present age is weary of such contention. So far as the Government of Palestine can have influence over these matters, it has steadily discountenanced all such disputes; it has endeavoured to reduce trifles to their true proportions; it has taken every opportunity to encourage union and harmonious co-operation.[44]

By maintaining the millet system, Samuel and Bentwich claimed continuity with Ottoman tradition; by extending it, they defined dissent in Palestine as merely an expression of primitive religious squabbles and positioned themselves and the mandate government as a modern institution above the medieval fray.

Their approach was by no means systematic. Despite Bentwich's claims of scientific precision and logic, the application of a wide variety of legal principles to the system during the first years of the mandate resulted in a chaotic "hodge-podge of rules and regulations."[45] The sheer volume of legislation passed by the mandate government multiplied the confusion. By the end of the 1920s, nearly as much legislation was being enacted annually in Palestine as in the whole of Britain; more than 380 ordinances in total were passed between 1920 and 1930, not including regulations and notices.[46] Some legal changes were codified in the Palestine Order-in-Council of 1922; many others, as in India, were promulgated on an ad hoc basis through the judgments of courts.[47] By 1930 one colonial official described mandate land law as "an unintelligible compost of the original Ottoman laws, provisional laws, judgments of various tribunals, Sultanic firmans, administrative orders having the force of law overlaid by a further amalgam of post-war Proclamations, Public Orders, Orders-in-Council, judgements [sic] of various civil and religious courts, Ordinance, Amending Ordinances, and Orders and Regulations under these."[48]

Bentwich's and Samuel's contradictory ideas about the millet system and Ottoman law, then, led to a confused mass of edicts and orders that frequently conflicted with one another. But however incoherently arrived at and applied, their deployment of a "status quo" policy with regard to the millet system and their expansion of the political meaning of communalism would permanently change the nature of religious identity in Arab Palestine.

ALTERNATIVE IMPERIAL STRATEGIES:
THE VIEW FROM THE PERIPHERY

Some officials in the British administration in Palestine openly reviled this approach to the reform of Ottoman law. Among the most vocal critics of Bentwich's actions was Edward Keith-Roach, who became Palestine's Public Custodian of Enemy Property in 1919 and went on to serve as assistant district commissioner in Haifa and district commissioner in Jerusalem. He previously worked for three years in India as an employee of the Mercantile Bank of India and served as a transport officer in Egypt during the war.[49] His views on the legal reforms of the millet system demonstrated an alternative British sensibility honed in Egypt and shared by other British officials in Palestine, like Ronald Storrs and Harry Charles Luke, whose concepts of governing the Arab Middle East arose out of an imperial philosophy developed in the colonies rather than the metropole.[50] During the 1920s Keith-Roach and his compatriots became increasingly opposed to Bentwich's concept of retraditionalizing Palestinian law and his romantic (and, Keith-Roach and others thought, pro-Zionist) approach to the creation and running of Palestinian legal institutions.

In Keith-Roach's memoirs he limited his recollection of Bentwich to a note that the attorney general's "qualifications for the post were somewhat shaky because some years before he had written a book in favour of Zionism."[51] But during the early years of the mandate, Keith-Roach was one of the most vocal critics of Bentwich's policies, which he regarded as muddled, misguided, and incompetent. Keith-Roach and a number of other like-minded colonial administrators viewed Bentwich's reforms as going far beyond his purview; they wanted an attorney general who would impose an English order on the legislative structures of the mandate state without attempting to introduce what they viewed as additional complications by taking into account previously existing systems and codes. Ironically, given Bentwich's determination to reverse the French influence on Ottoman legislation, Keith-Roach associated him with an undesirably French philosophy of law. "Mr. Bentwich views the law," he wrote, "from a French standpoint . . . the very school of law which he made his special study is international law and he is singularly unsuitable for the position that he holds."[52] This point of view met with sympathy in the Colonial Office, whose main legal adviser backed up Keith-Roach's objections and laid out an alternative path for legal reform in Palestine: "[Bentwich's] tastes lie in the direction of foreign rather than English jurisprudence. No one suggests for a moment that English Law should be forced wholesale upon Palestine, but it is desirable that Palestine legislation should proceed in form, etc., if not always in substance, on English lines and that its general tendencies should be British rather than foreign."[53] Here was an imperial legal approach that differed substantially from the India-derived "status quo" model favored by Bentwich and Samuel.

The retraditionalization of Palestinian law was not the only issue between the attorney general and his critics. Keith-Roach, Storrs, and a number of Bentwich's other critics opposed Bentwich's pro-Zionist stance and wanted him removed for his political views as much as for his universally acknowledged legal incompetence. Storrs' comments on Bentwich expressed a common sentiment: "I . . . cherished an admiring friendship for an Israelite who, with all his talents, was indeed without guile. Unfortunately Bentwich was not only the son of an original *Hoven Tsyion* but the author of a book on Zionism which, though written before, came out after his appointment . . . It is not often that too great love of a country proves a bar from dedicating to it the maturity of one's experience and qualifications, but such was the pathetic fate of Bentwich."[54] The anti-Zionist (and frequently anti-Semitic) assistant civil secretary E. T. Richmond, later director of antiquities in Palestine, echoed this sentiment in a letter to Samuel: "No opinion emanating from the Legal Secretary or his entourage or from any one dependent in any degree on the favour of his Department will at the present time be regarded as other than suspicious by a very large majority."[55] In the Palestinian context, the split between "field" colonial officials and those whose careers were based in Britain quite often manifested itself, among other things, as an anti- versus pro-Zionist divide.

With regard to the millet system, however, these two camps occupied more or less the same philosophical position, viewing Palestine as fundamentally divided by religion. Keith-Roach commented that Palestine suffered from a form of "nationalism" based on religion.[56] Harry Charles Luke concurred, writing, "Whether Jerusalem be regarded as indeed a city of living faith or, in the words of a well known modern writer, as merely the swarming of sects about the corpse of religion, each member of a particular community regards it as his duty, perhaps not unnaturally, to bear witness for that community with all his might. Unfortunately, his conception of his role is determined by the secular tradition of the place, a tradition of incessant struggle on the part of each sect or religious body to maintain its footing against its rivals."[57] Storrs, too, agreed with this assessment, adding that "Moslems are far more orthodox here than in Egypt—so is everyone, worse luck."[58] These essentialist understandings of religious identity—shared by British officials as different as Keith-Roach, Luke, Bentwich, Storrs, and Samuel—represented the philosophical underpinnings of the British decision to maintain and indeed strengthen the millet system, and they served to justify the mandate government's promotion of religious identity as a long-standing and inevitable mode of legal organization in Palestine.

THE EMPIRE, WORLD ISLAM, AND THE NEW MUSLIM MILLET

The most important and radical step in the extension of the millet system and the communalization of Palestinian political life was the redefinition of the Muslim community as a millet. For Palestinian Muslims, Samuel's government argued, the simple continuation of the millet system under British rule posed problems because the Muslim community had never had independent religious structures; its Islamic courts and institutions had been part of the central Ottoman authority. Under the mandate, what had once represented privilege became a disadvantage, since Muslim institutions incorporated into the central authority were now overseen by British rulers while separate Christian institutions remained under the control of Arabs.[59] Samuel therefore decided to extend the millet system to the Muslim community, creating Muslim religious courts and institutions and re-imagining the Muslim population as the largest and most influential millet in Palestine.[60]

This decision was supposed to appease the Palestinian Muslim community, whom the British feared for their supposed influence on the Muslim population of Britain's most valuable colony, India; but it had other justifications as well. The redefinition of the Muslim community as Palestine's largest millet defined Muslim law as separate from British civil law and divided the Muslim from the non-Muslim communities in Palestine. More crucially, it went some way toward circumscribing Palestinian Arab autonomy by defining it as communally organized, driven by textual religious tradition rather than Western legal models, and limited to matters of personal status and family law. The millet system was now being imagined as a mode of colonial control in both the international and the domestic realms.

The British made the decision to redefine the Palestinian Muslim community as a millet in the context of well-established assumptions on the part of the Colonial Office and the Foreign Office about the international connections of the Muslim communities in Palestine.[61] In creating a Muslim millet, the Colonial Office assumed that it was placating international Muslim sentiment and thereby defusing potentially dangerous Muslim opposition that could threaten British holdings in India.[62]

There were, in fact, a few instances of anticolonial cooperation between Palestinian and Indian Muslims. In 1931 the presence of the Indian Muslim political activist and thinker Muhammad Iqbal in Palestine excited nervous comment among the British.[63] In 1933 the Palestinian nationalist leader Hajj Amin al-Husayni made a fund-raising trip to India—which was, however, not particularly successful.[64] At the Arab Parliamentary Conference in Cairo in 1938, an Indian delegation made a number of speeches expressing solidarity with Palestinian Muslims, including one by ʿAbd al-Rahman al-Siddiqi stating that "the Lesson of this Congress should be that Muslim ought to treat Muslim questions from a Muslim point of view without distinction of nationality."[65] The delegates made statements to the effect that if Britain refused the demands of the congress with regard to Palestine, Indian Muslims would "sanction and put into effect such anti-British measures as the boycotting of English goods and non-cooperation in general with Great Britain," including a campaign against enlistment in the Indian Army.[66] These examples of contact and cooperation, while rare, served to fuel British fear about international Muslim challenges to their rule in India.[67]

The Colonial Office and the India Office viewed the new Muslim millet in Palestine as in some ways representative of, or at least closely connected with, worldwide Islam. The British created the Palestinian Muslim millet to appease what they assumed was a strong religious feeling among Palestinian Muslims, who through their international connections could pose a threat to Britain's colonial holdings in such far-flung places as Egypt, Malaysia, and, above all, India. Broad imperial considerations dictated a policy of conciliation toward a British concept of worldwide Islam.

THE INVENTION OF MUSLIM TRADITION: COMMUNAL COURTS, THE GRAND MUFTI, AND THE SUPREME MUSLIM COUNCIL

The most immediate practical ramifications of this decision to reinvent the Muslim community as a millet had to do with the Palestinian judicial system.[68] State courts dealing with matters of personal status now became Muslim courts, basing their judgments on shariʿa law and exercising jurisdiction only over Muslim citizens. (Previously, although the ecclesiastical courts had been allowed jurisdiction over members of non-Muslim communities under the millet system, there had been numerous cases in which non-Muslims were subject to the state courts and Muslim "common law.")[69] The new Muslim courts maintained absolute jurisdiction over all matters of personal status, in opposition to Christian and Jewish courts where matters of personal status other than those specifically defined as falling within their purview (marriage, divorce, alimony, and wills) could only be decided with the consent of all parties involved.[70] Muslim courts, unlike their Christian and

Jewish counterparts, were still under government supervision. They used the newly defined "Mohammedan Law of Procedure," published in 1919, which represented a modified version of Ottoman procedure. A further ordinance published later that same year provided that the courts should use the Ottoman family law as the basis for their decisions, disregarding any aspects designed for non-Muslim communities.[71]

Along with changes to the court system, the British began to create specifically communal institutions to represent Palestinian Arab Muslims to the mandate government. The foundation of the Supreme Muslim Council and the appointment of Hajj Amin al-Husayni as its head represented Samuel's attempt to formulate a communal model of representation for Palestine that would allow for the easy inclusion of the European Jewish presence and would also—more crucially—defuse nationalist tensions by confining political action to the communal sphere.[72]

The power of the mufti of Jerusalem (the Islamic cleric charged with oversight of Jerusalem's Muslim holy sites) was limited during the Ottoman period; it increased exponentially when the British discovered an ally and assistant in Kamil al-Husayni, who had served as mufti since 1908. The mandate government bestowed on him the new title of Grand Mufti (*al-mufti al-akbar*) as well as viewing him as a kind of official "representative of Islam in Palestine."[73] When Kamil al-Husayni died, the Husayni family spearheaded a campaign for his half-brother Hajj Amin al-Husayni to replace him; they were eventually successful, even though he came in fourth in the elections held to choose a new mufti. By this stage, the British had come to regard al-Husayni, like his predecessor, as representing all Muslim interests in Palestine and to think of him as a potential collaborator.

Complaints about a non-Muslim government heading Muslim awqaf and shari'a courts flooded the mandate government after Samuel took office. In August 1921 a Muslim conference was held at which leaders demanded complete autonomy for Muslim religious institutions. These kinds of complaints were only a part of the torrent of demands and protests pouring in to the mandate government from Palestinian Arabs, and they must be viewed as part of a broader protest against British mandate rule and the policy of the Jewish National Home. Nevertheless, as Uri Kupferschmidt points out, the Muslim community's desire to "administer its Shari'a and waqf [singular of awqaf] affairs were certainly a genuine element."[74]

Samuel saw this element as an opportunity to channel Muslim political participation into limited communal outlets. To this end, he declared that the government wanted to "establish a body representing the country's Muslims in order both to assure them complete control over their religious endowments and that the Muslim community might feel that the Shari'a courts were being supervised by people of its own choice. The Government does not wish to take the place of the Sheikh ul-Islam."[75] He created the Supreme Muslim Council in December 1921.

Samuel's description of the council suggests that the British were merely maintaining the Ottoman system without interfering in Muslim affairs. Elections for the SMC followed the pattern of Ottoman council elections, reinforcing the idea that the SMC represented nothing more than a continuation of the Ottoman system.[76] This kind of language situated the idea of a Muslim council within a colonial narrative of a long and storied history of sensitivity to Muslim religious autonomy.

In reality, the SMC represented a type of institution wholly new to Palestine. Samuel described British policy regarding the SMC and its powers as "based on the Turkish precedent except for the fact that we have been far more generous."[77] Essentially, the SMC took over the authority previously vested in both the Seyhulislam (the chief religious post within the Ottoman government) and the Ministry of Justice in Istanbul, but the British did not adopt the former Ottoman institutional controls of these institutions. Consequently, the SMC operated much further outside the government than had either of its Ottoman predecessors.[78] The SMC had substantial autonomy in running courts and awqaf, even while the salaries of all its officials, as well as the *qadis* (judges) it appointed, were paid by the government. This was part of what Kupferschmidt calls an "ingenious . . . legal fiction" that allowed the SMC to operate as a government body in terms of its administration of the shari'a courts but as a private organization in all waqf affairs. An order in 1921 laid out this system: "The Rais el Ulema and members of the Council shall receive salaries from the Government in consideration of their services in connection with the affairs of Sharia Courts and they shall also receive an allowance from Wakf Funds for their work in other Moslem affairs."[79]

Samuel himself admitted that the workings of the SMC represented a departure from the previous system, noting that there was no Ottoman precedent for the powers of appointing and dismissing judges of religious courts to be placed in the hands of a Muslim council; but he decided that "the circumstance in Palestine and the natural desire of the Moslem Community to exercise autonomy in their religious affairs appear to justify this new departure."[80] Under the scheme, the power of the local communities, the district council, and the shari'a courts, all of which had enjoyed substantial autonomy under the Ottomans, declined substantially.[81] Samuel placed Hajj Amin al-Husayni in the presidency of the SMC, an appointment that meant that al-Husayni became at once *ra'is al-'ulama* (head of the *'ulama*, the class of clerical scholars) and al-mufti al-akbar, Grand Mufti.[82] Samuel also made the decision not to require periodic reelections for the presidency, permitting al-Husayni and his supporters to make the claim that the position was a life-time appointment.

Not all British officials supported this approach. Harry Charles Luke, now the assistant governor of Jerusalem, was astonished at the range of the SMC's autonomy, saying at one point that "the constitution and these regulations involved a delegation to the Supreme Muslim Council of jurisdiction so extensive and powers so wide as to be to some extent almost an abdication by the Administration of Palestine of responsibilities normally incumbent upon a Government."[83] By 1934 even Bentwich was noting that the system was under attack not just from British officials but also from the Muslim community for "the financial responsibility of the Government and judicial irresponsibility of the Council" and that it was known generally in Palestine that "the courts and judicial patronage are used for political purposes, and that the religious judges do not enjoy true judicial independence."[84]

The SMC owed its existence in great part to Samuel's commitment to Muslim pacification on the communalizing Indian model. Samuel—and the British administration more generally—believed that Muslim loyalties were to their coreligionists above all and that therefore Muslims were best dealt with on a communal level by offering freedom of worship and control of Muslim religious institutions. In the British interpretation, Muslim communal loyalties outshone political, economic, or social interests and crossed regional and economic lines, and the support of Muslims around the world was essential to successful rule in India as well as the Middle East.

Samuel also conceived of the Supreme Muslim Council as a way to deflect nationalist energy into a limited, communally based institution. He explicitly expressed this notion in correspondence with then-foreign secretary and former viceroy of India George Curzon in 1920, during the early stages of negotiation for a Muslim representative council. "The establishment of an elected Council of four concerned with purely religious matters," he wrote, "will, I think, meet the desire of the Moslem population for some representative body, and may serve to check any agitation for political autonomy."[85] In the years following the formation of the SMC, the policy was deemed a successful one. Sir John Shuckburgh, the assistant undersecretary of state, wrote in 1926, "The institution of a Supreme Muslim Council has, on the whole, been one of our most successful moves in Palestine. It practically gave the Mohammedans self-government in regard to Moslem affairs."[86] Samuel and his supporters in the Colonial Office envisioned the SMC as channeling Palestinian Muslim political energies into communal rather than nationalist expressions.

A Muslim body designated with the oversight of religious affairs seemed the ideal way to appease nationalist opinion while undermining any moves toward a nationalist Arab forum that might challenge the political basis of the mandate itself. Consequently, the question of whether the SMC constituted a government arm was deliberately left unanswered when the council was founded. As late as 1935, British officials were still debating this point; a government advocate writing to the attorney general noted, "In my view the Supreme Moslem Council in its capacity as controller and administrator of the Sharia Courts is (the same as those courts) a government department and that in every other respect it is a private body." On the position of the muftis, he wrote, "It would appear to be prima facie evidence that if someone receives a salary from Government, he is a government official; but against that the fact that his appointment and control is not in the hands of Government, makes his position quite anomalous."[87] In the early days of the SMC, this kind of ambiguity was convenient; the SMC could be represented as an independent body representing Arab public opinion, or it could be viewed as a part of the mandate state apparatus.[88]

In British parlance, the Supreme Muslim Council was necessary not as a political outlet for the Arabs but to correct the religious problem that a Christian power was now in charge of traditionally Muslim institutions. Its autonomy, though very broad in the administration of the shari'a courts and awqaf, did not extend to representing the Arab community on issues relating to the political legitimacy of the mandate or the governmental structures introduced by the British. The British intended the council to serve as an example of progress toward eventual Palestinian self-determination without actually offering the members of the Palestinian Muslim community any secular political power. They also hoped it would function as a Muslim equivalent to the Jewish Agency, without having to be consulted on issues that did not relate to the religious functioning of the community. In creating the SMC, Samuel deliberately reified communal identities as a central aspect of politics in Palestine.

UNINTENDED CONSEQUENCES: COMMUNALISM, THE SMC, AND THE RISE OF ISLAMIC POLITICAL NATIONALISM

Almost immediately, Palestinian Arab leaders began to appropriate these new forms of communal organization for their own political ends in ways unanticipated by the British administration. After the founding of the SMC, Hajj Amin al-Husayni and his Muslim supporters quickly left behind the secularizing nationalist discourse, in which Arab Christians had participated with enthusiasm, in favor of an Islamist political rhetoric.[89] Al-Husayni skillfully played on British fears of international Islamic uprisings and emphasized his own religious leadership to British officials. At the same time, he a role and rhetoric for the SMC that had political implications far beyond what the British had imagined would be the scope of a communally based organization.[90]

Hajj Amin al-Husayni belonged to a wealthy landowning family, a number of whose members had served as muftis and mayors in Jerusalem; he had an early religious education and attended al-Azhar University in Cairo (although he did not finish his degree) before serving as an officer in the Ottoman army during World War I.[91] This particular family background and religious education led him to view religious and political power as essentially interconnected. Moreover, he was well aware that his power depended on British support and his claim to power rested largely on the British perception that he represented a traditional kind of Islamic authority recognized by Palestinian Muslims.

The new organization of the SMC excluded Christians formerly at the center of nationalist politics (like Najib Nassar, Ya'qub Farraj, the 'Isa cousins, and 'Isa Bandak) who had previously participated with enthusiasm in the multireligious discourse of various nationalist organizations. Reactions against the transition from Ottoman to British overlordship and growing opposition to the increasing Jewish presence in Palestine also helped to fuel an upsurge in Islamic religious feeling and expression during the first years of the mandate, leading eventually to the Wailing Wall riots of 1929.[92] This combination of circumstances allowed for the emergence of a modern Islamic political rhetoric and symbolism under al-Husayni and the newly formed Supreme Muslim Council, which differed substantially from the much more secular nationalist expressions (promoted primarily by now-excluded Christians) predominant during the first few years of the mandate.

Two of al-Husayni's major efforts in the first decade of his tenure as mufti demonstrated his conception of himself as a political figure within Palestine but also as a spokesman for Palestine within world Islam. His campaign to emphasize and publicize the celebration of the Muslim festival of Nebi Musa in Jerusalem and attract an international Muslim audience for its celebration was intended to affirm his own status as a religious leader and reposition Jerusalem as a city of central importance to global Islam.[93] Similarly, al-Husayni's organization of an international Islamic Congress in Jerusalem in 1931 served to reinforce his standing as a religious as well as a political leader and to remind the British of the potential strength of world Islam. The Colonial Office's decision to allow al-Husayni to hold the congress, based on the British supersensitivity to international Muslim opinion, showed the shrewdness of al-Husayni's approach. At the same time, it confirmed the ways in which the British sectarian approach was meant to undermine the expression of a broader Palestinian nationalism; al-Husayni had to agree that the congress would not become a vehicle for the expression of anti-British feeling and its delegates would not be permitted to mount a claim to total Palestinian Arab independence.[94]

The SMC and the broader political faction headed by the Husayni family developed an Islamic rhetoric that reinforced its position as both a religious and a political body.[95] By 1935 this model was fully operational; in a meeting of al-Husayni's political faction (known as the *majlisi*, in reference to Hajj Amin's position at the head of the *majlis*, the council), the resolutions included an appeal to Muslim leaders and chiefs throughout the Arab world to assist with the Palestinian cause and to hold a religious conference each year or when necessary, as well as political resolutions to campaign and use boycotts against land sales and immigration.[96]

During the 1920s and 1930s, Islamic language gradually replaced secular nationalist rhetoric in the opposition faction as well. The opposition party (*al-mu'arida*), led by the Nashashibi family under the leadership of the mayor of Jerusalem, Raghib al-Nashashibi, held its own rival Islamic congress in December 1931; it also founded a political organization, intended to correspond to the majlisi's Islamic Congress, called Hizb al-umma al-islamiyya (Party of the Islamic Nation).[97] When the opposition congress met, it focused on protesting the corruption and financial irresponsibility of the SMC and requested that the Department of Justice take over the operation of the SMC and the appointment of qadis to the shari'a courts. The opposition's attacks on the SMC and Hajj Amin al-Husayni also took the form of accusing him of neglecting Islamic holy sites; one accusation, that the SMC had desecrated a Muslim cemetery in Jerusalem by constructing a quarry over it while building the Palace Hotel, was widely repeated and seems to have been particularly effective at undermining al-Husayni's authority.[98] These examples of Islamic political rhetoric beginning to dominate an organization that still included many influential Christians demonstrates that the British-encouraged communal organization of the SMC began quickly to set the tone for nationalist political discussion among Palestinians, resulting in the almost total dominance of religious and sectarian language over the earlier explicitly multi-religious nationalist discourse by the mid-1930s.

A few Palestinian Arabs—most notably Hamdi al-Husayni, editor of *al-Sirat al-mustaqim* newspaper and an activist within the nationalist, pan-Arab Istiqlal (Independence) party—began in the early 1930s to challenge this sectarian model as a construct of the British and a strategy for continued imperial dominance. The Istiqlal party, founded by a group of disaffected former majlisi members, was based on the principles of pan-Arabism, internationalism, and nationalism and was heavily influenced by the examples of

Gandhi in India and Saʿd Zaghlul in Egypt. Hamdi al-Husayni challenged both Hajj Amin and Jamal al-Husayni, suggesting that they were mere collaborators with the British government and that in focusing on local opposition politics and on sectarian divides they were preventing the emergence of a genuine Palestinian nationalism and were promoting continued British imperial power.[99] Hamdi al-Husayni and some of the other leading Istiqlalists began in the early 1930s to view British tactics in Palestine and in India as related and to advocate secular pan-Arabism as a viable alternative to British-constructed sectarian political identifications in Palestine. But as nationalist feeling grew, both the majlisi faction (leading the SMC) and the Nashashibi-led opposition gradually merged nationalist and sectarian rhetoric in their public appeals.

The British had failed to anticipate the gradual incorporation of nationalist fervor into al-Husayni's approach and the diminishment and eventual abandonment of his collaboration with the mandate government.[100] Now they began to deny that the SMC had any political significance or capability. In 1936 the authors of the annual report on Palestine and Transjordan attempted to absolve the British of responsibility for the SMC's actions: "It is not a political body, but an administrative body dealing with Moslem religious affairs. Insofar as it is representative, it is representative of the Moslems of Palestine in their religious aspect."[101] The British had wanted to placate Muslim Arab feeling in Palestine by creating a body that would take the expensive and troublesome administration of Muslim affairs out of their hands and offer an outlet for Palestinian nationalist feeling that would not pose a serious challenge to mandate rule. In creating the SMC they had defined religion as the most central marker of identity in Palestine—as well as the only road to political recognition from the mandate government—and thereby unwittingly assisted the emergence of a religious nationalism that had now begun effectively to employ Islamic rhetoric, in conjunction with a fervent anti-British and anti-Zionist nationalism, to oppose the mandate.

THE CHRISTIAN MILLETS AND THE EUROPEAN POWERS

The mandate government's approach to the Christian millets in Palestine differed radically from its policies toward the Muslim community, not least because the British suspected Palestinian Christians of being inextricably intertwined with potentially hostile foreign governments. Any intervention in the affairs of these communities would therefore carry with it a danger of increased European intervention in Palestine. Consequently, while the mandate government involved itself extensively in the construction of communal institutions for the Palestinian Muslim community, it made the decision early on to intervene as little as possible in Christian communal life.

This fear was based in a long history of Palestinian Christian ties to foreign governments, dating from the eighteenth century when Russia and France began to anoint themselves the "protectors" of certain minority communities in the Ottoman empire.[102] Despite its own past participation in such practices, Britain was now extremely wary of European threats to total British autonomy in Palestine arising from claims on behalf of Palestine's Christian citizens. Government activity in the Christian communities, therefore, was kept to a minimum to prevent unwelcome European protests or interventions in Palestinian affairs.

Despite the almost total withdrawal of Russian money and activism from the Greek Orthodox Church after 1917,[103] the British continued to be anxious about Russian influence in Palestine through Russian church institutions like the Palestine Orthodox Society and the Russian Ecclesiastical Mission. Corresponding about a dispute between pro- and anti-Soviet elements within the Greek Orthodox Church in Jerusalem in 1945 and the necessity for reaching an agreement with the Soviet government, High Commissioner Sir Alan Cunningham worried that it would "undoubtedly provide an opportunity for Russian interference, and for the consequent growth of the influence of the Soviet temporal power, as in the days of the Czarist regime."[104] Individual Arab Christians were marked as potential Russian allies; an entry in the British "Arab Who's Who" on Yaʿqub Farraj, for instance, carefully reported that he had at one time served as dragoman for the Russian consulate general.[105]

The British were anxious that the Greek government not exercise undue influence in Palestine through the Greek Orthodox Church. In discussing the potential revision of patriarchal law in 1930, G. W. Rendel, head of the Eastern Department in the Foreign Office, noted that the text of the mandate could pose problems for Britain if Greece attempted to intervene in Palestinian affairs on behalf of the Greek Orthodox community. "Although no doubt any attempt at intervention on the part of the Greek Government might be opposed on the ground that the Greek Government had no title to intervene," he wrote, ". . . such opposition would not necessarily be successful and, in the meantime, the Greek Government might have succeeded in creating a considerable amount of trouble."[106]

The Latin churches were under equal suspicion for being too closely associated with the Vatican and, secondarily, France.[107] The Vatican's extensive correspondence with the British government, often expressed as being on behalf of the Latin communities in Palestine, was met with great irritation. H. F. Downie of the Colonial Office noted in a memo of 1931 that this attempt at control sometimes extended beyond the Vatican to the Italian government, which "has on occasion endeavoured to assume the role of guardian of Latin and Catholic interests in Palestine."[108] Relations between the mandate government and Louis Barlassina, who became the Latin patriarch in 1920 and quickly established himself as both anti-Zionist and anti-British, were barely courteous. The political report for July 1921 already included a complaint about Barlassina, that "strong propaganda against the Government continued to emanate from the Latin Patriarchate," including a campaign against a proposed government school at Bethlehem on the grounds that its aim was "to turn the people into Protestants and to make them learn Hebrew."[109] Luke later described Barlassina as possessing "the temperament of an Inquisitor, something of the fanatical zeal of a Savonarola."[110] The British, consistently suspicious of attempts to influence British policy, continued to monitor the level of Italian interest in Palestine throughout the mandate. The Vatican's vocal anti-Zionism and its opposition to the project of a Jewish National Home in Palestine increased British wariness of Italian and papal intrusions into colonial affairs.[111]

The British were similarly suspicious of French interference. Upon the British takeover of Palestine, the French government tried to negotiate the official continuation of its role of "protector" of the Latin communities, an attempt sharply rebuffed by the British.[112] In 1921 Wyndam Deedes, chief secretary to the high commissioner, complained of French attempts to influence policy in Palestine: "When one meets them they are friendly enough, but they do do such extraordinary things, they cry 'Christians in Danger from a Pan Islamic and Bolshevist Movement' and then do their best to make trouble for us — they really do! I can give you no proofs but feel sure of it."[113] The French protectorate over the Catholic communities was officially terminated in 1924, but French authorities continued to correspond with the British government in Palestine over issues affecting the Latin communities throughout the mandate.[114] These and other incidents seemed a demonstration of the strength of the ties between the Latin Christians of Palestine and their would-be "protectors" in Italy and France and made the Arab Latin Catholic population automatically suspect.

Concern for the reactions of outside powers affected every aspect of the British consideration of the Christian populations in Palestine. As early as 1917, for instance, a proposal by the Anglican bishop in Jerusalem, Rennie MacInnes, to repossess all buildings in Palestine (particularly mosques) that had originally been Christian churches and to restore them to that purpose met with hearty opposition on the grounds that it would not only arouse the anger of Palestinian Muslims but might also provoke angry reactions from "the Catholic and Orthodox churches, supported by their French and

Russian patrons."[115] In 1934, when the Executive Council discussed the idea of subvention to the Jewish and Christian religious courts in Palestine (requested by the Vaad Leumi, the governing council of the Jewish community), the secretary of state suggested that the ideal solution would be to arrange for the administration of religious law by civil courts and to allow the religious courts to operate "with concurrent, and not exclusive, jurisdiction." The Executive Council responded by agreeing that this would be "in principle desirable" but refused to enact the suggestion because of the likelihood that it would arouse opposition "from Moslem interests elsewhere and the Catholic Powers."[116] The tendency of the Vatican and other Catholic institutions to object to British changes to the Ottoman "status quo" acted as a significant disincentive for the British to involve themselves in issues relating to the Christian communities.[117] Indeed, the urge to avoid confrontation with the Vatican was so strong that the Foreign Office considered aborting the archbishop of Canterbury's proposed trip to Jerusalem in 1931 following Vatican objections.[118]

The British also worried about the status of foreigners under the new millet system. Although they did not want to resurrect the complex logistical operations of the capitulations system, they maintained its essence by allowing all Christian foreigners to be judged by the law of their own nations in matters of personal status.[119] By contrast, Muslim foreigners in Palestine fell under the jurisdiction of the shari'a courts. This prevented protest and intervention from other European powers on behalf of their citizens resident in Palestine.

The English evangelical interest in Zionism reinforced this reluctance to take action on issues relating to the Christian communities in Palestine. Evangelical British groups, far from interesting themselves in the doings or the survival of Arab Christians, tended to be strongly pro-Zionist and commit their resources and energy to furthering the "return of the Jews." Historically, Britain had claimed a "protectorate" not over indigenous Arab Christian communities but over Protestants and Jews in Palestine.[120] Ongoing Arab Christian attempts to engage the sympathies of the British government in Palestine and the British public in the metropole were therefore often doomed from the start by their foreign associations and by strong British evangelical ties to the Zionist movement.

The British reluctance to deal with the Christian millets was in large part due to concerns about Christian ties to foreign governments and entities and the intervention of those powers in Palestine. Christians in the metropole, who might have been expected to maintain an interest in their coreligionists in the "Holy Land," were instead focused on their role as promoters of Zionism; consequently, there were very few ties between Christian groups in

Britain and Palestinian Arab Christians. British officials like Deedes, Rendel, and Downie viewed the Arab Christian communities in Palestine as little more than dangerous outposts of European religious organizations intent on undermining the British mandate authority from within.

BRITISH ATTITUDES TOWARD THE CHRISTIAN MILLETS: OTHER FACTORS

Other British conceptions of the Palestinian Arab Christian communities buttressed the decision to leave aside the Christian millets in colonial policy making. First, the mandate government tended to consider the Christian communities necessarily marginal in a Muslim-majority nation. Second, many British officials thought the Christian communities were irreparably fragmented by ancient and primitive theological and denominational disputes and therefore incapable of representing a unified political front. Furthermore, the British viewed the urban, middle-class elite to which most Palestinian Christians belonged as a serious threat to the stability of the colonial state.

The British tended to view Christians as an "insignificant minority in the country," as one official political report put it;[121] many colonial officials thought that all over the Muslim Middle East, Christians were totally disenfranchised by virtue of their religion. A communiqué from the consul at Damascus about the Cairo Arab Congress of 1938, for instance, noted, "The Christian Fares al Khoury's [speaker of the Syrian parliament] plausibility and eloquence should not be allowed to create the impression that he wields any useful influence in the Moslem Arab world."[122] A similar note was struck in discussions of Lebanon; in 1938 the consul general at Beirut wrote that popular feeling about Palestine had become heightened to the point that "even the Christian Arab papers of Beirut, the editors of which cannot be expected to have the same sympathy with the Moslems of Palestine as the Moslems of Syria and the Lebanon, have to adopt as violent an attitude on the subject as do the Moslem papers if they wish to sell."[123]

In the Palestinian context, this point of view often became extreme. In 1921 a Palestinian Arab delegation including the prominent Palestinian Episcopalian politician Shibli Jamal met with Winston Churchill of the Colonial Office in London. They requested that in the record of Palestinian Arab objections to British policy the word "Christian" be added to the word "Moslem." "Certainly," Churchill replied. "But . . . it is no good pretending that you are more closely united to the Christians than to the Jews. That is not so. A wider gulf separates us from you than separates you from the Jew. I am talking of the Semitic races."[124] For officials like Churchill, Christianity was wholly associated with Europe and the concept of an Arab Christian political presence was totally meaningless. Many officials in the Colonial Office were unable to believe that Palestinian Arab Christians could be genuine, loyal, and well-regarded participants in any Muslim-majority political movement.

The British also thought that the Palestinian Christian communities were hopelessly fragmented by primitive denominational and theological quarrels. This impression arose primarily from the various intercommunal disputes regarding the ownership, maintenance, and use of the Holy Places, the myriad arguments over which constituted one of the primary points of contact between the British government and the Christian churches in Palestine. A 1928 memo on "The Status Quo in the Holy Places" reported that

> the ever recurring difficulties and disputes arising out of the circumstance that the Christian Holy Places in Jerusalem and Bethlehem were not in one ownership but were shared and served by several communities . . . [meant that] the rights and privileges of the Christian communities officiating in the Holy Places had to be most meticulously observed and what each rite practiced at that time in the way of public worship, decorations of altars and shrines, use of lamps, candelabra, tapestry and pictures, and in the exercise of the most minute acts of ownership and usage has to remain unaltered.[125]

The British took it upon themselves to ensure that no community was favored over another and that "the most scrupulous care [was] exercised to ensure that in all cases of dispute existing rights are preserved unimpaired."[126] This decision focused British attention on the disagreements among Palestine's Christian churches, rifts that were often essentially between foreign clergy rather than local communities, and positioned the mandate government as a necessary mediator among the various parties; it also caused endless administrative headaches, as it required the mandate government to take on the monitoring of tiny details of upkeep and administration. Bentwich, recording a failed attempt to set up a commission to determine the rights of each church in the Holy Places, expressed a common British sentiment when he noted that "the feeling between Catholics, Orthodox, and Protestants, were too strong to be overcome."[127] These disputes, while real and often bitter, reflected the power struggles among the various European powers tied to Palestine's Christian institutions more than hostile relations among the local Arab Christian communities themselves.

Nevertheless, British officials from everywhere on the political spectrum recorded their beliefs that the Christian communities could never be politically united; they also tended to portray Christian intercommunal battles as petty, undignified squabbles. Keith-Roach, for instance, recorded his recollection of a violent candlestick fight in the Church of the Nativity in Bethlehem between a Greek Orthodox monk and a Franciscan friar.[128] Luke wrote of a dispute between two churches over the placing of a chair at one of the Stations of the Cross that he recorded had led to one community being "assailed from the roof of the X convent with beer bottles and other missiles"; in another context he noted regretfully, "Unhappily, faction plays a large part in the life of the Christian East."[129] Storrs recorded an incident between the Latin patriarch and the Coptic Church in which the Copts retaliated against an incursion by a Latin procession by "emptying their slops out of the windows on to the exact spot upon which the Friday procession of Franciscans up the Via Dolorosa was accustomed to kneel."[130] The frequent involvement of other European powers or church representatives in these battles bolstered the concomitant British view that the Christian Palestinian churches represented outposts of various European rivals.[131]

These types of narratives reinforced the British concept of religion as more primitive and more deeply felt in Palestine than elsewhere and contributed to the conviction that intercommunal divides would always prevent the Palestinian Christian communities from acting as a body in the political realm.[132] The decision to present the mandate state as an impartial mediator, adhering to an Ottoman-derived "status quo," strengthened the idea of longstanding and bitter divisions among the Christian communities in Palestine and tended to deepen those divides by emphasizing historical disputes.

Beyond these reasons for neglecting and ignoring the Christian millets was the further rationale that elite Arab Christian leaders had very early demonstrated their opposition to Jewish immigration, a non-negotiable part of the British mandate, and their commitment to Palestinian Arab independence. In the years immediately following the war, many middle-class Christians in Palestine had already placed themselves in opposition to the mandate government by allying themselves with Faysal and the Southern Syria movement. Christian journalists like Najib Nassar and 'Isa al-'Isa had repeatedly expressed their opposition to Zionism in print. During these early years of the mandate, the Christians—particularly the Catholic communities—came under suspicion for their pro-nationalist and their pro-French positions. Prominent individuals from the Christian community like the 'Isas were labeled troublemakers for their membership in the Muslim-Christian Associations and for their anti-Zionist and pro-nationalist views; one report dating from 1919 referred to Yusef al-'Isa as "a very bad type of professional Politician."[133] Arab Christian journalists like Najib Nassar and the al-'Isas represented exactly the kind of secularized, middle-class, urban demographic that the British viewed as the most dangerous threat to continued imperial overlordship.

The deliberate neglect of the Christian communities resulted from a sense that they represented hostile European entities but also from the conviction that these communities were lacking in influence, hopelessly fragmented, and politically inflammatory. The British policy of non-interference in Christian affairs stood in marked contrast to their hands-on encouragement of Palestinian Muslim communal expression.

A POLICY OF NEGLECT: CHRISTIAN COMMUNAL INSTITUTIONS UNDER MANDATE

The military administration first discussed the political status of the Christian churches of Palestine in 1919. In consultation with a British Catholic priest named P. N. Waggett, it decided that the educational and personal autonomy that the religious communities had enjoyed under Ottoman rule should be continued and that churches should govern themselves as before. They would, of course, have to recognize the authority of the mandate government but should run their own affairs without application to the British except in extraordinary circumstances.[134] Under the Order in Council of 1922, the Christian courts, which had had only limited powers under the Ottomans as compared to their counterparts in Egypt, were assigned responsibility for cases involving wills and family issues, especially marriage, divorce, and alimony. They were allowed to provide an alternative to civil jurisdiction in other cases of personal status, an option that had not been permitted under the Ottomans. The judgments of the religious courts would be upheld and executed by "the processes and offices of the Civil Courts."[135] Only recognized millets, however, could maintain their own religious courts; other Christian communities had to apply to the established and recognized courts in matters of personal status.

In 1923 the British recognized the Greek Orthodox, Latin Catholic, Armenian Orthodox, Armenian Catholic, and Syrian Catholic communities as millets (as well as the Muslim and Jewish communities); in the next two years they also granted recognition to the Greek Catholic, Maronite, and Syrian Orthodox communities.[136] Recognition of this sort depended on the ability of each church to demonstrate that it had been regarded as a separate community during the years of Ottoman rule, thus providing a link between Ottoman "tradition" and British policy. This excluded very small denominations that could not prove their historical recognition, like the Copts.[137] It also excluded communities of more recent origin, most notably the small but highly educated and influential Protestant Arab community, whose members faced a host of legal difficulties during the mandate due to this British refusal to offer them religious community status.[138] Generally, however, as long as there was evidence that the Ottomans had regarded a denomination as a community, the British were willing to grant a church its own courts. These courts were set up to be as independent and self-contained as possible and to operate without British intervention. To this end, the British consistently refused requests to monitor and regulate the workings of the Christian courts despite repeated complaints of corruption and inefficiency.[139]

The Arab Christian communities responded to this deliberate neglect with vocal protests against the mandate government and constant requests for attention to their communal institutions. The maladministration of Christian ecclesiastical courts was a particularly common grievance. The Greek Catholic community in Acre submitted a list of complaints to the district commissioner in 1942 that indicated the court system had broken down altogether and was being run capriciously by a single person, the president of the court. "There is no law for the Court," community leader Rafful Khawwan wrote, "and the whole procedure is left in the hands of its president." He complained that there was no schedule of fees, that the president changed, dissolved, and reformed the courts at his will ("he can do this because there is no law for our community"), and that the president had been convicted of falsifying an immigration document.[140] The solicitor general refused to address the questions, suggesting that "the petitioners should be informed that their representations should be addressed to the appropriate ecclesiastical authorities."[141] There were numerous other complaints of a similar nature, and the mandate government received large numbers of letters from Arab Christians protesting that the mandate government's neglect had caused hardships and difficulties not just in the ecclesiastical courts but also in the administration of awqaf and schools.

Questions of mixed marriages were often problematic, and Arab Christians from every community wrote to the mandate government asking for clarification and reform of the laws concerning marriage and divorce. The mandate government did engage in conversations with Christian leaders about clarifying the law and revising the Religious Community Ordinance in 1935, to forbid churches from annulling marriages made in another church.[142] But many individual pleas, such as one relating to the dissolution of a mixed Greek Orthodox/Greek Catholic marriage, were rebuffed with such curt dismissals as "the matter is not one in which Government can intervene."[143] There were other complaints from Palestinians desiring to be married in a civil ceremony, for which there was no provision in Palestinian law.[144]

Further enabling the British to remain uninvolved, Christian courts did not have jurisdiction over foreigners, while Muslim courts had jurisdiction over all Muslims regardless of citizenship. Conversely, Arab Christians not belonging to a recognized millet had no recourse to a court of personal law. This caused a number of legal difficulties, particularly for the unrecognized Arab Protestants but also for a number of individuals not associated with any particular religious community. These sorts of discrepancies engendered a constant flow of protest from Arab Christians throughout the country.

The mandate government refused to acknowledge a problem. One report noted, "We understand that it is a basic principle in the system of government of the country to leave all religious matters to the various religious bodies to mandate for themselves. If these bodies mismanage their religious affairs the Government can and does do nothing."[145] This hands-off British policy regarding the Christian millets was designed to placate European interests and to prevent the mandate government from wasting energy, money, or resources on a segment of the population it believed to be marginal, internally divided, and essentially hostile. The reams of protest this neglect occasioned from every church community had little effect. Over the next three decades, then, Arab Christians would begin to look for new ways to constitute themselves communally and reinvent their Christian institutions and identities in order to be heard in Palestine's increasingly sectarian political landscape.

CHAPTER 3

THE ARAB ORTHODOX MOVEMENT

The aim of the Orthodox case is the independence of the community in its communal affairs and in the supervision of all its property so as to become a strong community with a definite and clear Arab influence, and so as to be able to deliver its national message in a full and suitable manner.

EXECUTIVE ORTHODOX COMMITTEE OF
PALESTINE AND TRANSJORDAN, 1946

By the mid-1920s, sectarian political institutions had become a primary venue for political action in Palestine. Arab Christians had been excluded from the main association for Arab political contact with the mandate state, the newly established Supreme Muslim Council. Hajj Amin al-Husayni had emerged as the most prominent Palestinian nationalist leader, based primarily on British interpretations of his credentials as a Muslim religious leader. Responding to these developments, leaders in the Arab Orthodox community now began to recast an internal church movement as a political cause tied to the organization, rhetoric, and goals of Palestinian nationalism. Through this redefinition of the Arab Orthodox movement as essentially political and nationalist, they proclaimed the Orthodox community's centrality to Palestinian politics and remade their religious community as a political entity.

A major conflict between the laity and the clergy had dominated the church's affairs since the late nineteenth century. Arab members of the Orthodox community, challenging the traditional Greek claim to ownership and control of the church, had long called for an Arabic liturgy and Arab representation in the higher reaches of the clergy as well as a greater share for the laity of the church's substantial land and economic resources. During the early 1920s, Arab Orthodox leaders began to make use of the organizational tactics and antiforeign rhetoric of the nationalist movement to work for the Arabization of their church and the strengthening of Ortho-dox communal institutions. In the 1920s and 1930s, the Jaffa paper *Filastin* lent the Arab Orthodox movement a specifically nationalist orientation by publicly recasting it as part of a broader movement for Palestinian Arab inde-pendence. After 1931 a dispute over the patriarchal election process led Arab Orthodox leaders to include a commitment to constitutional electoral reform and modern democratic political processes in their movement's platform. Although two of the most prominent members of the Arab Orthodox com-munity, Khalil al-Sakakini and George Antonius, an intellectual and civil ser-vant whose writings on Palestine were widely read in Britain and the United States, expressed opposition to this newly politicized approach, it had gained the support of most of the community by the mid-1930s.

This remaking of the Greek Orthodox controversy into a political move-ment, designed to highlight Arab Orthodox centrality to Palestinian nation-alism, represented an effort to respond to an increasingly sectarian politi-cal landscape. Arab Orthodox leaders, many of whom had been prominent actors in the multi-religious nationalist discourse of the late Ottoman and early mandate years, felt marginalized by the mandate state's focus on Mus-lim communal institutions and its deliberate neglect of Palestinian Chris-tians. In recasting their internal church movement as an integral part of a national struggle, Arab Orthodox leaders were trying to claim a role in a political system that was now clearly communally organized.

THE CONTROVERSY IN THE OTTOMAN PERIOD

The Arab Orthodox community represented the largest Christian denomi-nation in Palestine, making up nearly half of the Christian population.[1] The Christian populations of eight subdistricts had an Orthodox majority; in seven other subdistricts, including Jerusalem, Orthodox Christians made up the largest denomination.[2] Orthodox Arabs were quite integrated with the Muslim population, with large numbers in rural areas; they often shared fes-tivals and holidays with their Muslim neighbors. The leaders of the commu-nity tended to be well-educated, middle-class professionals, especially promi-nent in the fields of journalism, medicine, and teaching. Many of them—like Khalil al-Sakakini, ʿIsa Bandak, Yusef and ʿIsa al-ʿIsa, and Yaʿqub Farraj— were strong supporters of the fledgling Palestinian Arab nationalist move-ment as well as the Arab Orthodox cause. From the late Ottoman period, as we have seen, elites from the Orthodox and Muslim communities mixed freely in social and political settings as they began to build a new kind of modern urban middle class in Palestine.

The Greek Orthodox Church in Palestine itself, though, had long been foreign-dominated. The clerical hierarchy, who were entirely Greek and Greek-speaking, had for many centuries fostered strong ties to the Ottoman government that allowed them not only to consolidate control over many of the most important "Holy Places" in Palestine, including the Church of the Holy Sepulcher, but also to enjoy financial and administrative autonomy and freedom of movement and action throughout the empire. This pattern was not unique to Palestine; indigenous Orthodox Christians throughout the Ottoman Arab and Balkan provinces practiced their faith in a church administered and headed by Greeks and in which Greek was the liturgical language.

There were few challenges to this system of Greek domination anywhere in the empire until the mid-nineteenth century, when the laity in Bulgaria and Albania began to organize against the Greek church hierarchy. Lay leaders explicitly linked the liberation of their churches from Greek control with the expression of national (as opposed to Ottoman) identities. In 1893 the Arab laity of Antioch, following the Eastern European example, staged a series of uprisings and demonstrations that succeeded in putting an Arab on the patriarchal throne for the first time since the sixteenth century—a development that the Arab nationalist intellectual Sati' al-Husri hailed as "the first real victory for Arab nationalism."[3]

In Palestine, an all-Greek monastic order known as the Brotherhood of the Holy Sepulcher (sometimes called the Fraternity) headed the Greek Orthodox Church. Its members took vows of chastity and obedience but—significantly—not poverty. The monks understood their primary function to be the maintenance of the many Christian holy sites in Palestine, not the spiritual guidance of the Arab lay community. "The guardianship of the Holy Places," one patriarch explained, "was the real and original purpose of the Orthodox Church in the Holy Land, which (its members) had maintained, often with their lives, through many centuries of infidel domination. Their endowments were the result of foreign and not Arab munificence, and Christian ministrations, in the accepted sense, though admittedly important and desirable, were a supererogation beyond their primary scope."[4] Donations from the empire, particularly eastern Europe and the Balkans, funded the brotherhood and ensured continued Greek Orthodox dominance over the Holy Places despite challenges from Latin Catholic interests in France and Italy.

The Palestinian laity, who were ethnically Arab and Arabic-speaking, had neither rights nor responsibilities under this system. They were offered some financial support but were barred from becoming monks in the brotherhood (regardless of education) and had no role in the financial or administrative workings of the church. Arabs were allowed to serve as parish priests, but nineteenth-century commentators noted the poor education of these local clerical leaders and the pitiful remuneration they received. The Palestinian Arab role in the Greek Orthodox Church was usually limited to that of supplicant.

The late nineteenth century saw a number of lay protests against the Jerusalem patriarchate, resulting in a new Ottoman "Fundamental Law" in 1875 that brought changes to the rules for patriarchal elections. This new law gave the laity some minor rights but generally reaffirmed Greek control over the church. In 1908, following the promulgation of the Ottoman constitution and a lengthy period of negotiation, a vigorous and occasionally violent battle raged among the patriarch and his synod (governing council), the Ottoman government, and the Arab laity. The synod briefly deposed the Jerusalem patriarch Damianos for not opposing the demands of the laity forcefully enough; but he quickly returned to power due to lay protests, Ottoman pressure, and the untimely death of the man appointed to succeed him. In 1910 the Ottoman government tried to settle the question. It set up a Mixed Council (made up of six Greek and six Arab representatives) to help govern the church; the patriarchate would have to provide the council with one-third of church revenues to be spent on local schools, hospitals, and charities and allow any "qualified" Arab candidate to join the Brotherhood of the Holy Sepulcher. The Ottomans refused lay demands for greater Arab participation in the election of the patriarch and an acknowledgement that the Holy Places belonged to the whole community rather than the Greek hierarchy.[5]

Even these small concessions were never really implemented. In practice, no Arab was deemed qualified to join the order, and the church never granted more than an advisory role to the Mixed Council, which dissolved in 1913. By the end of World War I and the beginning of the mandate period, Orthodox Arabs in Palestine had made very little progress toward control of their spiritual institutions.

THE COMMUNITY, THE PATRIARCHATE, AND THE ZIONIST MOVEMENT

By the end of World War I the affairs of the patriarchate were in chaos. The fighting had been devastating; much of the countryside, including a great deal of church property, was in ruins. The war had cut the patriarchate off from one of its major sources of revenue, funds from the Balkans; worse, the Bolshevik Revolution and subsequent inaccessibility of the new Soviet Union meant the abrupt cessation of the significant sums from Russia upon which the patriarchate had always depended. More than 60 percent of its revenues, mainly from Russian governmental institutions and Russian pilgrims, had dried up, and Damianos made up the funds by taking out large international loans. By 1918 it was estimated that the patriarchate was more than 600,000 pounds in debt.[6]

In expectation of a British takeover of Palestine during the war, Jamal Pasha had moved the patriarch and the synod to Damascus. In their absence, a Committee of Management appointed to look after the interests of the patriarchate in Jerusalem contacted the government of Greece in hopes of effecting a solution to the financial crisis. At an extraordinary meeting, the brotherhood passed a resolution that "confid[ed] its fate entirely and without reserve to the Greek Government."[7] The Greek consul general in Cairo agreed to the proposal on the condition that Damianos be removed from power, and the brotherhood wrote up a formal request for deposition, accusing him of "pro-Turkish sympathies, reckless financial administration, arbitrary government and other offences,"[8] expecting that the Greek government would provide financial backing to the patriarchate upon Damianos' removal.

Lay protests drew the attention of General Edmund Allenby, now heading the British army in Palestine, who returned the patriarch and synod to Jerusalem and achieved a temporary reconciliation. But further upset followed when the brotherhood decided to solve the financial problem by taking out a large loan from the Bank of Greece, to be accompanied by considerable Greek governmental influence on the inner workings of the Jerusalem patriarchate. The brotherhood pressed for a set of resolutions, drawn up by a committee in Athens, that affirmed the Hellenic character of the patriarchate and made it accountable not only to the ecumenical Orthodox church but also to the Greek government. Damianos opposed the resolutions, as did the British, who saw them as a potential threat to British sovereignty over Palestine and especially Jerusalem. The British offered instead to finance the patriarchate through a loan from a British bank. The brotherhood agreed but simultaneously demanded Damianos' removal, accusing him of financial incompetence, suspicious ties to Russia, and unwillingness to recognize the Greek character of the patriarchate.

The new colonial government had an interest in making sure that the major religious institutions of Palestine remained functional; imperial policy throughout the empire demanded cautious treatment of religious institutions for fear of anticolonial rebellion. But the British had little familiarity with the issues involved here, and the avalanche of pleas and claims from the patriarch, synod, brotherhood, and laity baffled them. In 1921 the mandate government responded to the situation in classic imperial fashion by announcing a commission of inquiry to look into the problem. It appointed Sir Anton

Bertram, chief justice of Ceylon and a former judge of the Supreme Court of Cyprus who was considered an expert on the "Oriental churches," and Harry Charles Luke, the assistant governor of Jerusalem, to head the commission. They were charged with three tasks: reestablishing order in the Palestinian Orthodox church, deciding whether the brotherhood had the power to depose Damianos or make changes to the patriarchate, and offering recommendations on the best way to liquidate the patriarchate's substantial debts.

The commission determined that there was no authority within the church that could settle the dispute between the patriarch and synod. It declared that the synod had no rights under church law to depose Damianos and that for the moment, only "those members of the Synod who for the time being recognize the authority of the Patriarch shall for all purposes by deemed to constitute the Synod."[9] The best way to revive the failing establishment, Bertram and Luke decided, was to put control of its finances in the hands of a British-appointed committee "of liquidation and control."[10] Beyond these recommendations, Bertram and Luke noted that the British mandate government would shortly have to preside over the revision of the Ottoman Fundamental Law of 1875 dealing with patriarchal elections, thereby deciding what role the colonial administration would take vis-à-vis the Orthodox church. They recommended that the British assume all the powers of the Ottoman sultan, in case the government found it necessary to object to a candidate for the patriarchate, and that the civil courts should not have to arbitrate disputes within the church—both viewpoints consistent with broader imperial policy on the maintenance of religious institutions in colonial contexts. More significantly, Bertram and Luke stressed that the problem of the position of the laity in the church was bound to reappear and that they personally were sympathetic to lay claims that Arabs should be allowed to join the brotherhood and participate in church administration.[11]

Tensions between the laity and the patriarchate worsened substantially in the early 1920s when the Greek patriarchate issued statements of support for Zionism. To add to the conflict, the British/Greek commission that had taken over the church's finances sold substantial tracts of land in Jerusalem and its surrounds to the Zionist Palestine Land Development Company in 1923.[12] The land sales made the task of gaining Arab political ascendancy in the church seem immediately essential; Orthodox lay leaders, desiring to participate in the Arab politics of post-Ottoman Palestine, could not afford to be associated with an institution supportive of both large-scale Jewish immigration and British imperial control. The Arab Orthodox leadership now began to depict their Greek church hierarchy as a foreign oppressor along the same lines as the Zionists and the British and to employ nationalist and anti-imperial language in the struggle against the patriarchate.

During the early 1920s, community leaders began to reshape the Arab Orthodox movement into a political organization. They borrowed the organizational structures and terminology of the nationalist movement, convening
an Arab Orthodox Congress to discuss the issues at hand and appointing an
Executive Orthodox Committee to represent the community to the nation
and to the mandate government. These formulations were clearly modeled on
the Palestinian Arab Congresses and the Arab Executive that had emerged as
the major organizational structures of the nationalist movement in the early
years of the mandate. They rewrote their goals in the language of nationalism, making use of antiforeign rhetoric modeled on political expressions of
anti-Zionism and anti-imperialism.

When the sixth Palestinian Arab Congress was held in June 1923, Orthodox leaders including Ibrahim Shammas, ʿIsa al-ʿIsa, Jubran Iskandar Kazma,
ʿIsa Bandak, and Yaʿqub Bardakash presented it with a petition laying out
the issues confronting Orthodox Arabs in Palestine and asking the congress
for its support in the Orthodox struggle. All these men were middle-class,
well-educated, and familiar with European languages and politics; they had
participated enthusiastically in the nationalist activities of the early Palestinian Arab Congresses and were committed to an anti-Zionist platform and
to eventual Palestinian independence. Ibrahim Shammas of Jerusalem and
Yaʿqub Bardakash of Jaffa were both members of the executive committee
elected at the third Palestinian Arab Congress in Haifa in 1920. Jubran Iskandar Kazma was an agronomist from Nazareth; he spoke French, belonged to
the Muslim-Christian Association, and had participated in the delegation
sent to Paris in 1919 to present the resolutions of the first Palestinian Arab
Congress to the European powers. ʿIsa Bandak of Bethlehem was a well-
known journalist, as the founder and editor of the local paper *Bayt lahm* as
well as the nationalist publication *Sawt al-shaʿb*; he frequently represented
Bethlehem in political congresses, committees, and meetings. ʿIsa al-ʿIsa, as
the editor of the newspaper *Filastin*, was perhaps the most prominent member of the group. They were gratified to see the congress pass a resolution expressing support for their program of demands and recognizing the Orthodox issue as part of a broader national cause.[13]

In July 1923, encouraged by the sympathetic hearing they had received,
Orthodox leaders convened the first Arab Orthodox Congress in Haifa under
the leadership of Iskandar Kassab as president, Yaʿqub Farraj as deputy president, and Michel George Khouri as secretary. Farraj had already risen to
prominence within the national movement as a spokesman for the Arab

Orthodox community (he had acted as the Orthodox representative to the Administrative Committee of the Muslim-Christian Association in 1918) and over the next decade would become the Arab Orthodox movement's most committed and visible leader. Fifty-four delegates, representing all the dioceses, attended the congress. The use of these particular structures of representation and authority, modeled on the new institutions of the nationalist movement and involving some of the same people, was a major innovation and represented the first substantive step toward the politicization of the Arab Orthodox movement.

The congress laid out an ambitious program of reforms, intended as much as a formulation of a new Arab Orthodox identity as a plan for political action. Its first concern was to define the church as an Arab rather than a Greek institution. To this end, it called for the renaming of the patriarchate the Jerusalem Orthodox Patriarchate; the entrance of Arab members into the brotherhood and the clerical hierarchy; Arab administrative participation in the church's financial affairs; Arab control of church institutions like schools and awqaf; the formation of a Mixed Council with an Arab majority, to play an important role in administrative decisions, in patriarchal elections, and in admissions to the brotherhood; and an insistence on Arabic as the liturgical language of the church, the bishops, and the religious courts. These resolutions broadcast the Arab identity of the Orthodox community, casting it in opposition to the Greeks, who were "foreign of language and country . . . [and] have four centuries ago usurped the spiritual authority from the Arab Orthodox."[14] Such language recalled the antiforeign sentiments of the nationalist movement, linking the Greeks with both the Zionist and the British incursions into Palestine.

At the congress, representatives proposed ways to remake Orthodox communal institutions. They demanded the reorganization of the religious courts to provide for codified, Arab-dominated Orthodox judicial institutions and communal law, the formation of local councils to deal with community affairs, the publication of an Arab Orthodox magazine, and the organization of a yearly Orthodox congress.[15] They called for strong support for Orthodox institutions like awqaf, schools, and orphanages as an important manifestation of the Arab Orthodox presence in Palestine. While the courts and legal codes were being restructured, the congress suggested, local councils could temporarily assume their responsibilities and try cases in accordance with local shariʿa law.[16] The resolutions included a moratorium on land sales to Zionists for one year and castigated the patriarchate for its sale of lands to the Zionist Palestine Land Development Company.[17]

Immediately after the congress, Damianos worked to put together an opposing party that he advertised as representing a "moderate" point of view.

This party applied to the British government for recognition as an association in October 1923 and held meetings to discuss a less radical set of proposals for reform. Its proposals were published in a pamphlet in 1924 and included some of the main demands of the Haifa congress—the creation of the Mixed Council, the improvement of Orthodox educational institutions, and the right of Arabs to enter the brotherhood—but not the pro-Arab, anti-Greek sentiment or the commitment to the anti-Zionist cause.[18] Recognizing this as a patriarchal ploy rather than an authentic movement, the British acknowledged that the Haifa conference represented the majority Orthodox position but did not respond to the congress' demands.

Orthodox leaders continued to press the mandate government, declaring that as successors to the Ottomans, the British had an obligation to support the laity and maintain Orthodox institutions. A measure of desperation entered these pleas during the 1920s as Orthodox churches, courts, and schools began to collapse due to lack of funds, continued dissent between the laity and the clergy, and continuing loss of lands to European Jewish buyers. In 1929 the Orthodox Youth Club of Jerusalem wrote to the high commissioner protesting the patriarchate's continuing land sales, not least because its members feared the permanent impoverishment of the church: "sale is being carried out incessantly and we regret to say that the properties which are being sold are the best and most valuable Wakfs of the Patriarchate while had these properties been left for a short time they would procure a price three times as much as their present one . . . we beg Your Excellency to stop the sale immediately."[19]

They wanted lay representation on the financial commission and reforms of the religious courts. "This state has become very sad and deserves pitiness [sic]," they wrote. "Every illegal and anomalous action taken by those in charge of the Patriarchate and Community is considered a new blow added to the disasters and calamities of our miserable Community who has been destined for more than ten years to be under the shelter of Great Britain without finding any saviour or settlement of its cause."[20] The religious courts posed a particularly difficult problem, as the divisions between the laity and the Greek clergy were making it impossible to come to legal agreements. This situation was by no means limited to Jerusalem; letters from Orthodox communities throughout the country poured in, protesting that the British had failed in their responsibilities as successors to the Ottoman state and self-proclaimed upholders of the "status quo."

In their complaints to the mandate government, Arab Orthodox organizations emphasized the foreignness of the Greeks in language that recalled the antiforeign rhetoric of the nationalist movement. One letter from the Youth Orthodox Club of Jaffa in 1929 deplored the delay in reform caused by "the interference of foreigners" and protested that the issue should be addressed by the "local Government." The writers added a reference to the "attempts to turn all the holy places in this country, even the Awqaf and the tombs of our Fathers into Greek . . . By such deed and means in the past and in the present these Brethren have taken possession of the rich properties of the Patriarchate."[21] Complaints focused on Greek rapacity and greed, sometimes making charges of criminal activity; a letter from the Young Men's Orthodox Club of Lydda requested a government audit of the patriarchate, accusing it of the theft of large sums of money.[22]

THE BRITISH POSITION

Beyond the necessity of restoring order to the finances of the patriarchate, there was no consensus in the mandate government on how to deal with the upheavals in the Orthodox church, and the mechanics of the Eastern patriarchates and their monastic hierarchies were something of a mystery to most officials. Although a number of British officials believed that the laity had a just cause, they had decided that it was not in the interests of the British government to make changes to the "status quo," particularly in ways that might affect the administration of the Holy Places and thereby attract the attention of other European churches and governments. Further, while they supported the claims of the laity regarding church participation and entrance into the brotherhood to some degree, the British were wary of the antiforeign and Arabist language and the nationalist organizational tactics associated with the Arab Orthodox movement. In addition, the patriarchate had proven itself to be fairly pro-British and had supported both the mandate government and the Balfour Declaration. An Arab-run patriarchate was bound to be less malleable.

As the divisions between the laity and the patriarchate deepened, the government decided again on the familiar solution of a commission of inquiry. It was appointed in 1925 and headed once again by Sir Anton Bertram, who had overseen the earlier commission on the financial state of the patriarchate, and H. W. Young, who had served on the financial committee set up after the previous report. The commission's "report upon certain controversies," published in 1926, was essentially sympathetic to the aims of the Orthodox laity without assisting their cause in any meaningful way. It expressed the opinion quite explicitly that the Arabs were in the right: "It is impossible not to view with feelings of sympathy the position in which these members of the Church find themselves."[23] Bertram and Young recognized the introduction of nationalist thought into the Arab Orthodox movement:

Like all young men of their time, they are full of the idea of nationalism, and cherish the language which united them with their fellow countrymen. They do not wish to abandon their Church; on the contrary, they are attached to its traditions and its rites. But they find themselves, owing to a peculiar historical development, subject to a monastery whose greatest pride is that it is composed of members of a race alien (or which they themselves consider alien) to their own.[24]

But the commission's report also stated that the mandate government had no authority to make changes to the 1875 Ottoman Fundamental Law that had defined the nature of patriarchal elections. Bertram and Young supported the establishment of the Mixed Council and the admission of Arabs to the brotherhood as well as the idea of making the adoption of Palestinian nationality a requirement of membership in the brotherhood. They proposed requiring that diocesan bishops speak Arabic, translating ecclesiastical law into Arabic, and appointing local councils to administer local affairs. Nowhere, however, did they suggest a more radical reworking of the patriarchate to redefine it as essentially Arab rather than Greek.

Bertram wrote a confidential report to be presented to the government alongside the published findings of the commission, in which he noted the scandals (mainly revolving around money and women) that had dogged many of the Greek members of the brotherhood and traced the Arab Orthodox movement to disgust with the monks' behavior: "The facts which we have mentioned indicated a certain ethical demoralization which excites the indignation of the better members of the laity and is largely responsible for the strong local feeling against the Patriarchate."[25] He reported that despite his sympathy with the laity, there was no possibility of immediate reform even along the modest lines suggested in the commission's official report, and he suggested that the first opportunity for real change would come with the election of a new patriarch. Since a new patriarch had to be recognized by the government to take power, the British could withhold approval until the synod accepted some reforms.[26] Despite the justice of the laity's requests, Bertram wrote, he did not think they would "press for early action . . . They realise that the new institutions which the report proposes, could only be successfully worked in cooperation with an enlightened and conciliatory Patriarch who wished to bring about a general settlement."[27] Due to the difficulties of changing the Fundamental Law and the cooperative nature of the laity, Bertram thought it most desirable that "a considerable interval should be allowed to elapse for the purpose of the discussion of the proposals of the report."[28] This secret dispatch hindered the reform movement by making the British extremely reluctant to act even on the modest recommendations of the commission, preferring to wait until the death of the current patriarch opened up an opportunity for more radical change.[29]

There were other factors at play as well. By 1922 the British could see that Palestinian Arab Christians would side with their Muslim compatriots on all issues relating to Zionism; they had no incentive to empower Arab Orthodox communal institutions that were bound to be hostile to both the British and the Zionists. They feared the interference of Russia and France, both of whom had styled themselves "protectors" of Christian communities in Palestine in the past. By comparison, the Greeks usually cooperated with the British government, and Greek stewardship of the patriarchate meant relatively few challenges to the British mandate government. Moreover, Anglican church leaders in Britain were generally sympathetic to the Hellenic patriarchate, a reflection of contemporary trends within English church circles to reach out to Eastern Christians.[30] Despite personal sympathy for the laity on the part of certain officials, then, the British made no moves to address the problems of the Orthodox community.

FILASTIN: ARTICULATING A NATIONALIST ARGUMENT

Newspapers owned and edited by Orthodox Arabs played a major role in reconceptualizing the Orthodox movement. Addressing both literate Palestinians (Muslims as well as Christians) and the British government, these papers presented Palestinian nationalism as a central component of the movement and portrayed the Arab Orthodox cause as an essential aspect of broader political organization against British imperialism and European Zionism.

Middle-class urban Christians had been at the center of the young trades of journalism and publishing in Palestine since their development in the late Ottoman period; nineteen out of the twenty-five newspapers appearing in Palestine in 1908 were Christian-owned.[31] Christian journalists devoted a substantial amount of space to the Orthodox conflict. Al-Karmil, founded in 1908 by the Orthodox-turned-Protestant journalist Najib Nassar, covered the situation of the church vis-à-vis the Ottoman authorities in the aftermath of the 1908 upheaval. Khalil al-Sakakini, committed to the Orthodox cause during this early period (although he was later to lose interest) founded al-Dustur in 1910 and commented on church affairs there. Later, during the mandate period, still more Christian-owned newspapers appeared. The Jerusalem-based Mir'at al-sharq (1919–1939), owned by a Muslim-Christian Association member named Bulus Shihada, who was also active in the Palestinian Episcopalian community, focused on nationalist affairs; for its first few years it was published in both Arabic and English. Bandali Ilyas Mushahwar began *Bayt al-maqdis*, a twice-weekly paper with a focus on moderate nationalism, in 1919. The same year, Yuhnan Dakart and ʿIsa Bandak founded *Bayt lahm*, a paper largely concerned with local affairs and with emigrant communities from Bethlehem in Latin America; three years later Bandak expanded his operation, publishing the more political and nationalist *Sawt al-shaʿb*.

The most important organ of Arab Orthodox thought appeared in Jaffa in 1911 and was titled *Filastin*, confirming its commitment to the idea of a Palestinian nation. *Filastin*, founded and edited by the al-ʿIsa cousins, demonstrated the existence of a strong strain of protonationalist feeling in Palestine from the late Ottoman period on; as Rashid Khalidi puts it, even the title was "indicative of the local patriotism that inspired [its] establishment."[32] *Filastin*'s promotion of new protonationalist conceptions of Palestine was central to its mission, but ʿIsa al-ʿIsa conceived it as having another, equally important role as a mouthpiece for the Arab Orthodox laity fighting a rearguard action against the foreign domination of their church and community. In the pages of *Filastin*, the twin purposes of promoting Palestinian nationalism and the Arab Orthodox cause intertwined. Al-ʿIsa created a new Arab Orthodox articulation of a nationalist argument in which the struggle against Zionism and the fight against the Greek Orthodox church hierarchy were understood as two parts of one broader Palestinian national project.

From its inception, the paper invoked constitutionalist language to support its political positions on issues as different as Zionism and the Greek Orthodox controversies. In their first editorial, the al-ʿIsas stated that their paper would be an independent publication rooted in the principles of the 1908 constitution, especially the idea of freedom of the press, and that it would champion the construction of a Palestinian national identity.[33] But advocacy for the Arab Orthodox laity was equally central to *Filastin*'s mission. ʿIsa al-ʿIsa later declared that the promotion and encouragement of the Orthodox cause had been his central motive in founding the paper,[34] and he described the Arab Orthodox movement, anti-Ottomanism, and the battle against Zionist encroachment as his three major political causes.[35] The Orthodox controversy was a central issue for *Filastin*, which began in the 1920s to promulgate the view that the struggle of the Arab Orthodox laity against the Greek clerical hierarchy and the Palestinian Arab struggle against Zionism were politically and philosophically related.

When the paper first appeared in 1911, it featured a regular column, "Shuʾun urthuduksiyya," devoted to Orthodox affairs. This tradition continued when the al-ʿIsas resumed publication of *Filastin* after the war; they opened the column to readers who wished to comment publicly on the situation in the church.[36] *Filastin*'s commentary focused around a few basic points: the commitment of Arab Orthodox Christians to their church institutions; the foreignness, greed, and immorality of the Greek hierarchy; the constitutional rights of the Arab Orthodox to participate in the institute of the patriarchate; and the continued inadequacy of the British response to the problem.

Like the other leaders of the Orthodox congresses, 'Isa al-'Isa initially considered the British mandate government to be the Orthodox Arabs' best hope for improving the position of the laity, but he quickly became disillusioned with the British response. Although enthusiastic when the financial commission was appointed in 1921, even suggesting that the commission's purview be expanded to include the moral conduct of the brotherhood and the patriarchate,[37] *Filastin* was bitterly critical when the commission made the decision to sell land to the Zionist development company. The paper castigated the British for ignoring the petitions of the Orthodox community, the recommendations of the Bertram-Young report, and the constitutionally guaranteed (both in the Ottoman "status quo" and the mandate itself) "civil and religious rights" of the Orthodox community.[38]

Filastin began to trace a relationship between the Arab Orthodox resistance to its Greek oppressors and the Palestinian resistance to Zionist intrusion. It suggested that there was a degree of cooperation among the Greeks, British, and Zionists in their oppression of the Palestinians: "These three mandatories have helped one another in depriving Palestinian Arabs of their rights."[39] This language suggested that the Greek oppression of Palestinian Arabs within the church had assisted the British and the Zionists in their imperial conspiracy against the Palestinians. Blows against the Greek hierarchy in the Orthodox church would therefore also serve to damage the British and Zionist machinery in Palestine. Al-'Isa argued in *Filastin* that the Orthodox movement was, at its core, a part of a broader struggle against the European imperial domination of Palestine.

THE PATRIARCHAL ELECTION AND THE
CONSTITUTIONALIST ARGUMENT

In 1931 Damianos died after thirty-three years as patriarch, opening up just the possibilities for change and reform that Bertram had foreseen. The laity immediately moved to renew their claims, announcing that they would boycott any patriarchal election that did not take account of the Bertram-Young recommendations. In the subsequent battle, Arab Orthodox leaders introduced another element into their movement that reflected the interests of the nationalist movement: a commitment to specifically modern electoral and constitutional reform.

The laity began by pointing out that the British commission had recognized the justice of their claims; that the patriarchate of Antioch had been inclusive of its Arab laity and clergy for many years; that the brotherhood's claim that the Holy Places of Jerusalem belonged to the Greek nation was not supported by either the laity or the British government; that the laity were willing to cooperate with British officials and to provide the money for some of their own local costs; and, most importantly, that the patriarchate should not be Greek but Palestinian. "The Arab Community," they stated, "regard [the claim of Greek ownership of the Holy Places] as groundless and arrogant. The Patriarchate is an Orthodox institution in Palestine. The Patriarch and the Fraternity are Palestinians. The Community is Palestinian and the Shrines are in Palestine."[40] This language reaffirmed Orthodox self-identification as Arab and Palestinian and warned that the brotherhood and the synod were threatening both Arab and British control of Palestine by claiming ownership of important land and sites in Jerusalem.

Ya'qub Farraj, in his capacity as vice president of the Executive Orthodox Committee, assured the community the committee would fight for Arab rights. He called for a unified front in the battle against a Greek-dominated patriarchal election: "Any aim the Community might attain would be only the result of the unity and firm stand on its part in all spheres of action."[41] In October 1931 Nakhleh Kattan (the president of a small organization known as the Arab Patriarch Party), Farraj, and Shukhri Deib presided over a meeting of Arab Orthodox priests and more than four hundred Orthodox notables in Jerusalem. Those in attendance resolved not to participate in the election unless allowed full representation and not to recognize any patriarch elected without the consent of the community. "An enthusiastic spirit presided over the meeting," *Filastin* reported, "which Nakhleh Kattan closed, as he opened it, by a word of thanks acclaiming the life of the Arab Patriarch."[42]

On November 28 the second Arab Orthodox Congress convened in Jaffa under the leadership of 'Isa al-'Isa (Farraj having been temporarily sidelined by accusations of weakness toward the Greek clergy) to address the question of the patriarchal election.[43] The concurrent Islamic Congress in Jerusalem, officiated by Hajj Amin al-Husayni, heard an appeal by Kattan and responded by publicly recognizing and congratulating the Orthodox congress as well as passing a resolution acknowledging the Arab Orthodox cause as part of the broader Arab nationalist movement.[44]

The synod, moving quickly in the hopes of preempting Arab demands, put together an electoral college and nominated three candidates in preparation for an immediate election. The British high commissioner, Sir Arthur Wauchope,[45] allowed the election to proceed despite Arab protests, saying that the British government would not intervene until after a new patriarch had been installed—meaning, as one observer pointed out, that the patriarchal election "had again to be conducted on the basis of that astonishing Law of 1875," without the participation of the laity.[46] The Orthodox press angrily continued to cast the Greeks as foreign interlopers; *Filastin* complained especially of the interference of the Greek consul general of Jerusalem, who was attempting to back the candidacy of patriarch Metaxaki of Alexandria.[47] A British press summary noted that a number of Arab newspapers were suggesting that the British decision not to intervene reflected a desire to unite the Orthodox with the Anglican church.[48]

Arab Orthodox leaders now began to emphasize electoral rights within the patriarchate, achieved through official British channels, as a primary goal of their movement.[49] In appealing the British decision not to intervene, the leaders of the Orthodox community of Jerusalem pointed to the Antiochan precedent but also drew heavily on the language of secular constitutionalism. Even by the standards of the 1875 law, they argued, the Arab community was now inadequately represented in the electoral institutions, and they demanded the immediate revision of the law to bring it in line with the Antioch constitution "to ensure to the community their full rights in conformity with the election laws of the other Patriarchate."[50] They defined these claims in constitutional terms: "It is needless to stress the fact that the right of election is one of the most important constitutional rights."[51] The Arab Orthodox movement now included a new emphasis on an intracommunal, modern, democratic, Western-style electoral process based on a modernized version of Ottoman law—concerns that reflected the simultaneous quest of Palestinian Arab nationalists for some form of legislative representation in the mandate state.

THE FAILURE OF THE MOVEMENT AND THE APPOINTMENT OF TIMOTHEOS

When his pleas to both the British and the Greeks were unavailing, Farraj appointed a team of lawyers to prevent the Greeks from proceeding with the election without Arab participation.[52] This time, Orthodox Arab leaders made no radical arguments and avoided any hint of nationalist language. Instead, their argument hinged on the appropriate legal interpretation of the Ottoman regulations of 1875 and emphasized the recommendations of the Bertram and Luke report.[53] The case went to the Supreme Court of Palestine in January 1932, and Farraj's lawyers prevailed.

In its decision the court recorded its disappointment with the lack of cooperation from the patriarchal representative Archbishop Keladion, who refused to appoint a legal representative to appear before the court on the grounds that he did not recognize the court's jurisdiction over the synod and the brotherhood. The justices noted that "in this connection we desire to express our appreciation of the ability with which Dr. Eliash [counsel for the Orthodox Arabs], although as will be seen we do not adopt all his arguments, placed with us much clearness and fairness his clients' case before us,"[54] and they chided the government for doing so little to implement the Bertram-Young recommendations. According to the court, the Secretary of State for the Colonies was the legal successor to the Ottoman Grand Vizier and had inherited that office's responsibility for administering the affairs of the Orthodox church. Accordingly, Archbishop Keladion's appointment as *locum tenens* (interim patriarch) was invalid, as it had not been properly confirmed; further, the high commissioner had, by allowing the election to proceed, "misconceived his powers."[55] Keladion therefore might remain in his position only as long as it took to make preparations for a new patriarchal election in which the laity would be allowed to participate. The court criticized the mandate government for the way it had treated the laity and ignored the recommendations of the Bertram-Young report. "We know nothing," the justices wrote, "of the reasons which, after the administration had gone out of its way to appoint the Commission, led apparently to the pigeon-holing of its report and of its recommendations for nearly seven years, but . . . [a]n indefinite continuance of such circumstances is a matter which all responsible persons would be bound to view with regret."[56]

Filastin celebrated the judgment with extensive coverage of the statements of the court and the vindication of the Arab Orthodox position.[57] In the aftermath of the decision, the Executive Orthodox Committee continued to emphasize its use of legal channels and the importance of the community's electoral rights. The committee met with the high commissioner, Sir Arthur Wauchope, in the aftermath of the decision to urge immediate action; Farraj told the high commissioner that "the recent High Court judgment is clear as to the necessity of Government intervention. . . . The demands they were making were small and reasonable."[58] By contrast, Executive Orthodox Committee member Anton Attala pointed out, "the pride of the Fraternity was great; for instance they had refused to recognise the jurisdiction of the High Court in the recent case,"[59] thereby challenging the authority of the mandate government.

Wauchope responded to the court's scolding with irritation ("Palestine government was not party to the proceedings and Judgment has created very difficult position"[60]) and proposed that the secretary of state designate the high commissioner head of church matters in Palestine and allow the election to proceed.[61] London disagreed and upheld the decisions of the court.

Finally, in 1934 Wauchope issued a public statement that no patriarch would be confirmed who had not fulfilled the demands of the laity.[62]

The government now began to draw up a draft ordinance to replace the 1875 Fundamental Law, but in view of the ongoing tensions in Palestine and the pressing issues of Arab-Jewish conflict, the British had decided to "confine their intervention to a minimum" and were unwilling to press for a solution.[63] Their weak attempt to find a compromise resulted in a 1934 draft bill scorned by the Orthodox press; the *Arab Federation*, an English-language paper founded by prominent political activist Imil Ghori, quoted Farraj as saying, "The action of the government in publishing the new bill, after years of study and investigations, is in full agreement with the noted Arab proverb: 'The mountain has suffered birth pains, and borne a mouse.'"[64] There was now little faith in the government's intervention; Yusef al-'Isa and 'Uda Qusus, in a memo on their meetings with the executive committee and the patriarchal representatives, wrote, "We must in conclusion admit that the problem shall surely be trusted to the Government and that the Patriarchate and the Community shall have to enjoy what the two cats enjoyed of the piece of cheese on which they disputed one another."[65]

By 1935 the divided synod had agreed on Timotheos as patriarch-elect and had begun the process of installing him. The draft ordinance had gone no further, despite pressure from the laity and a number of bitterly critical articles in the Arab Orthodox press. Wauchope was theoretically sympathetic to the laity and friendly with Farraj, whom he described as "very helpful and moderate and willing to co-operate with Government."[66] He also made a point of consulting with the well-known writer and diplomat George Antonius, who was by this time no longer working for the British government but remained an important sounding board for Wauchope. At Antonius' suggestion, Wauchope met with the patriarch-elect, Timotheos, and the chief secretary of the patriarchate, Archmandrite Epiphanios, and found them both obdurate in their opposition to lay rights. "At the end of 2 hours," Wauchope wrote, "I rose in my chair and in my wrath said I was profoundly disappointed and dismayed at the regrettable lack he had shown of any approach to a spirit of good will or conciliation. I said I should not forget his statement that the Convent had the power and would part with none of it to the laity."[67] But this sympathy did not translate into action, and the Orthodox committee's attempts to prevent the election failed.

With the nationalist movement gaining steam and Palestinians across communal lines increasingly committed to Palestinian Arab political independence, the antiforeign aspect of the Orthodox argument had become central to a broadly based Palestinian Arab Orthodox movement, and the leadership had the support of Arab Orthodox communities all over the country. Even Wauchope noted in a missive to London that he thought "the statement that their Executive [the Executive Orthodox Committee] represent the view of about 90 percent of the lay community to be not far from the truth."[68] Tens of local Orthodox organizations sent telegrams to the high commissioner opposing Timotheos; clubs in Nablus, Jaffa, Acre, Lydda, Jerusalem, Ramallah, Tul Karm, Bethlehem, Gaza, Haifa, Ramleh, Bayt Jala, and Nazareth contributed to this barrage.[69] These messages not only conveyed opposition to the election but also explicitly expressed solidarity with and confidence in the Executive Orthodox Committee.

Farraj once again turned to British legal channels, filing a motion to have the election declared null and void on the grounds of irregularities in the election process. This time, however, the decision went against him. The court declared that since Timotheos had yet to be officially appointed by the successor to the Ottoman Grand Vizier (that is, the Secretary of State for the Colonies) he remained only patriarch-elect, and therefore the court was unable to pronounce on the validity of his election. Although the case ended in defeat for the Arab Orthodox community, the British felt uncertain about backing the synod and did not immediately confirm Timotheos' election.[70]

The leadership continued its efforts to persuade the mandate government to intervene. In 1937, in the aftermath of the previous year's general strike that marked the beginning of the Great Revolt that would continue until 1939, a new British commission (known as the Peel Commission, after its head) came to Palestine to determine a future path for Palestine's Arabs and Jews.[71] Farraj submitted a detailed grievance to the commission in which he emphasized the importance of religious institutions to Palestinian life and the Orthodox community's inability to participate through their own communal structures. He pointed out that the mandate had agreed that it would supervise the religious communities in Palestine as was necessary "for the maintenance of public order and good government" and that one of the first acts of the mandate government had been to address organizational issues relating to the Muslim and Jewish religious communities. The mandate state's neglect of the Orthodox Arabs, Farraj argued, was now causing their community's disintegration. "In particular," he testified, "the Ecclesiastical Courts are not properly organized and the administration of justice therein is far from being satisfactory. Orthodox children are denied any religious education. The revenue of the endowments and properties of the Jerusalem Church are collected and spent by the clergy without any proper control or consideration to the welfare of the Community which is the chief beneficiary."[72] In the sectarian landscape of colonial Palestine, he was arguing, functional communal institutions were a civic necessity. The breach between the laity and the hierarchy and the mandate government's policy of non-interference in Christian affairs therefore had serious legal and political ramifications for members of the Arab Orthodox community.

OPPOSING THE NEW IDENTITY:
GEORGE ANTONIUS AND KHALIL AL-SAKAKINI

This new Orthodox approach—recasting the Arab Orthodox movement as an essentially political movement integral to Palestinian nationalism—did not go unopposed. Two men who were arguably the Arab Orthodox community's most prominent members, George Antonius and Khalil al-Sakakini, had serious reservations about this campaign to reinvent the Palestinian Orthodox community as a political entity. Antonius, although he was in many ways sympathetic to the movement, thought that the incorporation of Palestinian Arab nationalism into Orthodox communal self-identification was counterproductive and would inevitably lead to the collapse of the institutions (particularly the schools) that were for him the community's *raison d'être*. Al-Sakakini, on the other hand, came to believe that communal political identifications were themselves inherently problematic and rendered it impossible for Christians of any denomination to integrate themselves fully into Palestinian national life.

George Antonius was a Lebanese-born, British-educated intellectual, civil servant, and diplomat who had worked in the Palestinian civil service during the 1920s and became famous in 1938 with the publication of a still-influential history of Arab nationalism (and defense of Arab Palestine against Zionism) titled *The Arab Awakening*. He had interested himself in the Palestinian Arab Orthodox movement since the publication of the Bertram-Young report and kept up a friendly correspondence with Anton Bertram. Antonius occasionally spoke on behalf of the Orthodox community vis-à-vis the British government and acted as an informal adviser on the matter to Wauchope during the early 1930s. He positioned himself as an independent mediator able to interact amicably with all the parties in the dispute. "Although I do not belong to any committee or public body of the community," he wrote to Bertram in 1932, "I have found myself called, purely in my capacity as a member of the Church, into consultations with the principal actors in this controversy, both among the community and in the Fraternity . . . without committing anyone but myself."[73]

Antonius supported greater Arab participation in the church and criticized the brotherhood for its unwillingness to compromise, while praising the Arab community leaders for displaying "a remarkable moderation and a real willingness to discuss the questions at issue in a spirit of conciliation."[74] Nevertheless, he thought the nationalist approach was a mistake. Antonius supported Meletios, the Greek candidate for the patriarchate, on the grounds that Arab control of the church was vastly less important than the renewal of the patriarchate as a functional institution and the revitalization of its communal institutions. "It is true that he [Meletios] is an ardent Hellene, and that his activities in the past have been marked by a resolute determination to oppose the claims of the community," he wrote, ". . . [but] he is by far the ablest candidate on the list; and, personally, I feel quite prepared to run such risks as his Hellenism may carry, for the sake of the certain gains to the moral life and material strength of the Fraternity which his election would undoubtedly mean."[75] Antonius went on to suggest forcefully that Arabization was less important than the restoration of the community's institutions and political functions: "I have tried to impress upon my friends on the Committee of the community that good order, discipline, and financial soundness are as important assets, to say the least, as Mixed Councils, Arab bishops, and so forth."[76] Antonius' conviction that the functioning of church institutions was more important than their Arabization was decidedly at odds with the position of Farraj, the 'Isas, and many of the lay leaders of the Arab Orthodox communities.

Khalil al-Sakakini's view on the Orthodox controversy was very different. From the time of the upheavals in the patriarchate in the late Ottoman period, al-Sakakini was deeply committed to the welfare of the Arab Orthodox community. Although he was not himself religious, he felt strongly connected to the community through social, political, and business ties. His diaries reveal an active commitment to the cause of Arabizing the Greek Orthodox church and patriarchate from 1908 on; he maintained extensive contacts with the leaders of the movement and lobbied for change in Jerusalem and Istanbul. In 1913 he was excommunicated for authoring a pamphlet titled *Al-Nahda al-urthuduksiyya fi Filastin* (The Orthodox Renaissance in Palestine) in which he excoriated the Greek patriarchate and extolled the virtues of the Arab Orthodox movement.

By the end of the Ottoman period, however, he had begun to lose interest in the project. In 1914 he declared that he would no longer support the Orthodox movement and disassociated himself from his church: "I cannot remain under the leadership of this corrupt and degenerate priesthood, I cannot be a member of this degenerate community . . . I am not Orthodox!"[77] This turnaround represented disillusionment not only with the Orthodox community but with the very idea of communal identifications. "If nationalism is to love life," he wrote in 1915, "then I am a nationalist. But if it lies in preferring one religion over another, one language over another, one city over another, one interest over another, then I am not a nationalist."[78] For al-Sakakini, a humanist, Western-influenced, essentially secular thinker, communal identifications threatened rather than complemented nationalism. He rejected the idea of sectarian organization as a mode of political participation.

During the mandate, al-Sakakini gradually moved still further away from the notion that a minority religious community could be a viable political entity. His progressive nationalist program, exemplified in the curriculum of his Dusturiyya school and in his educational theories, was based on notions of secular Arabism and Palestinian nationalism and had no place for communal institutions. As communal identifications in Palestine strengthened under the influence of mandate policy, al-Sakakini saw only the exclusion of Christians from Muslim institutions. He began to view the politicized Arab Orthodox movement as essentially problematic and to see Islamic political identity in hostile terms. In 1932 he expressed his views on the damaging effects of communalism in a now-famous statement to his son Sari: "No matter how my standing may be in science and literature, no matter how sincere my patriotism is, no matter how much I do to revive this nation . . . as long as I am not a Moslem I am nought."[79] Eventually he became so disappointed with the extent to which religious identifications had become politically central in the mandate state that he refused a public position, the directorship of the Arabic broadcasting service in Palestine, on the grounds that he was not Muslim. For al-Sakakini, communal identifications were incompatible with nationalism and destructive to unity—a point of view directly opposed to that of the Orthodox movement's leaders.

Leaders like Farraj, the 'Isas, and 'Isa Bandak viewed the entwining of communal and nationalist identities as a viable way to create a central political role for Orthodox Arabs in Palestinian politics. All these men were heavily involved in Muslim-led nationalist parties as well as the Orthodox cause; they had worked in both a communal and a nationalist context for many years, saw the two movements as essentially similar, and were able to convey this point of view to the Orthodox clubs and societies that petitioned the mandate government on their behalf during the 1920s and 1930s.[80] Antonius' rejection of a nationalist element in communal identity and al-Sakakini's rejection of a communal element in national identity represented a departure from the views of the Arab Orthodox leadership.[81]

Although Orthodox leaders continued to promote the Arab Orthodox cause, by the time Timotheos was finally issued the *Berat* (the official document confirming his appointment as patriarch) in 1939, the movement had lost much of its momentum, overshadowed by increasing Jewish-Arab hostility and the 1936–1939 Great Revolt. In July 1938 the synod had disseminated a new statute that followed the Bertram-Young recommendations in certain respects but included an absolute refusal to legitimize the possibility of an Arab patriarch. Consequently, all the participants in the second Arab Orthodox Congress, who had expressed their commitment to the idea of an Arab patriarch along the lines of Antioch, refused to recognize Timotheos. At the Conference of Orthodox Youth in 1935, the participants made a pledge not to acknowledge him as patriarch until all their claims had been satisfied.[82]

In 1941 the British signed off on another Orthodox patriarchate ordinance that essentially repeated the position of the previous one: the formation of mixed and local councils but no provision for the more radical demands of substantial Arab membership in the brotherhood and an Arab patriarch. The Orthodox communities in many parts of the country were now in total disarray, and numbers had dropped as members emigrated or joined another church. The Orthodox community in Haifa wrote to the patriarch in 1943 to bemoan the state of the flock:

> Many villages have been left without parish priests to take charge of their spiritual needs. Even towns lack such priests who command respect and are worthy of their robes. The only persons ordained by the Patriarch were unworthy individuals who were unable to subsist and chose to bargain with His Church for the lack of any alternative occupation. The state of affairs in the ecclesiastical courts is lamentable whilst the grievances sustained by the public are more to comment on in this short report . . . The Palestine Orthodox Community shrinks with shame at the humorous gestures made by the cultured western communities regarding the low standard of our parish priests.[83]

In September 1944 the leadership convened a third Arab Orthodox Congress in Jerusalem to repudiate the 1941 ordinance. It was attended by 150 members from Palestine and Transjordan; 'Isa Bandak served on its executive committee, along with Sam'an Daoud, Hanna Salama, Anton Attala, and Ya'qub Jmai'an. Their letter to the chief secretary of Palestine informing him of the resolution of the congress to oppose the ordinance was considerably less detailed and forceful than previous efforts. The congress' second resolution (after rejecting the ordinance) empowered the executive committee of the congress once again to open negotiations with the mandate government and the patriarchate.[84] "Our Committee," secretary Sam'an Daoud wrote,

> earnestly hopes that in the light of (a) developments which took place since the date of this letter (b) Government's experience of the uncompromising attitude of the Patriarchate under whose administration the Patriarchate and the Community are deteriorating and (c) the resolution of the Congress which found itself unable to cooperate with the Patriarchate on the basis of an Ordinance which gave the foreign clergy all powers and hardly any to the representatives of the laity: in the light of all these considerations it is hoped that Government would reconsider its decision and save the parties concerned from the dead lock.[85]

There was still a residual sympathy for the Orthodox cause among some Palestinian Muslims; Tawfiq Saleh al-Husayni, president of the Palestine Arab Party, wrote to the high commissioner to support the congress saying that "the Palestine Arab people as a whole are anxious to see the case of the Arab Orthodox Community settled, sympathize with that Community and with its case and support its just and right demands . . . The Palestine Arab Party joins with the Orthodox members of this Arab nation, and requests Government . . . [to] guarantee to the Arabs their rights and assure them of their interests and of their holy places and Awqafs."[86] The mandate government did not respond.

Finally giving up on the British, Orthodox leaders now turned their attention toward the leaders of the Arab world. In 1946 a party of Arab Orthodox representatives presented their case to the secretary of the newly formed Arab League asking him to support them and presenting their case in Arab nationalist terms. In their letter to 'Abd al-Rahman 'Azzam they described the long history of Arab Christianity in Palestine before the Greek incursion;[87] they blamed the Ottomans for supporting the Greek clergy against the Arab population—"like any imperialistic state, they helped them against the Arabs"—and represented their struggle as an Arab "revolt" against "foreign elements [that had] appropriated all the rights and property of the community."[88] They went on to designate the Orthodox struggle as an integral part of the Palestinian cause: "We as Arabs and our case being both nationally and politically an Arab affair present this humble petition requesting from your honourable League and from the Arab States participating in the League sympathy for our case by embracing it as an indivisible part of the general Palestinian case."[89] They justified this statement by saying that the Orthodox community was the largest one after the Muslim, that Muslims would be stirred by the "racial policy" of the patriarchate, and that the Orthodox aim was "the independence of the community in its communal affairs and in the supervision of all its property so as to become a strong community with a definite and clear Arab influence, and so as to be able to deliver its national message in a full and suitable manner."[90] There could be no clearer statement of the ways Orthodox leaders had tried to integrate their cause into the Palestinian nationalist movement and reinvent their religious community as a politically significant entity.

'Azzam's response was mildly sympathetic; he forwarded the letter to the British embassy in Cairo, "hoping that it will receive [London's] good consideration, with your kind attention and support."[91] But by this stage, the Muslim leadership in Palestine was in a state of serious disarray and could do little to express solidarity with the Orthodox movement. The expressly nationalist orientation of the movement had also now alienated the British government. Sir Harold MacMichael, the new high commissioner who oversaw the brutal crackdown on Palestinian Arab nationalist leaders in the later stages of the Great Revolt, stated in 1944, "The leaders of the lay community have now formally 'rejected' the Ordinance . . . [T]he extreme party among the laity show no desire for a reasonable settlement but are endeavouring to make of the Ordinance a political issue in alignment with Arab national ambitions."[92]

As Palestine moved toward political crisis in the final years of the mandate, national feeling overtook the Orthodox cause. At a meeting of Arab Orthodox clergy in Jerusalem in 1947, the main concern was not the patriarchal issue but expressions of support for Palestinian nationalism and vehement opposition to the proposed partition of Palestine into Arab and Jewish states. Reverend Ya'qub al-Hanna spoke of the meeting as a "lull before the storm," declaring that "the hour has struck to participate with the people in repelling the dangers encircling the dear homeland."[93] The conference's primary decision was to send out three telegrams. The first went to the Arab Higher Executive, the committee led by Hajj Amin al-Husayni that was directing nationalist activity and policy, expressing "absolute confidence" in its leadership and announcing "to the whole world the cooperation of the Arab Orthodox Community, in weal and woe, with its sister, the dear Muslim community." The second was to the secretary general of the Arab League and sent "greetings of glorification and appreciation for your attitude which is fraught with heroism towards the Palestine case." The last, to the high commissioner, declared that the community "supports the faithful leaders and the Arab Higher Executive and rejects partition categorically, announcing its preparedness to safeguard Palestine's Arabism and the Holy Places at any cost."[94] The Arab Orthodox cause, though not forgotten, was now subsumed in the calamity facing the whole of the Palestinian Arab population.

Arab Orthodox leaders like Ya'qub Farraj, the al-'Isas, 'Isa Bandak, and Imil Ghori had tried to present a movement for Arab control of their church as an essentially nationalist struggle with implications for the political fate of Arab Palestine—an approach that arose in response to colonial policies and foreign interventions that enshrined religion as a political and legal category. But in re-creating the Arab Orthodox community as an identifiable bloc with specifically communal political goals, they had also unwittingly helped to further the construction of a sectarian political landscape in Palestine.

They had not, however, succeeded in their goal of reinventing the Orthodox community as central to Palestinian Arab nationalist politics. Now, in this increasingly sectarian atmosphere, some of these same leaders would look to make Palestinian Christianity more broadly into a viable political identity.

APPROPRIATING SECTARIANISM: THE BRIEF EMERGENCE *of* PAN-CHRISTIAN COMMUNALISM, 1929–1936

It is a well known fact that under the Turkish Regime the Christian Community had full representation, not only in Municipal Councils but also in all Administrative and Judicial bodies. Such practice was practically followed since the British Occupation, and especially maintained in Municipal Councils.
No reasonable Christian can see any reason why Government should deviate from this Constitutional rule or practice. On the contrary, the Christians feel that such right which was acquired by tradition cannot be withheld from them without prejudicing their Civil and Religious rights.

MUGHANNAM MUGHANNAM, ARAB EPISCOPALIAN LAWYER,
RAMALLAH, 1934

In the mid-1930s the mandate government began to entertain the idea of creating a national legislative council in which Palestinian Arabs would take part.[1] This was the mandate government's second attempt at constructing a legislative council; the first had failed in 1923 after the Arabs organized a successful boycott of the elections. During the course of the revived public debate over the form and nature of Palestine's legislative structures, Arab Christians across the political spectrum came to support the idea of Christian communal representation in municipal and national legislatures. This new sense of Arab pan-Christian solidarity culminated in 1936 with a cross-party Christian expression of support for a communally elected legislative council—the first time in Palestinian history that Christians of all denominations presented themselves as a single, coherent political bloc.

This unprecedented pan-Christian alignment arose as a consequence of a new sense among Christians that their political existence in the mandate state was under threat from the increasing Jewish presence in representative institutions of all kinds. During the 1930s, Jewish leaders were beginning to argue for "racial" as opposed to communal representation in Palestine's political institutions. In their view the legislative system should be based on an equal balance of Jews and Arabs—"parity"—in the representative institutions of the mandate state, instead of a three-way franchise of Jews, Muslims, and Christians. Influenced by the Jewish leadership, the British began to abandon or modify the sectarian political models the colonial state itself had originally constructed. This shift in policy tended to result in a net loss of Arab representation as Arab Christians on various municipal and regional legislative bodies were replaced with Jewish members. Under these circumstances, Christians quickly recognized the idea of sectarian representation as a potential weapon against Zionist influence in Palestine; separate representation for each religious community—Muslim, Christian, and Jewish—could give Arabs a two-thirds majority in any legislative institution.

Arab Christian leaders therefore began advocating for communal legislative representation. As well as promoting the idea as a possible defense against Zionism, they redefined sectarian representation as a modernizing, progressive approach introduced by the Ottomans. During the early 1930s, Arab Christian leaders developed a new political rhetoric that explicitly associated sectarian representation with ideas of modernity and nationalism and depicted new British policies of "racial" representation as backward and primitive.

This approach successfully (if briefly) brought a number of Christian elites into cross-party agreement. Ultimately, however, this move toward sectarian representation as a mode of political participation was no more successful at reintegrating Christian elites and communities into the center of Palestinian politics than the endeavor to make their presence felt through the Arab Orthodox movement. The new Christian solidarity was more a temporary political alignment than a deeply rooted common identity; the leaders who spearheaded this collective Christian action remained dedicated to their various parties, political platforms, and individual religious communities.

Eventually what emerged from this flirtation with the idea of Palestinian pan-Christian solidarity was a kind of Arab Christian internationalism, represented especially by the new Arab Centre in London. This institution drew on mission connections, international networks of (disproportionately Christian) Palestinian expatriates, and European Christian institutions to defend the cause of Palestinian nationalism in an international forum. Its founder, 'Izzat Tannus, used his Christian connections to create an international network through which he could appeal for support for the Palestinian nationalist cause.

During the course of the legislative council negotiations, Palestinian Arab Christian leaders appropriated the idea of sectarian political organization from the colonial state and reinvented it as a tool of anti-Zionist and anti-colonial political argument at a time when the British themselves were beginning to move away from the idea of communal representation and toward "racially" based franchises of Jews and Arabs. Elite Palestinian Arab Christian leaders deployed the concept of communal identities, which the British had encouraged as a means of colonial control, to argue for an Arab majority in Palestine's representative institutions. They redefined sectarian representation as an Ottoman-invented mode of modernization and progress, contrasting it with the backward approach of the British colonial state. Further, Arab Christian elites deployed their religious identity for their own political purposes, drawing on Christian institutional contacts to promote Palestinian nationalism in the West. In these few years, Palestinian Arab Christians appropriated the colonial idea of sectarian representation, using it to serve their own nationalist and anti-Zionist agendas.

LEGISLATIVE REPRESENTATION: INITIAL CHRISTIAN ALIGNMENTS

Since the legal and representative structures of the mandate system were based on the principle of communalism, Christian participation in the two main political factions (the majlisi, associated with the SMC and led by the Husayni family, and the mu'arida, the opposition, headed by the Nashashibi family) was inevitably conditioned by some level of sectarian awareness. Nevertheless, no specifically Christian political consciousness had emerged; leaders who identified themselves as members of a Christian community aligned themselves with a number of parties. While Christian activists like 'Isa al-'Isa, Bulus Shihada, and Ya'qub Farraj were loyal to the Nashashibis' opposition faction, other prominent middle-class Christians like Imil Ghori, 'Izzat Tannus, Michel 'Azar, and Alfred Rok were affiliated with the Husaynis.[2] During the early 1930s, when political parties began to proliferate in Palestine, other Christian leaders joined splinter groups; Shibli Jamal and 'Isa Bandak, for instance, became active representatives of the Khalidi-run Reform party, and George Mansur (later one of the founders of the Arab Workers Society) and Salim Salama joined the more radical, pan-Arabist Istiqlal party. When the issue of communal representation on a legislative council came to the fore, then, Christian nationalist leaders were involved in all the main Arab political organizations in Palestine.

In June 1928 the seventh Palestinian Arab Congress sent a letter to the British government demanding a parliamentary government in which Arabs could participate.[3] In 1929 Jamal al-Husayni (representing the SMC and the

Husayni majlisi faction), Fakhri al-Nashashibi (nephew of opposition leader Raghib Nashashibi), and Awni ʿAbd al-Hadi (former Ottoman parliamentarian, member of the SMC, and associate of the Husaynis) met with the high commissioner, Sir John Chancellor, to suggest the form a new legislative council might take.

Al-Husayni, al-Nashashibi, and al-Hadi envisioned a body of fourteen officials and fifteen members—ten Muslims, three Jews, and two Christians—and went so far as to present Chancellor with a list of suggested names for the Muslim and Christian members; Yaʿqub Farraj, the Arab Orthodox leader from Jerusalem, and Mughannam Mughannam, a well-known Palestinian Episcopalian lawyer in Ramallah, were to represent the Christian communities.[4] Chancellor was seemingly amenable to these suggestions, and in June 1929 he brought the proposal to the colonial secretary.[5] The proposal was tabled two months later with the outbreak of hostilities over the Buraq (Western Wall) in Jerusalem.

When the issue arose again the next year, British proposals for a new legislative council elicited a positive response from Arab leaders across the political spectrum but especially from prominent Christians. Under ʿIsa al-ʿIsa, *Filastin* defended the shift in its position since a legislative council had been mooted eight years earlier: "It might be thought that some of the Arabs would allege that the Legislative Council now offered them is the same as that rejected by them in 1922. To such persons we now say that the spirit of the policy has been completely changed . . . Let us resort to the means which will lead us to the full independence for which we long."[6]

Two days later, however, the paper had moderated its tone and began to examine and find fault with the specifics of the proposal, suggesting that its form prevented the Arabs from full representation. The article noted that the council would be composed of ten appointed officials, of whom three would be Jewish, alongside eight Muslim and two Christian elected representatives. *Filastin* viewed this as a "gross injustice" since not only every district but also every Christian community would have its own opinion on various matters and needed representation; it suggested doubling the number of representatives, even if it meant halving the pay associated with the positions. Nevertheless, it noted, the proposal was likely to be viewed positively by many Arabs even without these changes.[7]

Filastin was not representing the unified stance of a multi-denominational Christian lobby at this stage; its focus was on obtaining sufficient representation to allow for the presentation of different points of view. The idea of Christian representation, for the moment, remained community-based. *Filastin*'s comments did, however, demonstrate the inchoate concept of communalism as a weapon in the war of numbers against Zionism; the suggested expansion of Christian representation was subtly presented as guaranteeing a wider Arab majority on the council.

The Bethlehem paper *Sawt al-sha'b*, edited by the Arab Orthodox community leader, politician, and journalist 'Isa Bandak, sounded a similar note. Although its writers had some reservations about the specifics of the legislative council proposals and about the permanence of the pro-Arab turn in British policy, they opined that the Arabs should immediately and without hesitation accept the idea of a legislative council, as any kind of representation to the British government would be better than the present situation in which the Arabs had no voice at all.[8] Like *Filastin*, *Sawt al-sha'b* noted that the situation had changed drastically since 1922 and that while the purpose of the legislative council proposals then was to force the Arabs to accept the Balfour Declaration, the idea now was to move toward Palestinian self-determination; cooperation with the British did not imply any relaxation of the claim to independence.[9] *Sawt al-sha'b*, then, demonstrated a commitment to representation as an essential step toward political modernity and eventual autonomy for an Arab Palestine.

Although there was interest in the proposals from Muslim political leaders as well as Christians, the Muslim-owned and Husayni-backed Jerusalem paper *al-Jami'a al-'arabiyya* was less effusive than its Christian-run counterparts, pointing out that the proposed form of the council actually gave the Arabs less political power than the one mooted in 1922 in that its members would be appointed whether or not Arabs decided to vote in the elections. "The course of events in this country under the British," the paper declared, "does not record, as far as the Arabs are concerned, any display of mercy or compassion . . . British policy in Palestine is still based on threats, violence, intimidation, dispossession, and eviction."[10] Legislative representation in itself did not necessarily indicate progress; the council might easily represent continued colonial dominance and brutality. For supporters of the Husaynis' majlisi faction, representation on a legislative council was a less pressing concern since they already had a certain level of representation to the British government through the Supreme Muslim Council. But for the editors of *Filastin* and *Sawt al-sha'b*, current representation was nonexistent; even a flawed system seemed better than none.

The arguments made by *Filastin* and *Sawt al-sha'b* did not suggest a unified political position among Christians; indeed, one of *Filastin*'s main arguments was that more representatives were needed because the various Christian communities would have different opinions on the questions discussed in the council. But they both expressed a strong feeling that Palestinian Arabs were increasingly going unheard and that any form of representation, however limited, was preferable to having no voice at all. In assuming—and not challenging—the continuation of mandate policies supporting communalism, *Filastin* was beginning to articulate the idea that communal representation could help build up Arab numbers in mandate institutions that included Jews. *Filastin*'s articles featured a repeated use of the phrase "Muslims and Christians" to indicate the Palestinian Arabs; this offered a subtle reminder of the multi-confessional nature of Palestinian nationalism, confirmed the continued Christian commitment to the Palestinian nationalist movement, and suggested that communal representation was a natural mode of operation for the proposed council. Christian elites were beginning to think that communal representation could offer a safeguard against Jewish domination of mandate-sponsored institutions as well as against their own exclusion from the process of representing the Palestinian Arab viewpoint to the British government.

The strong Jewish opposition to the legislative council proposals and the Zionist Executive's decision, in August 1930, that it would refuse to participate in the council if it were formed led the British to shelve the idea, focusing instead on trying to resolve the issues surrounding immigration and land purchase. Chancellor remained interested in the council, but he had difficulty convincing the Colonial Office to share his enthusiasm. In February 1931 London refused him permission to announce progress on its formation and responded very coolly to his explicitly stated opinion that the legislative council should be formed immediately.[11] The matter was postponed due to the formation of a new government (with a new colonial secretary, the Conservative Sir Philip Cunliffe-Lister) and Chancellor's resignation as high commissioner. By this time a general Palestinian Christian support had begun to emerge for the idea of communal representation in a national legislative council, on the assumption that it was a necessary step toward eventual independence.

COMMUNAL VERSUS RACIAL IDENTIFICATIONS:
THE BRITISH DEBATE

By 1930 sectarian representation was thoroughly ingrained in Palestinian politics. The legislative council proposals of the early 1920s had involved sectarian representation; the various commissions appointed by the British to investigate problems in Palestine invariably included representatives from each of the three religious communities; the Supreme Muslim Council was enshrined as Palestine's most important Arab representative body; and municipal representation was now communally organized. Responding to these colonial structures, both the majlisi faction and its most important political rival, the Nashashibi-run opposition, had begun to use Islamic symbolism and rhetoric to define their messages for both the Palestinian Arabs and the British. The Christian communities, excluded from the SMC and to some degree marginalized in the newly Islamicized opposition, had likewise begun to look for communally organized political outlets, initially revolving around protests at the neglect of their communal courts, schools, and awqaf. Even the emergence of the nonsectarian Istiqlal (Independence) party in 1932 and its explicit disavowal of al-Husayni's Islamic rhetoric in favor of a secular pan-Arabism with links to Iraq, Syria, and Lebanon serve to demonstrate the extent to which sectarian political identities had infiltrated Palestinian Arab politics by the early 1930s.

But having done so much to channel political activity into sectarian institutions, the British now began to change their minds. Continued Jewish immigration, combined with a collapsing economy and increased pressure on rural land, led to a series of demonstrations in 1933 that involved the majlisi and mu'arida factions, crossed sectarian and social lines, and included large numbers of rural peasantry as well as the elites and notables who had been the face of Palestinian political action during the 1920s.[12] This demonstration of Arab solidarity, combined with Hajj Amin al-Husayni's failure to raise substantial sums of money during his tour of India in 1933, undermined the British conviction that sectarian divisions represented the primary mode of political identification in Arab Palestine.[13] At the same time, the leaders of the European Jewish community were pressing the British to enshrine a policy of "parity," by which they meant equal representation of Jews and Arabs regardless of population numbers.

Responding to these shifts, the British now began to move toward a system that categorized Palestinians by "race" rather than religion. In 1932, in some notes on the proposed constitution for Palestine, Cosmo Parkinson of the Colonial Office compared the situation in Palestine with that of India, Kenya, and Ceylon: "Assuming that differentiation by religions is to be abandoned, the obvious line of differentiation is race; in any event the fact that the establishment of the Jewish National Home is one of the obligations of the mandate seems to imply, whatever cooperation may come about in time between Arabs and Jews, an indefinite perpetuation of racial distinction on politics. . . . It is recommended that for Palestine a communal franchise should be adopted."[14] By "communal franchise" Parkinson meant the production of two categories, Jews and Arabs, reserving the possibility of a separate grouping for the Druze. By the mid-1930s, then, having encouraged the emergence of a political identity based primarily on religious affiliation and expressed through newly formed millet-based institutions, the British had changed their minds and were now leaning toward collapsing the Muslim and Christian Arab communities into a single "racial" identity for political purposes.[15]

From the early 1930s, then, the British began to use racial categorizations alongside sectarian classifications to interpret and formulate government policy. In data on the population, the workforce, and government hiring practices, the categories "Arab" and "Jew" began to replace the previous labels of "Muslim," "Christian," and "Jew."[16] This new approach became especially clear in 1931 when the Palestine census included a category of self-reported ethnic identity for everyone except the country's nomads; 79.8 percent reported themselves to be Arab, and 18 percent categorized themselves as Jews, with 2.2 percent falling into the category "other."[17] In the published census, however, the focus remained on religion, with the population figures noted for the Muslim, Christian, and Jewish communities but also for the Druze, Baha'i, and Samaritan populations.[18] Clearly, this transition was by no means immediate or absolute, and debate over sectarian versus racial identifications would continue in both British and Palestinian Arab circles during the next decade.

The new high commissioner, Sir Arthur Wauchope, initially cited Jewish opposition and Arab unreadiness as reasons to postpone further discussion of the legislative council for another year.[19] But during the early 1930s the increasing unrest in Palestine led him to consider reviving the proposal in hopes that a council would "at least give all classes a means of expressing their views and grievances and lessen the temptation to adopt unconstitutional means."[20] In 1932 he asked George Antonius to draw up a proposal for a new constitutional government involving a representative legislative council.

Antonius' proposal became the site of British discussion about how to define the various franchises in Palestine. Commenting on the draft, Colonial Secretary Philip Cunliffe-Lister noted to Wauchope that the "original proposal had been that the basis of election should be religious" and suggested that it might be changed to a "racial" franchise, using the categories of Arab and Jewish rather than Muslim, Christian, and Jewish.[21] Wauchope opposed all versions of communalism, favoring instead the "modern" solution of territorial representation. Writing to Cunliffe-Lister in 1934, he declared that it would increase "stereotypes [of] racial and religious divisions and indeed would make more difficult the process of coming together which we wish to encourage in the future. Consequently I prefer the method . . . of arranging the constituencies so that each community will secure a fair representation, yet establishing the principle of an electorate by localities."[22] The British were reconsidering the principle of communal representation just as the Palestinian Arab Christian leadership was beginning to see it as a potential weapon against Zionism.

THE MUNICIPAL COUNCIL DEBATES

With the question not settled, Wauchope and his superiors in London determined that the mandate government should address the issue of municipal representation before beginning the process of forming a national council. In 1934 the mandate government undertook to overhaul the Municipal Corporations Ordinance in Jerusalem, experimenting with a territorial rather than a communally organized franchise. The ensuing debate featured a series of protests on the part of various representatives of the different Christian denominations about the loss of Christian representation on the council. In the course of the arguments, Arab Christian leaders began to formulate a new understanding of the idea of sectarian representation, associating it firmly with political "modernity." They presented communal representation as a modern political right, an essential component of an Ottoman program of modernization and advancement. The British revocation of that right, they argued, represented a political step backward, away from modernity and progress. This reclamation of the idea of sectarian representation as an integral part of a specifically Arab modernity cast the colonial state as a force for backwardness and primitive thought.

The municipal council in Jerusalem, put into place at the beginning of the mandate, had six members: two of each religious community, with a Muslim mayor and two deputy mayors—one Christian and one Jewish. In 1927 the mandate government made some adjustments to the system, doubling the number of members to twelve, with the proportion being determined by rate payments. This change meant the Christians lost one seat to a Muslim representative, but the basic principle of equality of each community was maintained and the mayoral system remained in place. The Municipal Corporations Ordinance of 1934 brought major alterations to this structure. Under the new rules, elections for the municipal council were to be held according to geographic divisions, and there would be only one deputy mayor rather than two.

This change occasioned protest from leaders of all the Christian communities. Yaʿqub Farraj, one of the leaders of the Arab Orthodox movement and vice president of the Arab Executive, was one of the first to remonstrate. (Part of Farraj's concern was personal, as he had previously served as the deputy mayor of Jerusalem and naturally did not wish to be deposed.) He met with Wauchope in February 1934 and wrote him a letter shortly thereafter enumerating the points he had made. "The Christians have every reason to fear losing their rights in representation," he told the high commissioner, "as no matter what efforts they exert in this respect, they cannot secure more than two Christian divisions by reason of their being scattered in different areas."[23]

Farraj presented communal municipal representation as an integral part of a modernization effort by the Ottomans and continued by the British; a reversal of this policy therefore stripped Palestinian Christians of their political rights. Ottoman precedent, he argued, provided a fair, modern, and just solution that the British themselves had accepted earlier in the mandate. Farraj explicitly linked the Ottoman-based "status quo" with the "rights," "justice," and "representation"—all words redolent of Western political philosophy—of the Christian population:

> One point I wish to invite Your Excellency's kind attention to and that is under the Turkish regime the Christian population was fully and adequately represented in both the Administration and Judicial Departments . . . In view of the preceding I humbly submit that Your Excellency will view with justice and equity the rights of the Christian communities in the Holy City which existed prior to the ratification of the Mandate for Palestine which acquired Status-quo characteristics relative to the period which elapsed and in which the Christian Communities were adequately represented.[24]

He also associated the communal principle with rhetoric of British justice and equality: "I do not wish to presume that Your Excellency, who is famous for justice and love of equality and far-sightedness will accept and allow that a community which has as many sacred places in this City if not more than any other community should not be adequately represented."[25] Farraj's deployment of such language, in English, was a subtle and skillful mode of suggesting that the Ottoman policies of communalism represented modernization and progress and that the British were taking Palestine backward by their rejection of these forms of political participation.

He even managed to deploy the British image of sectarian squabbling in Jerusalem as an argument for separate Christian communal representation. "If the principle of holding elections by dividing the Municipal area into divisions may have its advantages in England or other Countries," he wrote, "such a principle cannot be fairly applied in a City like Jerusalem, which is the cradle of the three religions and is the centre of perpetual religious and community contentions."[26] Farraj managed to appropriate imperial rhetoric about primitive sectarian quarrels as well as colonial language about justice, progress, and modernity in his arguments for communal representation.

Other politically engaged Arab Christians in different parts of Palestine shared Farraj's ideas. Very similar arguments are to be found in a letter about the changes in the municipal council electorates (not just in Jerusalem but also in Haifa and Jaffa) from another Christian member of the Palestinian elite, Mughannam Ilyas Mughannam. Mughannam, a Protestant,[27] was a lawyer who had emigrated to the United States before the war to study law; he served in France with the American Army during the war and returned to Palestine after the start of the mandate to begin a law practice in Ramallah. He was on the front lines of demonstrations in Jerusalem and Jaffa in 1933 alongside Jamal al-Husayni, Awni ʿAbd al-Hadi, and Alfred Rok. Mughannam became the secretary of Raghib Nashashibi's National Defense party in 1934 and was involved in the Arab Executive. His wife, Matiel Mughannam (Moghannam, in her own transliteration), whom he had met in the United States, was Lebanese American and became a central figure in the Palestinian women's movement during the mandate; her fame eclipsed his with the publication of her book *The Arab Woman and the Palestinian Problem* in 1937.[28]

Mughannam wrote to Wauchope in September 1934 to report that he had met with many of the "leading notables of the various Christian denominations" and that there was considerable unrest among them about the changes in the election law, with particular worries about the possibility of the appointment of a Jewish representative as the single deputy mayor. Like Farraj, he based his argument on the justice of the reformed Ottoman system, pointing to the British acceptance of the Ottoman legal structure until 1934. In describing and advocating for the maintenance of the Ottoman precedent he made even stronger use of language linking the Ottoman "status quo" to Western-style modern political representation, bringing in both the question of constitutionalism and the political responsibilities of the Palestine government under the terms of the mandate to preserve "Civil and Religious rights."[29] He went on to suggest that the change in the number of deputy mayors was accidental: "It must be presumed that this provision [for two deputy mayors] was inadvertently omitted from the Ordinance as finally promulgated as I am not aware that any person or body ever raised any objection to its inclusion in the Law, and certainly Government did not and will not intentionally deprive the Christian Community of that inherent right which is guaranteed to them by usage, traditional and Constitutional Law."[30] Mughannam thus managed to describe the British reversal of policy not just as an antimodern rejection of constitutionally guaranteed political rights but also as a manifestation of outright incompetence.

A number of prominent Latin Catholics used similar language to oppose the changes to the municipal election process in Jerusalem. Arguing that broadly defined Christian representation on the council was insufficient, as Orthodox members would not necessarily protect the interests of the Catholic Church, the Latin Patriarch Louis Barlassina and a number of Arab Catholic leaders demanded that a Catholic be appointed to the council to represent their community. Barlassina wrote to Wauchope several times to point out the Ottoman precedent for the inclusion of a Catholic council member and their inevitable loss of representation under the new plan due to the geographical dispersion of the Catholic population of Jerusalem. More than a year after the elections had taken place he was still protesting: "I feel really mortified to be obliged to insist again on my request regarding a Catholic member of the Municipal Council, I realise however the painful consequences that will arise both here and outside Palestine should this right not be recognised."[31] Leading Arab Latin Catholic laymen supported Barlassina's protests, writing to the high commissioner to support Barlassina's position and asking him to "safeguard the rights of the Catholic community, the importance of which Your Excellency is well aware."[32] Barlassina and the Arab Catholic leaders presented the idea of guaranteeing representative rights for the Catholic community as a bounden duty of a modern state, based on the Ottoman precedent.

The British, however, associated the idea of communalism—which they had themselves promoted in Palestine—with an innate and primitive Arab religiosity. The district commissioner of Jerusalem, in a letter responding to these protests, noted, "The plea for equal representation of the three principal religious communities on the Municipal Council of Jerusalem has already been reported to you . . . This principle would necessitate a reversion to communal elections. To this extent, the other two [Arab] communities would probably agree since communal thinking dies hard . . . In my opinion civic rights and responsibilities have nothing to do with religion."[33] British officials continued to describe sectarianism as a deeply rooted, primitive mode of political engagement and to use words like "reversion" to suggest the ancient roots of sectarian identifications in Palestine.

Although Christians of different backgrounds used similar language to protest the mandate government's change in policy, they were not altogether united. The debate over municipal representation also referenced disagreements within and among the different church communities and in particular the controversy raging in the Orthodox church. Keladion, *locum tenens* of the Greek Orthodox patriarchate, wrote to the government to express opposition to the changes and to support the maintenance of the Ottoman system and the traditional Christian privileges, but his priorities were not those of the

Arab Orthodox laity. Nakhleh Kattan, president of the Orthodox Renaissance Society in Jericho and a prominent figure in the Arab Orthodox movement against Greek domination of the church, protested the municipal elections not on the grounds of a loss of Christian representation but because of the influence of the Greek patriarchate in the process of electing Christian representatives. He objected to the inclusion of George Said, a highly placed employee of the patriarchate, as a member and threatened an Arab Orthodox boycott of elections: "Does Your Excellency agree now to the appointment of the Chief Clerk of the Patriarchate as a member of the Electoral Committee, so as to raise an assumption that the members of the Orthodox Community have no one who could properly represent them except the employees of the Greek Orthodox Patriarchate, which has trespassed on the rights of the Arabs? We have boycotted the elections of the patriarchate and we shall boycott the Municipal elections, if necessary."[34] For Kattan the issue of lay control of the church took precedence over the issue of Christian municipal representation, and arguments for a broadly based Christian communalism were less important than the balance of power within the Orthodox community. Although a consensus was beginning to emerge on the importance of separate Christian communal representation, Christian unity on the issue was by no means absolute.

SECTARIAN REPRESENTATION AS A TOOL OF ANTI-ZIONISM

Advocacy for communal representation now became a tactic in the continuing struggle against Zionist encroachment. Farraj and his colleagues were concerned not that Christians would be overpowered by the Muslim community but that their representation would shrink vis-à-vis the growing Jewish presence. They publicized this aspect of the debate in terms that subtly but clearly suggested to the Arab population that communal representation could guarantee an Arab majority in municipal and national legislative institutions.

Farraj made this argument very clear in his writing on the subject. The Christians, he wrote, were "well aware of the Jewish greed to swallow up the Municipality gradually aided by their strong influence in Government circles. . . . In other words the rights of the Christian communities should not be sacrificed for the interests of the Jewish Community and I do not think that Christians will ever accept to lose their rights in representation in their country in favour of a foreign community who have known political aspirations."[35] For the British government's benefit, Farraj argued that this was merely a communal and not a national issue, suggesting that while the Jews represented a unified political force, Christians were interested only in local issues of preserving their communities' property and welfare: "Further still if the Jews insist on acquiring full representation in the Country for their various political parties who have a common aim and separation and that is to dominate the Country, the Christians on the other hand do not take into consideration political factors but are interested each in the welfare of his own religious community and thus representation of religious communities has far more superior meaning in the Holy City than political."[36] The district commissioner, though, recognized the national implications of communal representation, noting in response to Farraj's demands that it would "immediately be opposed by the Jews, since they demand, not equal representation of the three religions but of the two races."[37] At this point Jews represented approximately 17 percent of Palestine's population, with Muslims comprising 74 percent and Christians about 9 percent.[38] Mughannam also saw communal representation as a way to oppose increased Jewish influence in the municipal councils. He publicized Christian leaders' concerns that "in view of the limitation made in the Municipal Corporation Ordinance, Government might submit to Jewish Pressure and appoint [a] Jewish Deputy Mayor."[39] He attributed the decline in Christian representation under the new system to the increasing Jewish presence in Jerusalem, Haifa, and Jaffa: "It is sufficient however to state that Jewish Immigration and Naturalization of alien Jews have been the cause of reducing Christian representation in the Councils."[40] For Mughannam, as for Farraj, the idea of communal representation was attractive partly because it offered a potential weapon against increasing Zionist influence in the institutions representing the Palestinians to the mandate government.

Mughannam presumed the common interest of all Arab Christians involved, even assuring Wauchope of the unanimity of all Arab Christian leaders on the question of communal representation: "I assure Your Excellency that the views and suggestions expressed herein fully represent the general sentiment of all the Arab Christians in Palestine."[41] By this point the opportunity for interdenominational meetings of Arab Christian leaders to discuss the approach to the municipal council had created a modicum of political solidarity on the part of the Palestinian Arab Christian elites. These meetings of Arab Christian leaders from different church communities would recur in the context of the debates about a national legislative council over the next two years.

When the government finally announced its intention to form the legislative council in 1935, a broad consensus quickly emerged among Christian leaders of both political factions supporting the idea. This multi-church, interparty alignment supporting communal representation on a legislative council represented the first time in Palestinian history that elite Christian leaders of all communal and political affiliations presented themselves as a single, coherent political bloc. Although it was short-lived, it demonstrated the extent to which sectarian thinking had come to dominate colonial politics in mandate Palestine.

By 1934 Wauchope felt considerable pressure to reopen the legislative council issue. Continued conversations with the Colonial Secretary Philip Cunliffe-Lister resulted in a template for a council in which elected members (seven Muslims, one Christian, and two Jews) would make up a majority; the council also would include four officials and three appointees. The two men agreed on the necessity of a British-Jewish veto power and after some discussion decided to give the high commissioner the right of veto rather than establishing a British-Jewish majority on the council that would allow a coalition to overrule any undesirable Arab decisions.[42] Although the British were still using communal language to describe representation in mandate institutions, pressures from the Zionist movement were leading them to think primarily in terms of a "racial" politics of Arabs and Jews.

In 1935, in response to a suggestion from Raghib Nashashibi, Wauchope officially announced the British mandate government's intention to set up a council. Growing Arab discontent with the British approach to the issues of Jewish immigration and the self-government of Palestine led Wauchope to this step; he saw the council as a way to conciliate Arab leaders, whose continued cooperation was necessary to maintain British interests in Palestine, while also demonstrating to the Permanent Mandates Commission in Geneva a gradual move toward self-government. "The value of a Legislative Council may well be open to doubt," he wrote to London in August 1935, "but the need for fulfilling our pledge of 1930 grows more acute each year ... apart from pledges, apart from the clear understanding of both communities that Government intends to proceed with its proposals, the evil results, were we to give way now in deference to Jewish protests and threats of non-cooperation in the election, would be as deplorable as they undoubtedly would be lasting."[43] In proceeding with the legislative council negotiations, Wauchope was attempting to appease the Arab communities of Palestine and gain some measure of cooperation.

The proposals envisioned a limited role for the council, which would not have the capacity to discuss matters relating to the mandate itself, that is, the issues of further European Jewish immigration and land purchase in Palestine. Wauchope, though, took the idea seriously, seeing in it an opportunity to build trust between his government and the Arab political establishment, both the Husayni and opposition factions. One official recalled Wauchope's sincere commitment to the legislative council project: "He exaggerated the importance of his very jejeune proposals . . . My remembrance is that the powers of this Leg. Co. would have been so restricted in respect of everything that really mattered—immigration, land sales, police, and internal security—that they would have had little to offer even the most right-wing Arab nationalist. But I'm sure Wauchope took them seriously."[44] He added that Wauchope was "a tremendous romantic" with "a touching but quite serious belief that [the problems of Palestine] could be solved by the establishment of good personal relations" between him and Hajj Amin al-Husayni on one hand and the Zionist leader David Ben-Gurion on the other.[45] Wauchope's notions of the value of personal relations with local elites and a pro forma legislative council to introduce "natives" to the concepts of parliamentary government both derived from British imperial policy of the previous century.

The majlisi vacillated on the idea of a legislative council during the course of the discussions. A British intelligence account opined hopefully that the lukewarm Husayni leadership was realizing that the council might provide a useful influence on legislation as well as an opportunity to "obtain the sympathetic support of the Eastern Governments represented in the League of Nations which will regard criticisms emanating from an official body in a different light to the reports received from political parties."[46] But disagreements on the form and the processes of the council continued; the *majlisiun* were unwilling to commit themselves, and the Istiqlal party expressed outright opposition.

Ya'qub Farraj met with Wauchope in July 1935 to discuss the proposals. His support for communal representation had nothing to do with an opposition to the proposed Muslim representation on the council; he made his support for his Muslim compatriots clear. Like them, he considered the number of Jews on the council to be too high and wanted it capped at four rather than five. He also sided with them on the issue of women members of the council, telling Wauchope that "both Moslem and Christian" had no objection to Jewish women being allowed to vote, but there was a "most strong objection" to their serving on the council.[47] Farraj's enthusiasm for communal representation owed nothing to a sense of threat from the Palestinian Muslim community.

Rather, Farraj used the now-solidified idea of communal representation as a weapon against Jewish numbers. Wauchope reported that Farraj

> did not claim Parity on behalf of his community, but that if Government allotted members of the Legislative Council on the principle of Parity, then he would remind me that there are three communities in Palestine each with a claim of its own, historic and otherwise, and if the principle of Parity is adopted for one, then he felt sure, Government in all fairness would apply the same principle to all three communities even as used to be the practice in former years for the Municipality of Jerusalem.[48]

Communal representation had become a potential weapon in Palestine's war of numbers.

In a further step toward a multi-denominational Christian bloc, Francis Khayat, a judge with the Palestine Supreme Court and an active member of the Greek Catholic community, made the suggestion that the high commissioner should convene a committee of Christian representatives, "which could advise the High Commissioner on behalf of the Christian community as a whole."[49] This striking suggestion indicated the extent to which the communal idea had taken hold in Palestine under British rule. Christian representative organizations had previously been organized by church; the idea of a pan-Christian committee as an advisory board to the mandate government had never before been mooted. Khayat made a number of other suggestions indicating new possibilities for interdenominational Christian cooperation as well as expressing continued anxiety that the Catholic retain some kind of separate representation. He advocated a system in which the Orthodox and Catholic communities would alternate in electing the Christian member and proposed that the high commissioner should appoint a second nominated member as a representative of the Christian minorities.[50] Continuing the theme of a modernizing Ottoman program, Khayat noted that the alternation of Orthodox and Catholic members had an Ottoman precedent: "In the constitution of the Administrative Council of the Vilayet of Jerusalem etc. under the Turkish Law and in the District Council of Jaffa it is laid down that the member should be alternately one Orthodox and one Roman Catholic."[51]

Jewish leaders immediately and publicly rejected the idea of a council, but discussion and debate continued among the Palestinian Arab parties. Although Wauchope reported hopefully that "if no unforeseen and extraneous factors arise the great majority of the Arab population will be prepared to co-operate with Government in the establishment and working of the Council,"[52] a number of prominent leaders raised concerns over the details of the proposition. The Reform party, led by Dr. Husayn Khalidi, had already agreed to the council in January, but when the Nashashibis' National Defense party came out with official support for the proposal in March 1936, it was only with a number of caveats, criticisms, and reservations. The National Bloc, led by 'Abd al-Latif Saleh, agreed to the proposals in April, again with a number of reservations. The Palestine Arab Party (led by the Husaynis) continued to prevaricate.

The new pan-Christian alliance now emerged in full force. Farraj, who was affiliated with the Nashashibis, collaborated with Alfred Rok of the majlisi faction to hold meetings of Christian community representatives all around the country to discuss the question of Christian representation on the legislative council and support for the mandate government's initiative. Alfred Rok was a wealthy citrus farmer from Jaffa whose family was firmly tied to the Husaynis. Like Farraj, he had acted as a Christian (Greek Catholic) representative to the seventh Palestinian Arab Congress in 1928; he was a member of the Palestine delegation to London in 1930 and became vice president of the Husaynis' Palestine Arab Party in 1935. His association with Farraj, who was just as firmly linked to the Nashashibis, marked these gatherings as occurring across party lines. This move was quite unprecedented in the history of Christian communalism in Palestine; never before had there been a nationwide effort to bring together elite Christian leaders of all communal affiliations to discuss an issue of national politics.

In March 1936 these meetings resulted in a policy. Farraj and Rok wrote to the high commissioner to inform him of the solidarity of this Arab Christian sector:

> Although the proposals made do not fully satisfy the desires and wishes of the Arab population of whom the Christians form an integral and indivisible part and are not adequate to protect their interests, nevertheless the Christian consensus of opinion is unanimously in favour of accepting the Legislative Council, it being understood that the Arab population shall have the right to claim wider powers for the Council and stronger Arab representation. This request is based upon the fact that, although the Christians were a minority at that time, the representative rights of Christians were officially recognized in all Government Offices during the Turkish regime.[53]

They added that the Christians should have three elected and one appointed representative on the council, an increase over the current proposal.

For the first time, Christian leaders were presenting the mandate government with the idea that Christians represented a separate, unified political bloc characterized by a consensus based on shared communal interests. This unprecedented display of solidarity from Christians of different communities on a political issue drew fire from *al-Liwa*, the newspaper of the Husaynis' Palestine Arab Party, for its abandonment of the national cause in favor of sectarian politics.[54]

Wauchope interpreted these types of interventions from members of the various Christian communities as a simple expression of primitive sectarianism but also as a latent communal fear of Muslim domination. After a meeting with the Zionist leader Moshe Shertok in July 1935, he reported to Colonial Secretary Malcolm MacDonald that Shertok had requested "communal" elections on the basis of race rather than religion and that he had replied that "this would not be fair on Christians who definitely look on themselves as a minority needing representation vis-à-vis the Moslems."[55] In reality, of course, this new enthusiasm for communal representation on the part of the Christians was a carefully calculated response to the sectarian policies of the British mandate state. These elite Christian leaders had managed to appropriate the idea of communal representation to serve their own anticolonial and anti-Zionist ends.

THE END OF THE PROPOSALS AND CHRISTIAN PARTICIPATION IN THE DELEGATION OF 1936

To the disappointment not only of the Christians but of many Muslims as well, Zionist pressure in both Palestine and London led to the rejection of the legislative council following a debate in the House of Commons in March 1936. Lord Lugard, in considering how to approach the issue of self-government at the meeting of the Permanent Mandates Commission in Geneva, wrote, "The recent riots seem to afford a reason for deferring the pledge to the Arabs [for a council] without loss of prestige to Sir Arthur Wauchope, while the Jews for their part as we know are strongly opposed to it."[56] Opposition to the proposal and the public denigration of Arab goals in debates in the House of Lords and the House of Commons shocked the Palestinian Arab leaders, who had not anticipated such a display of antipathy. Wauchope tried to convince the colonial secretary to proceed with the proposal, to no avail.[57]

At Wauchope's suggestions, however, the colonial secretary decided to invite an Arab delegation to London to present the Arab point of view to the British government.[58] This move was intended merely to placate the Arab parties involved; there was no suggestion on the part of any British official that there would be an effort to revive the legislative council proposals. The leadership of all five of the parties with which Wauchope had been negotiating accepted the offer. This moment represented the last significant, unified effort on the part of Palestinian Arab nationalist leaders to work within the confines of the mandate and gain their points through conversation with the British.

As April 1936 wore on, the prospect of the delegation grew fainter due to rising suspicions of British motives and discord among the various parties regarding the makeup of the proposed delegation. During the weeks of argument, Arab Christian leaders, regardless of party, continued to press the issue of the legislative council, with a sense that the immediate establishment of a communally organized official legislature represented the last chance for a multi-confessional modern Arab state to emerge in Palestine.

This stance was clearly articulated by the Christian lawyer Ilyas Koussa of Haifa, who on April 9, 1936, wrote an open letter to Wauchope that was published in *Filastin*: "I apprehend that the invitation [for the delegation] is a deliberate manoeuvre to protract the establishment of the Legislative Council in view of the strong opposition recently raised by the pro-Jewish members of the two Houses in London . . . I feel bound to say that having regard to the circumstances in which the invitation was made the opinion savours of an unpleasant intention."[59] Nevertheless, he remained committed to the legislative council and suggested that the British were not only favoring the Jews over the Arabs by preventing its creation but also opposing their own principles of justice and honesty.[60]

This letter was an expression of the Nashashibi position as well as a declaration of continued Christian support for the legislative council, and elite Christian leaders generally continued to participate in the argument over the makeup of the delegation primarily through their party organizations. The coalition of party leaders who had been meeting with Wauchope initially agreed that the delegation would be made up of six representatives and would include one Christian—a suggestion that appears to have originated with Wauchope rather than with any of the Palestinian leaders.[61] The Palestine Arab Party suggested sending three of its representatives (solving the Christian problem by including Alfred Rok) accompanied by one leader from each of the other three parties (the opposition, the Istiqlal, and the Reform party), a suggestion that was met with anger from the other leaders.[62] A demand came for more Christian representation from supporters of the Haifa lawyer Hanna ʿAsfur, but his claim to a spot on the delegation arose from his leading role in the Palestine Arab Workers Society and in the railway union negotiations, not from his religious affiliations.[63] Other groups likewise demanded representation; the Arab leadership was at an impasse and appealed to Wauchope for assistance in determining the makeup of the delegation. Wauchope refused to arbitrate the quarrel.[64] When the disturbances leading to the strike broke out on April 20, the Arab leadership called a meeting and decided to call off the delegation's visit to London. "It is not in the public interest," they wrote to Wauchope on April 22, "that such a delegation should go at the present moment, in compliance with the expressed desire of the nation and in view of the state of anxiety and disorder which now prevails in the country."[65] With a major revolt looming, the temporary Christian alignment that had emerged over the legislative council had no further opportunity to press its case.

ARAB CHRISTIAN INTERNATIONALISM: 'IZZAT TANNUS AND THE LONDON ARAB CENTRE

With violence breaking out, a divided leadership, the loss of the legislative council idea, and the increasing power and numbers of the Jewish immigrant population in Palestine, some elite Arab Christian political leaders decided that Palestinian Arab nationalists had to reach an international audience, particularly a British domestic one. In June 1936 two Christian members affiliated with the Palestine Arab Party decided to travel to London, at their own expense, to present the Arab case and defend the idea of a legislative council. 'Izzat Tannus, an Arab Episcopalian doctor and majlisi political activist from Nablus, proposed the idea of an unofficial delegation to London to Hajj Amin and Jamal al-Husayni to "argue our just case to the British Government and, also, to tell our story to the British people who had never heard of it before from the right people."[66] The Husaynis agreed, and Tannus and his friend Shibli Jamal (also an active member of the Arab Episcopalian community) accompanied Jamal al-Husayni to London in June 1936 on an unofficial delegation that was described to the British government as a representative body "entrusted with the task of presenting the Arab Case before the British People."[67] Shortly thereafter, they were joined by Imil Ghori, who spearheaded a number of meetings with various British officials in the London government.

In his interviews with Lord Plymouth and the colonial secretary, Ghori did not mention the Christian support for communal representation or even focus on the legislative council; his main arguments dealt with immigration and in particular his suggestion that immigration should be suspended until the results of the proposed Royal Commission of Inquiry (under Peel) were known.[68] Tannus and Jamal were likewise focused on the questions of nationalism, immigration, and land. In his repeated meetings with Malcolm MacDonald, Tannus argued for allowing Hajj Amin al-Husayni, who had fled

Palestine, to return, a suspension of Jewish immigration, amnesty for Palestinian rebels, and further negotiations with Arab leaders.[69]

Tannus, Jamal, and Ghori used this trip to develop a program of international diplomatic outreach. This new program had three aspects to it. First, the members of the delegation were intent on providing a Palestinian Arab narrative to London and Geneva to counter the Zionist narrative that they perceived as dominating discussion of the issue in both places. This message focused on Muslim-Christian Arab solidarity and the political, economic, and social sophistication of the Palestinian Arab population; it was intended to underscore the intellectual modernity and political cohesion of Arab Palestine, a middle-class vision shared by many elite urban Christians. Second, it involved setting up a center for the dissemination of pro-Arab material in the metropole, a project that drew on contacts with English missions and Christian church connections for its realization. Third, it involved the active promotion of the Arab cause throughout Europe and the United States, primarily through contacts with church organizations and expatriate Palestinian Arabs, a disproportionate number of whom were Christian. The years of the revolt saw Tannus, in particular, drawing heavily on his own Christian background and connections to spearhead an international campaign for Palestinian nationalism.

The unofficial delegation to London and Geneva focused on the themes of Muslim-Christian unity in Palestine, general Arab solidarity with the Palestinian Arabs, and the political and intellectual sophistication of a Palestinian Arab population trying to defend its constitutional rights. Before arriving in London the delegation stopped in Paris, where it met with a Syrian delegation made up of Hashem al-Atassi, Faris al-Khouri, Sa'adallah al-Jabiri, and the Lebanese nationalist Riad al-Sulh, who, Tannus explained, "accompanied the delegation, not as a delegate, but as an Arab enthusiast, indicating that the Arabs were still one nation."[70] The theme of Arab solidarity was important for the international image Tannus, Jamal, and Ghori were attempting to project. They began their sojourn in London by meeting with a number of Arab officials, including the ministers of the Iraqi and Saudi Arabian legations, who came to the Palestinians' hotel on the second day of their visit to offer support and help them draw up a program.[71]

As well as meeting with a number of British officials, the delegation produced a pamphlet titled "The Palestine Case" that Tannus believed was the first Arab document about the Palestinian cause published in the United Kingdom. He deplored the slowness of the Palestinian Arabs in producing propaganda aimed at a British audience: "This is a frank admission of our backwardness in the very important field of information and propaganda. I must admit again that it was wrong of the Arab people of Palestine to depend only on their indisputable natural rights to their country and on the Covenant of the League of Nations which decreed their self-determination."[72]

Tannus also wanted to use his time in London to set up an institution to defend the Palestinian cause within the metropole to the British government and a British domestic audience. In the summer of 1936 he managed to organize two bodies along these lines. The first was the Pro-Arab Parliamentary Committee, chaired by Lord Winterton (a friend of Faysal) and including Clifton Brown, Ernest Bennet, P.W.M. Pickthorne, and Douglas Reed as members. More important, he organized a number of pro-Arab British writers, journalists, activists, and missionaries to take part in the opening of an Arab Centre in London. The leadership of the new Arab Centre included such people as the travel writer H. V. Morton, who had written accounts of his biblically inspired travels in Palestine; the journalist J.M.N. Jeffries, a former Middle East correspondent for the *Daily Mail*; Frances Newton, the daughter of an English missionary who had lived in Haifa for most of her life and was heavily involved in church circles and the Palestinian nationalist cause; and the pro-Arab Lord Lamington. Tannus' associates in both organizations were drawn largely from mission connections and from a group of British Conservatives who maintained allegiances to the ideas of the World War I–era Arab Bureau (a British intelligence and propaganda operation run from Cairo from 1916 to 1920) and remained loyal to individual Arab notables like Faysal (now of Iraq) and Sharif Husayn. Some of these Britons, in fact, were expecting to see a more exotic group. Tannus recalled their first meeting with member of Parliament Colonel Douglas Clifton Brown at the House of Commons: "After half an hour's waiting, a gentleman walked up to us and asked gently who we were. 'The Arab delegation from Palestine' was our answer. 'I am extremely sorry for keeping you waiting,' he said very apologetically, 'I have been standing over there (pointing with his finger) for forty-five minutes anxiously waiting for the Arab delegation in their beautiful colorful Arab robes to enter the hall as I wanted to welcome them at the entrance.' 'Please come in' and he apologized again."[73] In the Arab Centre's productions, the Palestinian leaders' self-identification with modernity and progress contrasted oddly with the social and political positions of its primary British supporters, nearly all of whom were associated with colonial political positions much more typical of the pre-1919 era than of the interwar period.

Nevertheless, Tannus viewed the Arab Centre in London as important for furthering the Palestinian cause and tried to cast it as an institution with the backing of Palestinian Arabs generally and as a London branch of a unified Palestinian nationalist movement.[74] His mission connections and the numerous church connections of his British friends lent the Arab Centre an aura of

Christian internationalism of the kind that was growing all over the world during this period. In his efforts on behalf of the Palestinian nationalist cause, Tannus drew on as many international Christian connections as he could. In October 1938 he sent a telegraph to the Palestine Defense Committee in Damascus suggesting appeals to Christian groups around the world in response to the growing American Christian interest in Zionism. It was "essential," he thought, "that Patriarchs and heads of churches [in] Syria and Palestine cable British and American governments and churches urgently" with a message that could garner international Christian support for the Palestinian Arabs: "American churches favouring Zionism damages Christian prestige inseparable from Palestine Arab cause. Appeal realize [sic] Arab peoples' establishment of rights threatened by extermination by misguided Christian sympathy delivering Christ's heritage to Jews provokes Christian indignation. Please support Arabs faithful guardians heritage."[75] The Arab Centre tried other modes of appealing to international Christian feeling as well; one of Tannus' Palestinian compatriots at the Arab Centre, George Mansur, aimed at the religious instincts of evangelical Christians in England by telling a Liberal member of Parliament that "the Arabs, under Jewish influence, in the last ten years, have suffered from the demoralizing influence exerted upon them by Jewish publicans and the efforts of Jewish wine manufacturers to increase the consumption of alcoholic liquors among the population of Palestine."[76]

International Christian networks, Tannus thought, might provide a means of disseminating pro-Arab material to counter the powerful international associations of the Zionists. In June 1937 Tannus left London for the United States on what he described as a "propaganda mission" to alert American citizens to the Palestinian plight and raise money to support children orphaned by the fighting.[77] He arrived in New York as the guest of the Arab National League, a foundation of Arab expatriates (mainly from Palestine, Syria, and Lebanon) with a disproportionate number of Christians among the leadership. The documents to come out of this encounter, most notably a league memorandum for distribution to various national politicians and leaders of Arab-American communities throughout the country, continued to emphasize Muslim-Christian solidarity, efforts at peace, and Palestine's exalted position as the birthplace of Christianity in an attempt to appeal to American churchgoers. "To attempt to back a policy by armed force," the manifesto read, "is a reversion to the Dark Ages and an invitation to retaliate force by force . . . This appeal is addressed to all peace loving people to raise their voices to save the land where the Prince of Peace was born, to save it as a shrine to which Christian, Moslem and Jew may reverentially turn."[78] The desire to demonstrate Muslim-Christian solidarity was so strong, Tannus reported, that one Christian member (George Khayrallah, a doctor and scholar who had translated Omar Khayyam into English), "called himself 'Abu Ali,' in significance of Moslem Christian unity."[79]

In 1937 a small delegation from the Arab League visited the British embassy in Washington to present a memorandum detailing its position for the prime minister. The group consisted of Peter George, the Arab Episcopalian brother of *Mir'at al-sharq* owner Bulus Shihada; a Greek Orthodox man named Ayub; and the well-known writer and activist Amin al-Rihani.[80] This delegation, like Tannus' earlier delegation to London and Geneva, made its appeals on the grounds of the political unanimity of the Arabs and the international implications of the situation: "For the Arabs are all determined to defend their country to the very end . . . . In the interests of world peace, as well as the safety of the Empire and the good name of the British people, we earnestly hope that His Majesty's Government will grant the Arabs' reasonable and just demands and thus initiate an era of peace and progress in the Holy Land."[81]

Tannus and his associates in London and New York used their religious heritage and connections to drum up politically sympathetic contacts throughout Europe and the United States through Eastern church institutions and Western missionary connections. These attempts on the part of internationally oriented, well-educated Palestinian Christians in Palestine, London, and the United States to spearhead an international diplomatic appeal to Britain using church and mission networks as well as international political associations to spread a call for justice represented another Palestinian Christian attempt to appropriate the idea of communal identifications for anti-Zionist and anticolonial political purposes.

The struggles over municipal and legislative representation that dominated elite politics in the early and mid-1930s set the stage for the emergence of Christian sectarian alignments that had never before been a feature of the Palestinian political landscape. This new Christian solidarity transpired not because of a natural Christian opposition to a Palestinian Muslim political dominance but because many Arab Christian political elites felt that their civic participation had been seriously eroded by the burgeoning Jewish presence and the British invention of Muslim institutions to represent Palestinian Arab public opinion.

Two developments thwarted this Christian attempt to take a role in sectarian politics. First, Arab Christians began to deploy communal franchises and networks—once a tool of colonial control—as potential weapons in the war against Zionism at just the moment that the British began to abandon the sectarian political model they had developed in Palestine. But equally important, the failed legislative council negotiations contributed to the outbreak of a massive general strike that marked the beginning of a three-year period of mass revolt. Al-Thawra al-kubra, the Great Revolt, began in Nablus in April 1936 with a strike protesting land sales and Jewish immigration and quickly spread throughout the country. The revolt mobilized the Palestinian rural poor rather than the middle-class elites and the urban notables who until now had been the primary face of the nationalist movement; it arose more or less spontaneously, without organizational direction from the national political leadership.[82] This shift of political momentum from the notables and the professional classes to the rural peasantry caused a sudden, steep loss of influence for the elite urban demographic to which most Palestinian Arab Christians belonged, and it brought the brief era of Christian jockeying for a recognized communal position in Palestinian elite politics to an abrupt end.

CHAPTER 5

PALESTINIAN ARAB EPISCOPALIANS
under MANDATE

*I went with my mother to all the Anglican services as well as the
Orthodox ones. I knew some of the hymns by heart, some of them
translated by my uncle Elias and included in our hymnbook, such as
"Here comes the conquering hero", and "Lo, in the grave he lay." My
mother's Anglicanism was very important to her. It was the source
of her joy and outlook on life and she considered it as one aspect
of the renaissance of the Arab Christian world.*

NAJWA KAWAR FARAH, PALESTINIAN ARAB
CHRISTIAN WRITER, 1996

The Arab Episcopalian community to which 'Izzat Tannus and Shibli Jamal
belonged faced particularly difficult challenges in Palestine's newly sectarian political system.[1] It was a small but highly influential group whose long
ties to mission institutions conferred substantial educational and professional
benefits in the British-run mandate state. As converts to a European faith,
however, Arab Episcopalians began during the mandate to face accusations
of collusion and collaboration with the British occupying power and, by extension, with the Zionist movement. During the course of the mandate,
like other Palestinian Christians, Arab Episcopalians had to try to carve out
a space for themselves in Palestine's increasingly sectarian atmosphere; but
they also had to define themselves and their faith as authentically Palestinian
Arab and defend themselves against charges of treachery and betrayal.

In response to these pressures, Palestinian Episcopalians developed a self-
consciously Arab ecclesiastical organization based around the Palestine Native Church Council (PNCC), which acted as the political head of the Arab
Episcopal Church and promoted an autonomous Arab church independent
from the British Jerusalem bishopric. PNCC leaders wanted their organization and church to be recognized as a genuinely Palestinian Arab institu-

tion, equal in cultural authenticity and religious legitimacy to the Muslim community and free from foreign influence. They created a politically separatist, uncompromisingly evangelical Palestinian Arab church culture. Eventually the PNCC and its members began to encourage cooperation among the various elite Protestant communities in Palestine, Syria, and Lebanon and tried to promote a pan-Protestant Arab movement aimed at the exclusion of the British missions and the Jerusalem bishopric. This concept of a Protestant elite that spanned the Arab world owed a great deal to the internationalizing discourse of the Palestinian Arab middle classes from the late Ottoman period. Drawing on this discourse, Palestinian Episcopalian intellectual leaders produced historical and ethnographic scholarship designed to inscribe Arab Christianity at the center of an "authentic" Palestinian Arab culture and history.

The PNCC became the public face of the Arab Episcopalian battle for legal recognition from the mandate state as an official religious community, a status that conferred a number of important political and legal benefits. Arab Episcopalians attempted to formalize their communal position in the legal and political structures of the new British millet system, which had become central to the experience of Palestinian Arab political and civic participation in the mandate state.

During the late 1930s British Anglican support in the metropole for the Zionist project in Palestine caused a major breach between the Palestinian Episcopalian community and its British parent church. The church debate over Zionism led Arab Episcopalian leaders to use the PNCC and its Episcopalian international connections to promote anti-British Palestinian nationalism. Many Arab Episcopalians took the opportunity to disavow their connections with British mission institutions and the Jerusalem bishopric; some chose to emigrate or to abandon their faith altogether.

Like many other Arab Christians during the mandate, Arab Episcopalians sought ways to participate fully in the political, intellectual, and social life of a more rigidly sectarian Palestine. But Arab Episcopalians' unique status as converts to a British faith and the interest of their English church leaders in the Zionist project presented particularly serious obstacles to their quest for a viable communal role.

THE BEGINNINGS OF ARAB EPISCOPALIANISM IN PALESTINE

The newest Christian communities in Palestine, the Protestants, derived from European mission activity beginning in the mid-nineteenth century. The Anglican Church Missionary Society (CMS) began its activity in the Middle

East in the 1820s and sent its first missionary to Jerusalem in 1826. Early missionary interest in Palestine focused on the idea of the conversion of the Jews, an outgrowth of the messianic and revivalist messages of the Protestant "awakenings" sweeping across Britain and the United States in the early nineteenth century.[2] The London Jews Society (an evangelical Protestant mission organization that aimed to convert Jews) set up a permanent station in Jerusalem in 1833.

In 1841 a collaboration between the Church of England and the Evangelical Church of Prussia resulted in the first Protestant bishopric in Jerusalem, overseen by a former Jewish rabbi, Michael Solomon Alexander. The second bishop, the Swiss-born, German-speaking clergyman Samuel Gobat, set the tone for Anglican activity by focusing on education; during his tenure as bishop, forty-two Anglican schools opened in Palestine, and the first two Palestinian Arab priests were ordained. The collaboration between the Anglican and Lutheran churches lapsed in 1881 due to theological differences, and the Jerusalem bishopric became purely Anglican in 1887, when Bishop Popham Blyth took over the leadership of the new Jerusalem and East Mission. St. George's Cathedral Church, still the center of Anglican life in Jerusalem, was built in 1898. As in other parts of the Middle East, the initial focus on proselytizing to Jews and Muslims quickly gave way to ministering to Arab members of other Christian churches, particularly the Greek Orthodox.[3]

British mission organizations, unlike the Greek Orthodox patriarchate, tended to be interested in creating a class of indigenous Protestant missionaries. This idea originated with the prominent CMS secretary Henry Venn, who began in the mid-nineteenth century to promote the idea of independent local churches headed by a "native clergy." Venn's concept expanded in scope during the next two decades; the CMS slogan "Native Agency under European Superintendence" morphed by the 1860s into "a Native Church, the soul of a mission."[4] This more radical stance indicated the development of Venn's belief that Europeans would be an impermanent and transitory presence in the mission field, eventually leaving it altogether as a genuinely non-Western form of Christianity emerged.

Missionaries in Palestine thus took active steps to promote an indigenous clergy as well as an indigenous congregation. Bishop Samuel Gobat, influenced by Venn's ideas, made efforts to recruit Arab readers, teachers, and catechists from the beginning of his tenure and was responsible for ordaining the first Palestinian priests. As early as 1884 CMS organizers in London had suggested the formation of a local church council in Palestine to prepare indigenous Protestants for eventual church governance.[5] By 1908 there were sixteen Palestinian Arab priests assigned to congregations and numerous Arabs involved with running their congregations in other capacities.[6] In 1928

Reverend F. S. Cragg was still interested in the promotion of Venn's "native clergy" in Palestine, noting that it represented "a great opportunity in Galilee for the evangelization of Moslems. . . . There is no question that the native christians [*sic*] of Galilee are now ready to take their share in Moslem evangelization."[7] The minutes of a CMS meeting as late as 1933 continued to reflect Venn's vision: "The whole weight of the Mission should be thrown into the Native Church recognizing that ultimately upon it will rest the evangelization of this land."[8]

Nearly all Arab Episcopalians were converts from the Greek Orthodox Church. The CMS, promoting an evangelical reformist Protestantism, viewed Eastern Church traditions as degenerate, corrupt, and ritualistic and drew most of its Arab members from Orthodox churches during the second half of the nineteenth century.[9] Palestinian Lutheran minister Mitri Raheb's description of his grandfather's conversion to Protestantism in Bethlehem (before the split between the Anglican and Prussian churches), while anecdotal, probably represents a fairly typical conversion narrative:

> My orphaned grandfather Mitri was accepted into this Syrian Orphanage [the German Protestant Schneller School] in 1868. That is where he found a home after the death of his parents; that is where he went to school and learned a trade; and that is where my Greek Orthodox grandfather was confronted with the Protestant faith . . . [He] returned to his hometown of Bethlehem after graduating from the Schneller School and tried to be a faithful member of his Greek Orthodox Church despite his confirmation in the Protestant faith. But he missed the Protestant sermons, pastoral care, and instruction. As a matter of fact, conditions in the Greek Orthodox Church had degenerated greatly . . . After a confrontation with the Greek Orthodox hierarchy, my grandfather was compelled to join the Protestant congregation in Bethlehem, which had been founded in 1854.[10]

The issue of proselytizing to Eastern Christians, however, became a contentious one within Anglican church circles in the last years of the Ottoman Empire. In the early twentieth century Lambeth Palace was engaged in discussions of a rapprochement with the Eastern Christian denominations and did not wish to offend the Orthodox churches by trying to convert their members. Consequently, the Jerusalem bishopric put into place an official policy of not proselytizing to Orthodox communities. In 1922 the Anglican bishop in Jerusalem,[11] Rennie MacInnes, reported to Lambeth Palace that he had been visited by a group of six or seven Orthodox Arabs from Bayt Sahur who, disgusted with the state of affairs within their own church, came to MacInnes "with the request that I should take over them and all their families—some

800 people in number—as they had finished with the Greek Patriarch and wanted to become Anglicans. They accompanied this request with some very formal looking documents, with quantities of purple seals all over them, stating their case. It was not a very easy one to deal with as they certainly had some grievances and were very final and determined throughout . . . They came round every other day for some time."[12] Adhering to his church's new policies on converting members of the Orthodox church, MacInnes declined their request. As a result of this shift in policy toward the Eastern Christian churches, few converts were made from the Orthodox communities after the end of the Ottoman period.

By the mandate period, there were small but important groups of Arab Episcopalians in many of Palestine's urban centers, including Jerusalem, Ramallah, Ramleh, Nazareth, and Jaffa. The Arab Episcopalian community represented an elite who often benefited materially from an English education and was firmly situated within the middle and upper middle classes; records indicate that lay readers in the Arab Episcopalian congregations were mainly professionals—journalists, doctors, dentists, civil servants, and especially teachers. Large percentages of Arab Episcopalians were involved in education, particularly in the running of Anglican schools like the Bishop Gobat School and St. George's, and many of them had studied abroad; the PNCC sometimes funded study at the American University of Beirut for aspiring Arab clergy.[13] Women in the Arab Episcopalian community had an unusual degree of access to schooling and often worked as teachers in the mission schools.[14] "[Their] weight and standing in the business life of the country," Archdeacon W. H. Stewart wrote to the archbishop of Canterbury, "is much greater than their number alone would indicate."[15] Arab Episcopalians were themselves conscious of this status; as a prominent member of Ramleh's Episcopalian community, a civil servant named Nicola Saba, would later declare, "It has often been said that although the Evangelical Denomination in Palestine is numerically the smallest, it is in fact the greatest in influence and the best in quality . . . . There is no doubt in my mind that the members of the Evangelical denomination in Palestine are the most enlightened persons in the country."[16]

ARAB PROTESTANTISM AND THE PALESTINE
NATIVE CHURCH COUNCIL

Arab Episcopalians in Palestine brought up in evangelical missionary institutions drew their English religious influences from a dissenting tradition.[17] Their evangelical commitment, combined with their elevated social and educational status and their decades-long access to Western-style humanist education, created an intellectual culture characterized by, as Ussama Makdisi has put it in describing Lebanon's Butrus al-Bustani, "a locally rooted ecumenical humanism and a secularized evangelical sensibility."[18] This background strongly affected both their political and intellectual presence in mandate Palestine.

In 1905 Arab priests within the church began to agitate for greater self-governance and for the Arabization of the CMS missionary schools. These priests formed the PNCC as an Arab governing body to direct the missionary schools and have a certain amount of autonomy in social and educational church matters, although it remained under the CMS' spiritual guidance.[19] The PNCC, sometimes called the Council of the Episcopal Evangelical Church (Majma' al-kanisa al-injiliyya al-usqufiyya), comprised all the Palestinian priests, lay catechists of the Arab congregations, lay delegates elected by pastorate committees, and "visitors" nominated by the CMS. It met with all its members annually and had a rotating standing committee for issues that came up between meetings. The CMS undertook to provide a grant-in-aid to the council (initially 1,320 pounds for the year), to be decreased annually as the PNCC gradually took financial responsibility for the salaries of its members and its operating costs. The CMS-appointed visitors (all European missionaries, many involved in the Anglican schools), who did not have a vote but did have a voice and substantial influence, would have a presence on the council for as long as it continued to accept CMS funding. The regulations envisioned eventually turning over some of the CMS' property to the PNCC, but the society postponed the execution of this plan until later due to the "difficulties and dangers" of such a transfer under Ottoman law.[20]

Even at this early date, the PNCC associated itself with issues of cultural Arabism and took on a specifically Arab character that prefigured its later emergence as an expression of nationalist Arab Palestinian Protestantism. The regulations of 1905 excluded all non-Arab congregations—not only the English-speaking congregations of expatriate Europeans and Americans but also the tiny congregations of "Hebrew Christians," Jews who had converted to Christianity under the influence of European missions.

The Arab character of the PNCC and the church community strengthened during World War I, when all British missionaries were removed from Palestine. The newly selected Bishop MacInnes spent the first three years of his appointment in Egypt, leaving the church wholly in the hands of its Palestinian clergy and lay leaders. Although many of the schools and other institutions founded by the missionaries were closed or requisitioned by the Ottomans, the churches themselves continued to operate under Arab leadership. They were, however, objects of suspicion to the Ottoman government for their ties to British institutions. Canon Ibrahim Baz, a Palestinian Arab priest working in Jerusalem, recalled that during the war, Ottoman officers came to services every week and sat directly in front of the pulpit, in case of any anti-Ottoman remarks.[21] In the spring of 1918, as the war drew to a close, Ottoman officials took action against the church. Palestinian writer Najwa Farah describes the experience of her uncle Ilyas Marmura, pastor of the Nablus church (and later to become canon of St. Paul's Church in Jerusalem and chairman of the PNCC):

> One day, in the spring of 1918, they [Ottoman military authorities] descended on my uncle's house and searched every Bible and hymnbook. On the following Sunday the Turkish commander with his soldiers appeared in the front seats of the church to listen to my uncle's sermon. Then they arrested him along with other local dignitaries, imprisoned them and sentenced them to death by hanging. At the last minute, the sentence was changed to banishing the whole community—eighty of them—to the city of Urpha, near the Euphrates river in southern Turkey . . . they had to sell most of their furniture and take into exile only the clothes, bedding and cooking pots that they could carry.[22]

At least one other Arab Episcopal priest, Butrus Nasir of Jaffa, was imprisoned by the Ottoman authorities during part of the war.

The PNCC nevertheless carried on the work of the bishopric and managed to maintain most of its congregations with no European assistance for four years. Despite the requisitioning of all church property in Jerusalem except the actual church building, Ibrahim Baz continued to minister to the Jerusalem congregation throughout the war, and the secretary of the CMS further reported to London that "after the battle at Gaza a number of wounded English prisoners were brought into J[erusalem] and Mr. Baz obtained permission to act as Army chaplain to them."[23] Weekly services continued relatively uninterrupted in Jerusalem, Nazareth, Haifa, and Nablus despite the requisitioning of property and breakup of church congregations; congregations in Transjordan, Jaffa, and Ramallah continued to meet sporadically in private houses.[24] This wartime experience of total self-sufficiency solidified the Arab culture of the PNCC and its conception of itself as naturally bound for self-governance as an independent church.[25]

By the beginning of the mandate the Arab Episcopalian community had come to think of itself as an Arab church, culturally and institutionally separate—if not independent—from its British sponsor. Socially, the Arab Episcopalian churches remained close to the Orthodox communities from which most of their members were drawn, and the PNCC's congregations maintained connections with the Arab Orthodox leadership. The relationship between Orthodox and Protestant church communities was characterized by collaboration and friendship (sometimes against the wishes of the Greek Orthodox hierarchy) more often than by proselytization.

The mandate period saw a number of examples of local cooperation between PNCC congregations and Greek Orthodox churches. In 1918, for instance, Reverend Salih Saba of Haifa proposed that government schools and the Greek church be approached to allow Anglican priests to offer religious instruction to "children of both Churches."[26] In Nazareth, Canon As'ad Mansur assisted the foundation of a Sunday school within the Greek Orthodox Church.[27] 'Isa Bandak appealed for funds from the archbishop of Canterbury to alleviate poverty in the Orthodox community in Bethlehem on the basis of a shared Christian heritage; this request was supported by Bishop Francis Graham Brown.[28] Large numbers of Orthodox children attended Anglican schools, making up the majority of the student body in some elite institutions like St. George's and the Bishop Gobat School.

A number of Protestant Arabs sympathized with the Arab Orthodox movement for the Arabization of the Greek Orthodox church. Shibli Jamal used his Anglican connections to represent himself to the American Committee on the Preservation of the Holy Places as an official representative of the Jerusalem bishopric supporting the Orthodox cause, to Bishop MacInnes' considerable annoyance.[29] Arab priests Ilyas Marmura and Butrus Nasir, of Jerusalem and Jaffa, respectively, were also sympathetic to the Orthodox cause and opposed the English bishop when he requested that they visit the newly elected patriarch Timotheos to offer congratulations. Nasir refused to attend, but Marmura, under extreme duress, capitulated.[30] The expectation of Arab Protestant solidarity with the Arab Orthodox community was confirmed the following day, when *Filastin* published a scathing editorial condemning Marmura's actions: "We do not wonder at the Anglican bishop making such a call, as he moves in accordance with the policy of his English government, which does not agree with the feelings and interests of the people of Palestine. But we strongly blame the Rev. Ilyas Marmura, who is one of the sons of the country, for following his chief and not respecting the feelings of his native brothers, which we regard as an intentional offense to the national feeling."[31]

Clearly, the ties between Arab Orthodox converts to Protestantism and their original Orthodox communities remained strong, and proselytizing was much rarer than cooperation and assistance. Marmura confirmed his own continuing identification with the Orthodox community when he casually noted to CMS official Eric Bishop that he would be happy to be a practicing Orthodox Christian were it not for the laxity of Orthodox divorce laws.[32]

The missionary impulse was not a prominent aspect of Arab Episcopalian-Orthodox relations; by 1932 a CMS official noted that he was "impressed by the disappearance of the desire to proselytize to the different sects."[33] Najwa Kawar Farah remembered attending both Orthodox and Protestant services and notes that her mother viewed the Arab Episcopalian community in Palestine as part of a broader Arab Christian renaissance.[34]

Nevertheless, Arab Episcopalians developed an ecclesiastical culture in their community that was constructed in direct opposition to many elements of the Greek Orthodox practice as well as to the High Church rituals of some varieties of English Anglicanism. The PNCC's congregations celebrated a Low Church, evangelical, antiritualistic culture. The church's evangelical theology and its practice of strong lay participation in worship marked Arab Episcopalianism as something quite distinct from Orthodox—and High Church Anglican—traditions.[35]

The ecclesiastical culture that developed in PNCC congregations was self-consciously Low Church. The consistent use of the word "evangelical" in the PNCC's self-description indicated an attachment to reformist traditions that had begun in the early days of the CMS mission and owed something to the German evangelical influence in late-nineteenth-century Palestine. Arab Episcopalian church buildings were modest and spare, in keeping with evangelical tradition. Palestinian priests were referred to as pastors; for services, they wore plain black robes and a simple white surplice, in opposition to the elaborate Orthodox and Catholic garb as well as to the High Church robes of some British Anglicans. Outside services, Palestinian priests developed a specifically Arab Episcopalian dress involving the black suit and clerical collar of the British Anglican priests in combination with a red tarbush.[36] They used an Arabic translation of the 1662 *Book of Common Prayer* and held only the services of communion and morning and evening prayer, eschewing High Church traditions like evensong and evening communion, and rejecting the more ritualistic elements of British Anglicanism. This evangelical approach was at the center of Arab Episcopal—and, more broadly, Arab Protestant—self-identification, and the PNCC fought hard to maintain it despite the interventions of a British Anglican bishopric with very different theological approaches and ritual practices.

As early as 1924 the PNCC began negotiating for almost total independence from the British Anglican Church, not least to ensure the continued evangelical character of its CMS-trained congregations. It was willing to retain a connection with the bishop, who would perform confirmations and ordinations and represent the church to the government, but otherwise wanted the Jerusalem bishopric and the less evangelical church culture it represented to remain peripheral to Arab Episcopalian life in Palestine. PNCC leaders were particularly anxious that the bishop not have the right to impose the use of a different prayer book. (An attempt to replace the 1662 book with a new version, produced in 1927, met with evangelical opposition in England and elsewhere for its introduction of certain rituals associated with Anglo-Catholicism.) They also wanted guarantees that the bishop could not make changes in such sensitive areas as church ritual, dress, furniture, and the nature or times of services. Neither did the PNCC leaders want the bishop to have the right to appoint priests who might not share in the Low Church orientation to Arab congregations.[37]

For Arab Episcopalians this reformist, evangelical approach had several benefits. It reordered the church hierarchy, placing responsibility and control in the hands of the laity rather than the bishopric or even the clergy, and providing clear and central roles for congregants in church practice and organization—an approach in sharp contrast to the Arab laity's lack of influence and importance in the Greek Orthodox Church, from which most of these Episcopalians had originally converted. The focus on lay participation reapportioned control of the church from a mainly English upper clergy to a mainly Arab local priesthood, thus offering a high degree of freedom from what was inevitably viewed as a kind of clerical colonialism. It reflected the elite Palestinian interest in modernity; evangelical Protestantism, with its rejection of elaborate ritual and its focus on personal relationships with God, carried connotations of rejecting ancient rigid church hierarchies in favor of a modern, individualist approach to spirituality. The principle of lay control also offered a philosophical defense for the rejection of European control of an Arab church.

PNCC members were eager for it to be recognized as a fundamentally Arab community distinct from its English counterpart and self-identifying as both Arab and Palestinian. Editing a declaration from British church leaders in Palestine to the bishop establishing its position vis-à-vis the Jerusalem bishopric, they emphasized the Arabness of the congregations as well as their evangelical commitment (PNCC additions are in italics):

> We, the Clergy and members of the Church of England in Palestine who are of Palestinian *Arab* nationality, hereby declare *that we are using, and claim the right to continue to use, the present book of common prayer and articles of religion, without being liable to be called upon to accept any amended edition* . . . and we hereby declare that all property that is held by this Palestinian *Arab* section of the Church of England and is held in trust for the work of this Palestinian *Arab* section of the church of England, and cannot be alienated from or varied from work or purposes connected with the *said*

Palestinian Arab section of the Church of England *which body* is under the jurisdiction of the aforesaid Bishop.[38]

This remarkable document demonstrates the degree to which the Palestinian Episcopalian community was trying to define itself as specifically Arab. The label "Palestinian," which indicated all citizens of the country including European Jews, was not a sufficient identification; they wanted to be recognized as an indivisible part of an Arab polity in Palestine. Palestinian Arab Episcopalians focused on their community's Arab identity in other contexts as well. By the 1930s PNCC members like Jiryes Khouri, a civil servant in Haifa, were lobbying hard for the appointment of an Arab bishop and archdeacon of Jerusalem.[39]

This insistence on the community's Arabness caused major ruptures with the British ecclesiastical hierarchy. In the late 1920s Bishop MacInnes decided to regularize the position of his church. He envisioned welding all the Anglican communities and organizations in Palestine into a single self-governing institution, run along representative constitutional lines and subject only to Lambeth Palace. Coming during a decade characterized by the boiling-over of political tensions in Palestine and the exponential growth of anti-British feeling among Palestinian Arabs, however, the proposal's ultimate effect was to heighten the PNCC's commitment to an Arab church independent of its British sponsors.

The PNCC objected strongly to the plan's creation of seven district councils that would be defined geographically, the object being to encourage the mingling of British, "Hebrew," and Arab Episcopalians in the work of running the church. Palestinian Episcopalian leaders felt, first, that the new councils would replace some of the authority the PNCC enjoyed in running its own congregations, and second, that the forced integration with British and Hebrew Anglicans would compromise their church's Arab character. Here again, Arabism was central to the PNCC's communal self-definition. The PNCC did not want to belong to a global Anglican body; it wanted to be recognized as the head of an independent Palestinian Arab church.

MacInnes died suddenly in 1932. His successor, Francis Graham Brown, already witnessing the upsurge in violence and the deterioration of relations between Arabs and Jews in Palestine during the 1930s, was adamantly opposed to nationalism and spoke on several occasions against the intrusion of materialism, secularism, and national feeling into public life. He strongly resisted all manifestations of cultural nationalism in the Arab Episcopalian Church in Palestine.[40] When Lambeth Palace offered a revised version of the constitution calling for a dramatic integration of the PNCC into the workings and government of the Palestinian Anglican Church, Graham Brown accepted the proposal. PNCC leaders were furious and refused to cooperate further with the bishopric or the CMS on the project.

Instead, they decided to register as a charitable trust under the name Arab Evangelical Trust Association, using the PNCC rules as their charter. At this stage, even this modest move toward independence—originally suggested by MacInnes—aroused protest from the bishopric, which protested that the church objected to "any move which would involve or imply a top-to-bottom division of the Anglican Church on racial lines, or would confer on any one racial section a kind of 'millet' status."[41] On this issue the goals of the PNCC and those of the Jerusalem bishopric were at opposite poles. For the bishopric the reorganization meant the full integration and recognition of their community into a worldwide Anglican Church network. For the PNCC it meant a loss of autonomy and the subsuming of an Arab evangelical church culture into a High Church Anglicized one. The Arab Episcopalian battle against the diocese project indicated the depths of the community's self-identification as Palestinian Arab.

THE IDEA OF A PAN-ARAB PROTESTANT CHURCH

During the course of the mandate, Arab Episcopalian leaders seriously considered the possibility of breaking off from the Anglican Church to form an Arab pan-Protestant entity that would include Arab Protestant congregations in Syria and Lebanon as well as Palestine. Making and maintaining connections with other Arab Protestants in Palestine and other parts of the Levant seemed a potential solution to the perpetual problem of evangelical Arab Christian identity.

Relations between PNCC congregations and the Lutheran, Presbyterian, and Quaker communities were cordial and sympathetic. The PNCC lobbied the CMS to allow intercommunion and clerical exchanges with other Arab Protestants in Palestine without the special permission of the bishop, in direct opposition to Anglican canonical law.[42] In 1925, on the occasion of St. Paul's Anniversary Jubilee, the German Church and the Society of the Syrian Orphanage, the German missionary institution where Mitri Raheb's grandfather was converted to Lutheran Protestantism, donated twenty-five pounds, "acknowledging friendly relations existing between bodies."[43] The PNCC and the CMS agreed to leave the schooling in Ramallah primarily to the American Quaker mission school with which they cooperated and whose educational work they respected.[44] Arab Christians who ran secondary schools like St. George's and the Bishop Gobat School also kept in close contact with the American University of Beirut (formerly the Syrian Protestant College), which many of their students went on to attend. Eric Bishop of the CMS recorded that the missionary society had employed an Arab schoolteacher who was a Syrian Presbyterian, noting "how much in the Near East does not Anglicanism owe to American-trained Presbyterians!"[45] Relations were close between PNCC congregations and Lutheran, Quaker, and Presbyterian congregations in Lebanon and Syria as well.

Cross-denominational Arab Protestant ties strongly referenced a middle-class culture centered around access to premier educational institutions—especially the American University of Beirut, which came to be seen as the pinnacle of Arab Protestant educational accomplishment. This transnational community of Arab Protestants defined itself not only through a common religious affiliation but also through a shared commitment to middle-class values, in the context of an internationalizing elite Arab discourse that extended throughout the eastern Mediterranean.

These connections held promise for the eventual dissolution of the PNCC's bonds with the British Anglican Church and the formation of an evangelical Arab Protestant church including all the Protestant Arab congregations in Palestine, Syria, and Lebanon. In 1923, in the context of a discussion of the legal status of the PNCC congregations, the Palestinians were already thinking about a unified Arab Protestant church—"possibly Episcopalian, possibly not."[46] Some of the PNCC congregations had cultivated ties with the congregations of the American Presbyterian missions in Syria and were considering a broader Arab Protestant Syrian-Palestinian union. In 1924 MacInnes noted this trend in an interview with a CMS group committee, suggesting that "reasons for this were the lack of definite Church teaching in the Congregations, and the number of connexions that they had with the members of the American Presbyterian Mission. . . . [I]f they had the financial ability there would be real danger of their cutting themselves adrift from the Anglican communion, and establishing with the Presbyterians, a United Native Church free of outside control."[47]

In September 1924 the PNCC discussed the creation of a single independent Arab church from the Arab Episcopalian, Presbyterian, and Lutheran churches in Palestine and Syria if the Jerusalem bishopric was unresponsive to the council's requests for independence. Although there was considerable interest in this plan, it was not without its opponents. "Curiously enough," the CMS visitors to the meeting reported, "many of those who are against 'Unification' are the smaller Churches. Their reason however is that they fear that under such a scheme they would lose their own individuality and come absolutely under the control of a small coterie of the leading members of the larger Churches."[48] The plan was repeatedly resurrected throughout the mandate period despite these reservations and the unlikelihood of its practical implementation due to the PNCC's continued financial dependence on the CMS.

Part of the impetus for an emphatically Arab-centered church was the constant assumption of British superiority that emanated from the Anglican institutions in Palestine, even the pro–"native clergy" CMS. In discussing the appointment of a new bishop after MacInnes' death in 1931, CMS officials Algerman Ward and E. M. Bickersteth wrote that MacInnes had maintained successful relations with the Orthodox communities and avoided the disaster of an Arab Protestant separatist movement thanks to his clear understanding of the psychology of the Arabs: "He always maintained that the Eastern mind immediately said if approached with any request for help or cooperation, 'What is it that this person wants from me.'" The next bishop, they thought, needed to be "an absolute gentleman; this is always essential with natives, who spot the difference at once; a man prepared to work very slowly and get to understand the native mind and point of view."[49] This racist view extended to a deep suspicion of Anglican cooperation with the American Episcopal Church, whose activity in Palestine could threaten the work of the British: "The Americans might at the next vacancy propose an American, which would be fatal . . . it would probably be best that a pukka Englishman should be appointed."[50] This kind of attitude naturally affected the Arab members of the church. In the post-mandate period the Arab Episcopalian Bishop Riah Abu El-Assal deplored the psychological consequences of these views: "[Arab Christians] were taught that the English way, its traditions, and its peoples were more competent . . . it had a debilitating effect on Palestinian Christians."[51] Assumptions of cultural and racial superiority on the part of the British missions made an all-Arab Protestant church seem all the more appealing.

Beyond the cultural and theological sympathies of evangelical Arab Protestants of different denominations, as well as a rejection of the Anglo-centric viewpoint of some CMS and Anglican officials, part of the reason for this pan-Protestant, anti-Anglican approach was the increase in anti-Zionist and anti-British feeling among the Palestinian Arabs broadly. As the political situation grew more difficult and antipathy to British rule intensified, Arab Protestants naturally preferred to cultivate connections with other Arab churches rather than with British missions, which were often necessarily associated with the mandate government. As early as 1922 the CMS was expressing concern about the extent to which Arab priests were engaged in nationalist politics.[52] Reverend MacIntyre, a visitor at a PNCC meeting in May 1923, reported that the subject aroused passions among the Arabs present:

When matter was again raised in PNCC, sympathy of Council, both lay and clerical, was markedly in favor of the pastors' activities, and some pastors were most bitter. Present is critical time for native church, as nearly all are deeply concerned with present violent political propaganda against the Government . . . Missionaries, as Britishers, are thought to side with British Govt. against native population, and latter are not disposed to listen to advice or counsel from former.[53]

In 1931 MacInnes reported to the archbishop of Canterbury that the PNCC had "become very active, almost aggressive, owing to the Nationalist Movement among the Arabs in Palestine."[54] By 1934 Ilyas Marmura had become president of an organization called Majma' al-watani al-kanisi fi Filastin wa-al-Urdun (National Church Association in Palestine and Jordan), whose name suggested not just a union of Christians across the region but also an element of Arab national identity.[55] Unlike Arab Christians of other denominations, the status of Arab Episcopalians as converts to a British religion and their connections to British mission personnel put them under suspicion from other Palestinian Arabs. Many Arab Episcopalians viewed an independent Arab Protestant church as vastly preferable to a continued reliance on British missionaries, who were often associated with the policies of the mandate state and with advocacy for the Zionist movement.[56]

AUTHENTICATING PALESTINIAN CHRISTIANITY

Members of this middle-class, multi-denominational Arab Protestantism sought to normalize Christianity's place in Palestinian national identity. During the late Ottoman era and the mandate period, Palestinian Protestant church leaders produced histories and ethnographies that focused on recording Christianity's contributions to the "authentic" rural peasant culture of Palestine. Using the intellectual tools of their Protestant education, Ilyas Marmura and As'ad Mansur undertook scholarly projects that presented Palestinian Christianity as central to a nativist concept of Palestinian culture. This clerical scholarship represented a new attempt to defend the cultural authenticity of Palestinian Christians as well as carve out a role for the Palestinian Episcopalian intelligentsia as a mediator between educated Palestinians and Western scholars.

Ilyas Marmura in Jerusalem and As'ad Mansur in Nazareth produced histories and ethnographies of Palestine, Marmura in his studies of Palestinian Christian music and of the tiny community of Samaritans, Mansur in his still-important history of Nazareth. For both these men, recording and preserving the traditions and histories of Palestine seemed to fall within the purview of Western-educated Protestant Arabs who could negotiate both the traditions of the Palestinian peasantry and the scholarly language and dialogue of the West. Marmura and Mansur positioned themselves as interpreters of authentic Palestinian culture to the West, presenting Palestine as a land of ethnographic interest and pluralistic religious traditions.

Reverend Ilyas Marmura, canon of St. Paul's Church in Jerusalem, was a highly educated man who, one observer recorded, "possessed such a grasp and flow of spontaneous Classical Arabic that he never seemed to have a note when in the pulpit."[57] His early writing fell squarely within the rubric of traditional Ottoman Arab Palestinian poetry, drawing heavily on classical Arab motifs.[58] After the war and the imposition of the mandate, Marmura's ethnographic work took a number of forms, all of which inscribed Christianity at the center of Palestinian history and placed him in the position of interpreter of ancient Palestinian religious and cultural traditions to Western audiences. He collected Palestinian Christmas carols, displaying them to the British community as authentic Palestinian Christian musical rituals unadulterated by the accretions of later texts and traditions. "His carols," Marmura's friend Eric Bishop wrote, "do not go outside the text of Scripture, as has happened for so long in a western Christendom and in a manner that risks taking Christmas out of history and clothing the simplicity of Bethlehem in legend or in myth."[59] This type of ethnomusicological research focused on the Christian elements of "authentic" Palestinian folk culture but was also intended to showcase the centrality of Palestinian Arab Christian communities to the history of Christianity, rather than highlighting the biblical sites that were a more typical focus of Western Christian interest.

Marmura's primary scholarly interest, however, was in the Samaritans of Nablus, an ancient community organized around a monotheistic religion that they believed was the original faith of the Israelites. Marmura learned the liturgical language of Samaritan Aramaic and produced an Arabic translation of the Samaritan Pentateuch, which displayed the Samaritan and the Arabic in alternate lines.[60] In 1934 he produced a book on the Samaritans in which he described their history, their language, and their contemporary rituals as practiced in their small community near Nablus. Marmura's work on the Samaritans incorporated the work of various European scholars of religious history and was in turn influential for a number of English and German scholars interested in the history of the tiny community.[61]

Marmura was also interested in the preservation of Palestinian peasant folk culture, which he regarded as an endangered tradition. During the 1940s Marmura occupied the vicarage of St. Paul's Church in Jerusalem, located next to the Anglican-owned building that housed the Palestine Broadcasting Service. He befriended many of the broadcasters and staff there and suggested to ʿAzmi Nashashibi, who headed the station, an idea for a series of broadcasts on Palestinian folk tales. Nashashibi was enthusiastic, and the station sent out a call for listeners to contribute the tales they knew; Nashashibi managed to broadcast a few of these episodes before the building came under attack in 1947.[62]

Like many other middle-class Palestinian intellectuals, Marmura located cultural authenticity primarily in folk and peasant traditions, a global trend in this period, and was eager to preserve them in the scholarly record. His work also focused on placing Arab Christianity and the ancient practices of Arab Samaritans at the center of Palestinian history and biblical study. In his writings and intellectual activities he presented himself and his Protestant community as scholarly mediators between European academia, an educated Palestinian readership, and an "authentic" Palestinian peasant culture.

Asʿad Mansur, a native of the Galilean village Shef ʿAmru, worked in various CMS churches in Nazareth and the Galilee, eventually becoming canon of the Anglican church in Ramallah. He was credited with making the first Muslim convert to the Anglican Church in Palestine and sent several of his students to England to study theology at Oxford. His book *Taʾrikh al-Nasira*, published in Cairo in 1924, grew out of his diary and combined urban history with topography, geography, and anthropology. Like Marmura, he was concerned with preserving a record of histories and ways of life that seemed to be vanishing. "I hope that the citizens (*wataniyyun*)," he wrote in the introduction to his history, "will take greater care than before to record events in their diaries, which is a good thing for them to do and is a service to their descendants."[63] Mansur made the case that Nazareth was of particular interest to both East and West due to its unique biblical history and its centrality to Christianity.[64]

In part, Mansur's work on Nazareth constituted an effort to provide documentation of a long-standing Palestinian Arab engagement with the land, in reaction to Zionist claims.[65] But it also represented an attempt to contribute to a body of Palestinian scholarship in dialogue with European and Arab intellectual trends outside Palestine and to privilege the role of Christianity in the Palestinian historical narrative. In his focus on Nazareth he sought to demonstrate the pluralistic nature of Ottoman and mandate Palestine, the centrality of Christianity to Palestinian urban history, and the importance of Palestine and especially Nazareth for the international history of Christianity. In developing these three themes, Mansur deliberately engaged a Palestinian Arab audience while also carrying on a conversation with contemporary Arab and European authors.[66]

Mansur's urban history of Nazareth represented an admixture of history, archaeology, art history, geography, and topography and was influenced by European models in these various fields and responding to an ever-increasing European scholarly interest in Palestine. He began by describing Nazareth's geographical layout, with a particular focus on its neighborhoods, its buildings, and its markets. He included a number of photographs with his introduction; these images, reproduced in rather blurry half-tone, are postcard-style pictures with captions orienting the reader geographically, emphasizing Nazareth's churches and providing overlook views of the city from each direction. The two final photographs show, respectively, a rural village gathering and a city scene of collecting water from a streetside spring; both have ethnographic content to them, evoking a premodern peasant tradition.[67] The beginning of Mansur's book inscribed a multi-church, pluralist Christianity at the center of Palestinian history while also positioning the author as a mediator between European archaeological and historical scholarship and an educated Palestinian readership.

The first major section of the book offered a chronological narrative history of Nazareth, chronicling the fates of all its multiple communities under different political regimes and governments. Here, Mansur emphasized the pluralism of Nazareth as a city, discussing not only the Christian and Muslim communities but also the smaller communities of Jews and Samaritans in Nazareth, whom he presented as a natural object of ethnographic, historical, and religious interest to Westerners and educated Palestinian Arabs.[68]

For Mansur, Christianity was central to Nazareth's history, and his book includes a lengthy discussion of the city's churches and Christian sites. Focusing on the buildings and incorporating discussions of the architects and artists who built and decorated the churches, he discussed the European institutions and individuals involved with each church's community and explores the particular biblical associations of each church's location.[69] These capsule histories of each Christian building or site emphasize Nazareth's ties to Europe, a theme Mansur reinforced by including a number of photographs of Western-influenced paintings and sculpture in the Church of the Annunciation that served to suggest the long history of European interest in Nazareth's holy sites.[70] This part of his book repeatedly referenced Nazareth's special position in biblical narrative, discussing archaeological and historical attempts to locate places mentioned in the Gospels and the scholarly difficulties of such efforts.[71]

Marmura and Mansur produced their ethnographic and historical work in the context of a modern intellectual culture made up of people with a serious interest in European and Arab historical, political, and archaeological scholarship and a broad familiarity with the scholarly work on Palestine being produced in the West. Their contributions to this body of scholarship tried to inscribe Christianity at the center of an authentically Palestinian historical narrative. Marmura and Mansur deliberately positioned themselves as mediators between educated Palestinian Arabs and the European scholarly community. As clerical representatives of their Palestinian Episcopalian congregations, they were intent on transforming the liminality of their community into an established role as interpreters of Palestinian history, standing between Europe and the Middle East. Through their writings they were claiming a central role for themselves and their church communities in a national Palestinian Arab intellectual culture.

MANDATE POLICY AND THE PNCC'S BATTLE FOR LEGAL RECOGNITION

These intellectual efforts, though, could not solve the practical difficulties of being an Arab Protestant in Palestine. The mandate state, as we have seen, reinvented the millet system during the 1920s to make religious affiliation central to the interaction between citizens and the state. Palestinian Episcopalians, whose church the British government did not recognize as an official millet, lacked access to the official channels through which civic participation was possible. During the 1920s and 1930s this issue came to be central to the PNCC's mission and activities, and the problem of official recognition came to encapsulate many of the difficulties of being a Palestinian Arab member of a British-led Christian church.

In 1923, when the British admitted a number of churches as millets, they refused to grant recognition to the Arab Protestant communities on the grounds that the Protestants had not had millet status under the Ottoman system—an assertion the Protestant community strenuously refuted. In fact, the Protestant community indeed had been recognized in 1850 by Sultan Abdelmecid; the sultan's decree was even translated into English in 1854.[72] Either the British mandate government did not know of the legal recognition the Ottomans had bestowed on the Protestants or (more likely) it was influenced by pressure from the British Anglican clergy, who thought that millet status reflected a primitive vision of religion that would damage the standing of their mission church.

Because of the millet-inspired structure of the judicial system, the British refusal to recognize the Protestant community caused myriad legal headaches for Arab Protestants and soon became a focus of community organization. These problems became more intractable during the 1920s as the mandate government introduced a number of statutes reinforcing their decision to define the Palestinians communally. In 1928, for instance, a new education ordinance gave local authorities the power to levy an education tax, which would be refunded to recognized religious communities like the Greek Orthodox and Latin Catholic churches that ran schools; Episcopalians, by contrast, would have to pay the tax without receiving a refund. The status of church property was also an issue; when the CMS transferred some of its holdings to the PNCC, the council was not allowed to register its property because it was not recognized as a religious community.[73] In another instance, the PNCC representative for Acre, George Khoury, told the council that the Acre pastorate was refused a case for the collection of debts owed to the chairman of the pastorate committee because it was not registered as a charitable organization.[74] In 1933 the CMS wrote to Graham Brown on behalf of the PNCC protesting that Arab Episcopalians could not vote in municipal elections, the franchises for which were determined through membership in a recognized church community: "Some members in voting for the Town Council had actually to vote as Romans because they had no Government recognition of their own."[75] Further, non-Muslim Palestinians who did not belong to a recognized millet had no access to personal status courts and could not engage in litigation in matters of marriage, divorce, wills, or property.

These and other incidents led the members of the PNCC constantly to remind the bishopric and the mandate government that they had not faced these legal problems during the Ottoman period. Nicola Saba made the case to the CMS that the situation had been much better under the Ottomans: "At that time our community . . . enjoyed all rights and privileges exercised by other communities in the Ottoman Empire. We were actually represented in official circles—we acquired immovable property in the name of the community and we were exempted from Government and Municipal taxes on such property."[76] Reverend F. S. Cragg of the Jerusalem church quite correctly recognized that the PNCC's demands related primarily to the decision of the mandate state to encourage communal identifications as the primary mode of civic and political participation in Palestine: "The organization of this country is on a community basis. This is becoming more and more an element in the Palestine Constitution. Therefore it would seem desirable that some recognition of the Native Church, at any rate as a Community, should be sought."[77] In 1924 the PNCC began to marshal its case for presentation to the mandate government. Its leaders asked MacInnes to offer his support to their requests for legal recognition as a religious community, making the argument that the Episcopalian community, although never recognized as an official millet, had been granted the privileges of a religious community under the Ottomans and therefore deserved to be recognized by the British.

The efforts to have the Arab Protestant community recognized as a millet would be at the center of the PNCC's mission for the next two decades, giving the community and the council a political aspect and a sense of legal and political identity it had not previously possessed.

With the mandate government's promulgation of the Religious Communities Ordinance in 1926, the PNCC's members began to lobby in earnest, and they proposed a set of regulations in 1930. To both the CMS and the Jerusalem bishopric, the document seemed dangerously separatist. The CMS had early reservations about a clause explicitly denying it permission to own shares in the trust association that would deal with the community's property (the proposal included the provision that only native Arabic speakers were eligible).[78] MacInnes, in commenting on the draft to the CMS general secretary Wilson Cash, noted suspiciously that he saw in it a "general tendency towards exclusiveness, verging on separatism, rather than forming an integral part of a diocesan system."[79] Although Cash was more supportive of the PNCC's undertaking, he agreed that the proposed regulations were too separatist in their failure to acknowledge the spiritual authority of the bishop or the unity of the PNCC's congregations with the rest of the diocese. The PNCC proposal, Cash thought, did not "seem to make the Anglican Communion an essential element in the future of the native church."[80]

In these regulations, the PNCC leadership was trying to define the council as a legitimate Palestinian Arab communal body, equal to the other Muslim and Christian Arab communities and independent from foreign oversight. For Palestinian Arab Episcopalians, this was an issue of civic standing and nationalist commitment as well as religious independence. Within the mandate state, communal recognition was tied to voting, court hearings, tax exemptions, and municipal representation, among other legal and political rights. Moreover, Palestinian Arab Episcopalians wanted to make their ethnic and cultural commitment to Palestinian Arabism clear; they did not want to be viewed as a branch of a church associated with colonial occupation and the promotion of Zionist interests in Palestine. The problem of recognition highlighted the radical legal and political sectarianization of the colonial state.

The bishopric's response combined reluctance with mystification. MacInnes wrote to Cash that he could not understand the Arab insistence on separate recognition and saw "no advantage in this move other than prestige."[81] When MacInnes' successor, Francis Graham Brown, was consecrated in 1932, he was even more explicitly opposed to the PNCC's demands. In a meeting with the standing committee he outlined his objections to the proposal. The recognition of the Arab Episcopalians as a religious community, he thought, was a divisive move that might encourage the separation of other parts of the community from the diocese; it would also separate the PNCC's congregations from their counterparts in Transjordan, since this was under a separate administration. More important, however, was his objection that recognition as a religious community would involve a dangerous move backward into the Ottoman millet system. The CMS backed this objection, telling the PNCC, "The more the question of registration is investigated the more it appears to be a retrograde step, and a return to the policy of pre-war Turkish days. We feel that there is something better in store for the Native Church Council than a return to a system which had to be made because of the injustice of Turkish law."[82] Admitting that the legal position of Arab Episcopalians was a real issue, the bishop and the CMS suggested that the community constitute itself legally as a charitable trust rather than a religious community.

The PNCC response to this was hostile. The council's members angrily replied that their proposal had previously received the support of both the bishopric and the CMS and that they had been expecting continued support in return for their own willingness to participate in the process of diocesan organization. The idea of registering as a charitable trust to solve Arab Episcopalians' legal problems was dismissed out of hand; it would, Marmura stated unequivocally, be "undignified to appear before the government and the other churches as a company."[83] Nicola Saba seconded this feeling, noting that registration as a charitable trust would mean that police authorities would have legal access to church records, that district authorities would require the registration and continuous reports on all members, that membership would be age-restricted, and that property ownership would be limited to the actual financial requirements of the trust. "It is, of course, obvious," he added, "how unbecoming it would be for a religious community to adopt for itself the status of a society formed for other purposes than a religious one."[84]

For the Arab Episcopalian community, recognition was not only about legal access to courts and property; it also represented a legitimization of communal identity, which the mandate government had made central to the Palestinian Arab experience of civic and political participation. As a committee of PNCC members appointed to meet with the bishop explained in 1933, "The setting up of a Trust Board may meet a part of the needs of the Council which is the registration of its property but does not secure its constitution and existence as a religious community having *national rights*."[85] Najib Quba'in, chairman of the PNCC and later the first Arab Episcopalian bishop of Jerusalem, set out the PNCC's case clearly in a letter to Reverend Hooper of the CMS in 1935:

The Council has not been able to understand the cause of the aversion of the P.C. [the CMS' Parent Committee] to registration. How does it clash with the spiritual welfare of the Kingdom? . . . Above all it is a fact that no body can hold and dispose of public money unless it is registered with the Government.

. . . As a matter of fact our congregations are becoming impatient of this prolonged delay of their recognition by Government as a community and are already losing interest in the work of the church on that account. They feel that their existence as a church is by toleration and sufferance and not by right. Calling registration as a return to the policy of pre-war Turkish days does not move them or appeal to them in the least. It is a thing which they desire and wish to have as soon as they can. Then all other communities and Christian denominations of all sorts are officially recognized (Jews, Moslems, Greek, Orthodox, Roman Catholics, Copts, Abyssinians, Armenians, etc., etc.)[86] they can see no harm in or fault with registration. And here we must point out that we are not asking for ecclesiastical courts but for recognition by Government for the afore mentioned purposes.[87]

The PNCC set Mitri Hanna and Mughannam Mughannam to work on the possibility of taking the battle for recognition to court.[88] Jamil Habibi, a council representative from Haifa, focused on the Ottoman precedent for recognition. "The Evangelical Community," he said, "was founded during the Ottoman regime as an Ottoman Evangelical Community and as such it had a representative at Istanbul . . . . The law of Palestine and the mandate recognize the status of our Community."[89] A Jerusalem representative, Shafiq Mansur, requested that the PNCC look into the matter "from the standpoint of personal respect and national being."[90]

The British point of view was expressed in Eric Bishop's discussion of the language of new PNCC regulations in 1945:

I must confess to being somewhat disturbed at the substitution of the word "Community" in English for "Church." The latter is so much richer and more historically Christian; the former savours in this part of the world of "segregation" rather than "congregation." If *Church* can be retained without infringing any point of view—adjectivally would be sufficient whether in English or Arabic, I would be happier and most grateful. (The Arabic substitute has (for me) too much of a *sect* about it.)[91]

For Quba'in and the PNCC leaders, constitution as a religious community was essential for the legitimacy and functionality of Arab Episcopalian individuals in Palestine, not because of an atavistic attachment to the millet system but because the mandate was constituted to bestow civic privileges only through recognized communal channels. For British Anglicans influenced by contemporary church philosophy about the universal church, any legal or political definition of a church community was inherently problematic.

The use of the word "community" also reflected all the discussion in British official circles surrounding the innate sectarianism of Palestine—and, indeed, the Middle East generally—by people like Herbert Samuel and Norman Bentwich. Many British officials had decided that the legal separation of religious communities was uniquely appropriate for a region in which sectarian identities constituted a primary loyalty. The British contrasted the supposedly innate communalism of Palestine with a vision of the West as liberal and rational with regard to religious commitment. British Anglicans like Eric Bishop did not want these pejorative labels of "community" and "sect" applied to their own church, which for them fell squarely within the Western rubric of liberalism and rationality. The British Anglican leaders could not understand that in committing Palestine to a sectarian legal model, the British mandate government had made it impossible for Palestinian Arabs to operate without a clear, legally defined communal identification. Instead, they saw in the PNCC's proposals a desire to impose primitive Eastern concepts of sectarian division on an essentially Western church institution.

Negotiations continued into 1947, when the bishopric and the PNCC agreed on revised constitutional regulations that would allow for PNCC recognition within the framework of a bigger Anglican Church. The mandate government had difficulty processing this request, as there was no format for such an arrangement in any of the other religious communities; this in itself was a problem, as the PNCC leaders had objected in the past to being treated as a *sui generis* case, claiming that such special arrangements rendered their own recognition inferior to the status of the other established churches.[92] The battle over community recognition continued, unresolved, until the end of the year, by which time it was becoming clear that the focus on the legal recognition of the community by the Palestine government would soon be a moot point when the British abandoned the mandate.

A THREE-WAY BATTLE OVER ZIONISM: THE PNCC, LAMBETH PALACE, AND THE JERUSALEM BISHOPRIC

The battle over recognition was not the only difficulty Palestinian Arab Episcopalians faced. The Great Revolt of 1936–1939 opened up new questions of identity and belonging for their church community; as relations deteriorated and violence increased between the Palestinian Arabs and their British colonizers, Palestinian Episcopalian ties with British church institutions brought their own nationalist loyalties to Palestine under scrutiny. For the Palestinian Episcopalian community, the attitude of their British church leaders toward the revolt endangered their community's position, eventually leading some to question and even abandon their church affiliation.

In 1936 Palestine disintegrated into open revolt. The Great Revolt (al-Thawra al-kubra) mobilized the Palestinian rural poor rather than the middle-class elites and notables who had until then been the primary face of the nationalist movement. Although this shift of political momentum from the notables and the professional classes to the rural peasantry caused a loss of influence for the elite populations to which most Palestinian Christians belonged, there is little evidence of the sudden emergence of a deeply felt sectarian divide between Muslims and Christians in the context of the revolt.[93] Nevertheless, British Anglican leaders in Palestine tended to see an increased hostility between Muslims and Christians and to interpret it as a manifestation of a primitive sectarianism endemic to the region. "The Christians are not afraid of the educated Moslem or the Effendi class who live in the towns," Graham Brown wrote to the Peel Commission in 1937, "but they have come to realize that the zeal shown by the fellahin in the late disturbances was religious and fundamentally in the nature of a Holy War against a Christian Mandate and against Christian people as well as against the Jews."[94] This extravagant claim reflected the continuing British commitment to the idea that religious affiliation always trumped every other kind of loyalty among Palestinian Arabs.

The deteriorating political situation led the PNCC's leaders to begin to use the council as a forum to express Arab Episcopalian support for anti-Zionist and anti-British sentiments and to use their mission connections to publicize their political views. In 1936 Marmura, Quba'in, 'Izzat Tannus, and As'ad Mansur made their nationalist position clear in a PNCC-sponsored letter to the Archbishop of Canterbury Cosmo Lang. Their missive expressed Arab anger over the missteps of the British mandate government and the injustices of British treatment of the Arabs in Palestine; they noted the peaceful relations that had existed between Arab and Jewish communities in Palestine before the British mandate and requested Lang to intervene with the British government to stop Jewish immigration into Palestine.[95] This use of a church forum to promote a nationalist political stance worried a number of English CMS members, who saw in it another warning that the PNCC might leave the Church of England altogether. Eric Bishop noted in June 1936 that "many of them feel the injustice of the Government (British NOT Palestine) and the League of Nations so keenly that it would not take very much for a number of them to decide to cut their connection, not with Christianity, but with the Church of England, just because it is the Church of *England*."[96]

On the questions of Zionism and Jewish immigration, Arab Episcopalian community had the sympathy of many British missionaries in Palestine in both the CMS and the bishopric. Cash wrote to Marmura after receiving a copy of the latter's letter to Canterbury, "I think you have presented the case fairly, honestly, and with great restraint . . . As you know my sympathies in this controversy have all along been pro-Arab, and the present situation is the natural outcome of the policy developed over a period of years."[97] Graham Brown too was opposed to the project of a Jewish National Home. In a letter to the Jerusalem and East Mission in October 1936 he wrote, "Does not his [Jesus'] teaching of a spiritual Israel, really deny the basis of a 'National Home' in Palestine? In other words, the establishment of a 'National Home' in Palestine cannot be made to depend on the prophecies of the Old Testament, but rather on other grounds."[98] He received agreement from a mission leader involved with the World Missionary Conference, William Paton, who wrote to Graham Brown:

> I entirely agree with the position implied in your letter, that a Christian can hardly accept the view that Palestine is destined by the Will of God to be a home for the Jews. I agree entirely with you that the promises of God were fulfilled in Christ and that the transcendence of race and nation is an essential part of the Christian Conception of the Kingdom. We cannot therefore as Christians accept the view that in endeavouring to make Palestine a Jewish home we are faithful to the revealed will of God.[99]

But in 1937 Archbishop of Canterbury Cosmo Lang gave an address in the House of Lords in which he expressed support for the Jewish National Home based on sympathy for Jewish victims of anti-Semitism in Germany and a theological interpretation of the Jewish return to the Holy Land. Arab Episcopalians in Palestine responded to this speech with a tide of furious objection. A PNCC meeting in Jerusalem recorded that the standing committee read a letter from Marmura and his congregation at St Paul's protesting Lang's address and stated that the committee "was sorry for the painful effect the words of His Grace have had on the Arabs, and especially on the Christians, not only from a national point of view, but also from a religious point of view . . . all those who help in circulating this thought are met—especially by the Christians of Palestine—with abhorrence."[100] A group of Arab Episcopalians, joined by a priest from the Orthodox church of Jerusalem, visited Graham Brown to protest the archbishop's speech, objecting particularly to his use of the term "minority" to describe the Palestinian Arab Christians:

"The delegation asked His Lordship to inform the Archbishop of Canterbury that the Christian Arabs are a part of the Arab community and do not wish to be thought of as a minority in the country."[101] The Women's Arab Society, of which the Arab Episcopalian writer Matiel Mughannam was a leading member, published a letter protesting the speech in *Filastin* on July 24 and sent a delegation to the bishop to express opposition to Lang's statements.[102]

Prominent Arab Episcopalian intellectuals turned their efforts toward the production of English-language political tracts explaining the Palestinian position to the Western powers.[103] Tawfiq Kana'an, in his pamphlet on "The Palestine Arab Cause," was careful to link the nationalist position specifically to the Arab Christian communities. "We Arab Christians of Palestine," he wrote, "who were mostly educated in British schools and who are attached to the British people more than are any other Palestinians, admiring British justice, British manners and British policy, are those at present who hate most bitterly the unchristian policy of Great Britain."[104] Arab Episcopalians also strengthened their ties with the nationalist movement in the form of the Husayni political machine. In 1937 Hajj Amin al-Husayni asked Marmura to serve as the representative of the Palestinian national cause at the London celebrations of the fiftieth anniversary of the Jerusalem diocese, where Marmura tried to present the Arab Christian point of view to Anglican policy makers in the metropole.[105]

Marmura wrote a personal letter to Lang expressing the distress of Arab Anglicans at the archbishop's statements. In this epistle he suggested that there was a movement of Arab Christians toward converting to Islam as a mode of participating in the nationalist movement.[106] "It is described," he wrote, "as the result of despair expecting any good from the Christian west . . . They are shamed by their Moslem neighbors that no Pope, Archbishop or Bishop has raised his voice against the Zionist ambitions, whereas all the Moslem kings and princes and religious leaders have done their utmost to help the Arab cause."[107] He went on to say that other Arab priests had written to him on several occasions to tell of conversions to Islam and that he now believed that "some ten thousand Arab Christian young men chiefly of the cultured class are thinking of going over to Islam . . . Shall this be the crown of the missionary labours of a century in the Holy Land!?"[108] Demonstrating a shrewd apprehension of British Anglican priorities, Marmura added, "I am afraid that the Anglican church both British and Arab has lost its prestige which it has been gaining both among Arab Christians and Moslems as against Catholicism. However, that cannot be revoked."[109] He demanded the abandonment of the partition scheme, which he described as "disastrous" to all the Arab Christians in Palestine who would be abandoned to Muslim or Jewish overlordship, asking instead for a modified British mandate allowing for much reduced Jewish immigration. "Such a scheme," he wrote, "is the only safeguard for the preservation and liberty of Christians in the Holy Land."[110]

Although Arab Episcopalians were most deeply affected by this turn of events, Lang's comments also aroused protest from British Anglicans in Palestine. Graham Brown wrote to Lang to report on the disturbances his speech had caused, taking particular exception to the archbishop's derogatory comments about Hajj Amin al-Husayni and to his expression of support for including Jerusalem in a proposed Jewish state.[111] He collaborated with his education adviser Mabel Warburton, American chaplain Charles Bridgeman, and Archdeacon W. H. Stewart to produce a memo detailing the bishopric's position on the idea of partition. "The Jewish problem of Europe," the memo stated, "must be solved by the Christian powers at their own expense and not at the expense of Palestine." The authors were generally opposed to partition; if partition did occur, they said, it must recognize existing ethnic boundaries, reject forced population transfers, and provide a mandatory area "large enough to accommodate those who do not wish to remain in either the proposed Arab or the proposed Jewish state," as well as protect the interests of Palestine's Christian institutions.[112] For many leading British Anglicans in Palestine, Zionism and the idea of a Jewish state seemed to threaten Christian interests in the Holy Land.

The bishopric and the CMS likewise recognized that Zionism represented a threat to the Arabs who made up a majority of the Episcopalian congregations in Palestine, and their anti-Zionist position was partly based in sympathy for their Arab congregants. Graham Brown wrote to Lang in 1937 that "Christian Arabs are under no illusion as to their possible ultimate fate. Although they realise that under an Arab National Government it might mean for them submergence or at least discrimination and persecution, yet they would prefer an Arab regime to a Jewish one . . . . If the Mandatory can see its way clear to render real service to the Christian minorities, and pursue a long-term and unselfish policy, all will be well; if not, it were better to leave the Christians to get along as best they can with their masters."[113] There was no illusion on the part of Graham Brown or the CMS, as there was on the part of some British colonial officials, that Arab Christians were any less opposed to Zionism and a possible Jewish state than their Muslim counterparts.

Within Palestine, the British Anglican response to Palestinian Arab nationalism was generally a quiet sympathy. When Lang issued a statement condemning nationalism as an unworthy worldly commitment, he failed to win the wholehearted approval of his missionaries. Mabel Warburton wrote to Hooper in 1936, "It should never have come to this . . . Of course the immigration should have been suspended long ago, now it is being made a most serious issue. I am very sorry for the Christian Arabs, who find themselves in a great dilemma between their Christian principles and their national feelings."[114] Sometimes this sympathy appears to have translated into political activity against the instructions of the CMS and the mandate government. In a letter to Eric Bishop, Hooper noted,

> Having given a warning that we expect the missionaries in a Mission to act together as a body and to be guided by the advice received through their Secretary from the civil authorities, we cannot very well exert compulsion if an individual missionary prefers to fly in the face of these instructions and to trust his own judgment . . . It is not so much a question of being British or any other nationality; it is a question of the place of the individual in a civil state.[115]

Lang himself, on the other hand, demonstrated a very limited grasp of the damage he had caused to the Arab Episcopalian community: "I fear it is impossible for me to correct all the misunderstandings of my words which constantly occur in all parts of the world . . . If the Arabs are so afraid of the Jews and their financial power, it surprises me that they are not more ready to think favourably of a definitely Arab State from which they would be able to exclude the Jews which they certainly could not do if the Mandate in its present form, or even a modified form, were maintained. As for the Jews, I read Weizmann's speech at Zurich very carefully and I was impressed by its ability and statesmanlike outlook."[116] Anglican leaders in the metropole had no political sympathy for the small community their missionaries had fostered in Palestine.

For Arab Episcopalians, the support of many members of the missionary societies and the Jerusalem bishopric could not undo the damage inflicted by Lang's speech. "I don't think it wise," Nicola Saba wrote to the CMS,

> to end this note without some reference to the sufferings our congregations have to undergo on account of the theory now and anon expounded by certain dignitaries of the Church of England relating to the return of the Jews to Palestine. Although, as individuals, we do not believe that this doctrine agrees with our interpretation of the New Testament, there can be no doubt that, being in communion with the Church of England, we are as a body suspected of holding the same view. What makes it worse for us is that some of the missionary workers in Palestine stick to what is termed to be the declared doctrine of the Church of England. We are therefore not only looked upon as enemies of our own country, but as spies or agents for the British Government, who is solely responsible for the enforcement

of the Balfour Declaration, thereby breaking its promises to the Arabs of whom we form a part.[117]

Shortly thereafter, Saba, whose wife and children had spent the war years in London, tried to persuade the Arab Episcopal communities in the southern parts of Palestine to sell their lands and possessions and move en masse to Brazil.[118] Arab Episcopalians found themselves under suspicion for treachery and covert pro-Zionism despite the long-standing nationalist orientation of the PNCC and its vocal opposition to Lang's position. Even some British noted that the political stance of the mandate state and the metropolitan Anglican Church appeared to have damaged the standing of the Arab Episcopalian community: "In many people's minds missionaries are regarded as political agents and are therefore now associated with the move to make Palestine a National Home for the Jews. A popular word for Protestant Christian is 'Inglesi [English].'"[119]

Some Arab Episcopalians expressed their anger through political action within the church. When the bishop tried to restart talks on the constitution in 1938, the PNCC refused on the ground that "the present state of affairs in the country do not enable the Council to continue discussing the subject for the purpose of taking a resolution."[120] Members of the PNCC began to protest holding council meetings at the British Institute.[121] Jiryes Khouri, a town clerk in Haifa who was brought up Lutheran and took an active role in the PNCC during the 1940s, tried to bring back the idea of abandoning the Anglican Church altogether in favor of an Arab pan-Protestantism, eventually going so far as to suggest the formation of a pan-Christian Palestinian Arab church to protect Christian interests.[122] In April 1947 the PNCC, under the direction of Najib Quba'in, unanimously agreed to send a telegram to the United Nations in New York deploying Palestine's Christian history to call on Christians to support the Arab cause: "The PNCC meeting in Nazareth beseeches the U.N.O. in the name of Christianity and from the city of Christ to do justice in giving the Arabs of Palestine their National rights, to terminate the British mandate, to declare Palestine an independent country and to form a democratic Government immediately."[123] At the PNCC meeting at Nazareth and at the United Missionary Conference in Beirut in 1947, Quba'in and the other PNCC leaders demanded that the CMS turn over all its work (including schools, churches, charities, hospitals, and orphanages) to the PNCC, which would rename the CMS mission the "Mission of the Church"; they appointed Habib Khouri, a retired government inspector, chair of a new committee on running all the church schools.[124] Nicola Saba and Suleiman Tannus ('Izzat Tannus' brother) lobbied the CMS to transfer its land, offices, and personnel to the PNCC and appoint a Palestinian Arab assistant bishop.[125]

For many Arab Episcopalians, though, the damage was done, and rather than engage in further political activity through the church they began to discuss a more drastic measure: emigration out of Palestine.[126] The long-standing European connections, the Western schooling, and the multi-lingual educations many of these Arab Episcopalian clergy and congregants had received meant that emigration to Lebanon, the United States, or Europe was quite often a real possibility, one that became more attractive as Palestine descended into violence and the position of the Palestinian Arab Episcopalian community continued to decline. Latin America was also a popular destination; parts of Brazil, Chile, and Honduras had a century-long history of receiving Palestinian Christian immigrants.[127] In the years following the revolt, many Palestinian Episcopalians began to consider emigration as the only possible response to their disillusionment with their church and their damaged standing within Palestinian society.

As 1947 drew to a close, it became clear that many of the issues around which the Arab Episcopalian community had organized itself were becoming moot. The United Nations Special Committee on Palestine called for the end of the mandate and the partition of the country in August; on September 26, Britain announced its intention to withdraw; and in November the United Nations General Assembly voted for partition and the termination of the mandate. Palestinian Arab Episcopalians would henceforth be in the very different position of negotiating their legal, political, and cultural identity with their Arab neighbors and with the new state of Israel.

EPILOGUE: THE CONSEQUENCES
of SECTARIANISM

In 1917, just before Edmund Allenby entered Jerusalem and claimed Palestine for the British, Arab Christians seemed poised to take a central role in the construction of a post-Ottoman political order. By the time the mandate ended in 1948, they had nearly disappeared from Palestinian political life. At the same time, they also vanished from much of the historiography of modern Palestine. The colonial conflict that began with the 1917 British declaration of support for a Jewish National Home in Palestine was, by 1948, already being portrayed as partly a religious contest between Muslims and Jews for their shared "Holy Land," an interpretation that replaced its political and economic causes with an invented primordial religious origin and conveniently elided Britain's role in the making of the struggle.

British policy in Palestine, driven by imperial precepts developed in India and Africa, helped to create a new kind of sectarianism in Palestine that encouraged the emergence of Muslim political organization while discouraging the kind of multi-religious, middle-class, urban nationalism in which Christians were heavily involved. British officials developed a rhetoric of an innate Palestinian sectarianism that they used simultaneously to justify their own invented systems of communal organization and to decry the primitiveness of the Palestinian Arabs. This colonial discourse also served to rationalize the British refusal to allow Palestinian Arabs official political representation. The involvement of various European powers that had historically claimed "protectorates" over the Christian communities in Palestine and their ongoing interest in maintaining their privileges in the "Holy Land" through their church institutions further promoted the development of a highly sectarian atmosphere.

Palestinian Arab Christians reacted to this colonial interpretation of religious identity by reinventing their communal institutions as political entities in an attempt to maintain some influence and access to the state in the new system. In remaking their church communities as identifiable blocs with specifically communal political interests, Arab Christians were both responding and contributing to an increasingly sectarian political landscape. While the colonial construction of sectarianism did not manage to slow the progress of anti-imperial feeling or nationalist organization, it did succeed in driving a wedge between Muslims and Christians in Palestine and in redefining religious affiliation as a central aspect of political participation in the modern Middle East—a legacy that persists to the present day.

The British decision to exclude the Arab Christian population from Palestinian politics was made on the basis of immediate imperial interests. As the mandate proceeded, it became clear that this approach had another benefit. Gradually excising the Christian population from Palestinian Arab politics made it possible for British to cast the relationship between European Jews and Arab Muslims in Palestine as one of medieval religious hatred rather than modern political conflict. It suppressed discussion of the British role in creating a situation of discord and presented the British colonial government as a necessary mediator among warring parties in a Palestine hidebound by primitive religious feeling. This vision of the origins of the conflict and the necessity of Western mediation among Palestine's different religious groups has survived the demise of the mandate; it may well be among the most lasting legacies of British imperial rule in the Middle East.

PALESTINIAN CHRISTIANS FROM THE LATE OTTOMAN ERA TO THE END OF THE MANDATE: SOME CONCLUSIONS

The category of Palestinian Arab Christian began to take on a specifically modern political meaning during the late nineteenth century. The unprecedented growth of foreign institutions in Palestine and the internationalization of Palestine's affairs helped to promote new kinds of communal identifications in Palestine's Muslim and Christian communities. But simultaneously, these same forces assisted the emergence of a self-consciously modern political, social, and cultural space for Palestine's urban elites, both Muslim and Christian. When the British entered Palestine in December 1917, elite urban Palestinian Christians were beginning to consider the political implications of their religious heritage but were more interested in building up a modern, multi-religious Arab civil society.

The presence of so many Christian leaders in the Palestinian nationalist movement confused British dignitaries in London like Winston Churchill, who seemed unable to comprehend the presence of an indigenous Arab Christianity politically committed to Palestinian nationalism. In a more local context, mandate officials saw Palestinian Christian leaders contributing to the middle-class, urban, nationalist movement that they (quite correctly) considered a threat to British overlordship. Colonial policy makers in both London and Jerusalem, then, had incentives to separate Palestine's Christians and Muslims, especially as Palestinian Christian leaders began to draw on international Christian networks to rally support for their national cause against British occupation and the Zionist movement.

During the early years of British rule, Palestine's colonial occupiers reinvented religious affiliation as the basis for political, legal, and civic participation in the mandate state. This colonial strategy drew on models of British imperial rule in India and Africa as well as on similar efforts in Egypt and Iraq and in the French-controlled mandates of Syria and Lebanon. The British reimagined the Palestinian Muslim community as a millet and put into place legal and political structures that allowed access to the colonial state only through recognized communal channels. This system was designed to create a space for the growing European Jewish settler community in the governmental structure of Palestine while also discouraging the secular nationalist activity coming out of Palestine's new multi-religious middle class. This imperial approach reified sectarianism as a primary marker of political identity in mandate Palestine and had the effect of sidelining the substantial Christian population by defining it as a religious "minority."

In an attempt to regain their influence in this newly sectarian political landscape, Palestinian Arab Christians now began to conceive of their church communities in political terms. Arab Orthodox leaders, for instance, tried to recast the battle within the church between the Greek hierarchy and the Arab laity as an essentially political and nationalist struggle. They argued that their movement represented an effort to reclaim Palestine's resources and institutions from foreign influence and as such was a vital part of the anti-imperial and anti-Zionist Palestinian cause. In re-imagining their communal movement as an integral part of the national struggle, Arab Orthodox leaders put forward their religious community as a new kind of political entity.

Christian urban elites also began to formulate new modes of broader Christian political activity. During the 1930s, in the course of the negotiations between the mandate state and the Palestinian Arab nationalist leadership over representation in a legislative council, elite Christian political leaders tried to appropriate the idea of sectarian representation as a tool of anti-imperial and anti-Zionist activity. They formed an unprecedented (albeit short-lived) pan-Christian coalition, promoting the idea of communal representation in municipal and legislative councils as a way of guaranteeing an Arab majority in Palestine's representative institutions. Some prominent Palestinian Christian leaders began to deploy their Christian heritage as a weapon against Zionism in the West as well, using their church and mission connections to promote the causes of Palestinian nationalism and anti-Zionism in Europe and the United States.

The small but highly influential Palestinian Episcopalian community came under increasing suspicion during the course of the mandate for its membership in a British church and its connections with a totally discredited colonial government. During the mandate period, embattled Palestinian Arab Episcopalians campaigned for legal, political, and social recognition as a legitimate and authentically Arab religious community, but they also began to reject their British parent church and turned their communal institutions into venues for the promotion of nationalist arguments. When these strategies failed to rehabilitate their position within Palestinian Arab politics and society, many Palestinian Episcopalians began to turn to the more radical option of emigration, seeing it as the only possible reaction to the unfavorable political associations their religious affiliation had acquired.

All these movements and activities constituted attempts to maintain Arab Christian political and civic participation in the face of an increasingly sectarian political landscape in mandate Palestine. None of them was especially successful. Although individual Christians continued to hold influential positions within the nationalist movement, the political implications of membership in the Christian community had become mostly negative, and the British had deliberately targeted the multi-religious middle class to which most Palestinian Christians belonged as an enemy of colonial rule. By the time the British relinquished the mandate in 1948, their policies had largely succeeded in marginalizing the Palestinian Arab Christian communities.

PALESTINIAN ARAB CHRISTIANS AFTER 1948

The making of sectarianism in Palestine continued to affect the Christian population after the end of the mandate and the British withdrawal. During the 1948 war (known to Palestinians as al-Nakba, the Catastrophe), approximately 750,000 Palestinians were displaced and more than four hundred Palestinian villages were destroyed. The dispossessions of 1948 were especially disastrous for the Arab Christians of Jerusalem, nearly half of whom lived in the western neighborhoods of the New City and lost their homes and all their possessions with the incorporation of West Jerusalem into the new state of Israel. Christian institutions were likewise severely affected; 34 percent of the land Israel claimed in West Jerusalem was church property, and in the Old City (which came under Jordanian control after the 1948 war), many Christian churches and institutions suffered serious damage.[1]

Mass emigration quickly became the central characteristic of the post-

Nakba Palestinian Christian experience. After 1948, facing radically restricted economic and political opportunities, Christians emigrated out of the Palestinian territories at a rate twice that of the general population.[2] Palestinian Christians' ties to Western institutions, knowledge of Western languages, and relatively strong economic situations helped facilitate this mass exodus. As one commentator has noted, "A community with a high educational achievement and a relatively good standard of living but with no real prospects for economic security or advancement will most probably become a migrant community."[3] The Christian population in the Jordanian-controlled West Bank dropped precipitously in the years after 1948; in Jerusalem the Christian population fell by more than half between 1948 and 1961.[4] The outward flow only accelerated after the 1967 war and Israel's takeover of the West Bank and Gaza.

In the new state of Israel itself, the government made the decision early on to treat its Arab citizens as members of minority religious entities rather than as an ethnic minority in a secular state. Yehoshua Palmon, the first adviser on Arab affairs in the new state of Israel, suggested dealing with the remaining Palestinian population through the ministry of religions, thus preserving two primary tenets of the British mandate state: the inherent importance of religious distinctions in Arab society and the primacy of sectarian over national identifications for Palestinians.[5] As in the West Bank and Gaza, Christians emptied out of Israel en masse after 1948. They now constitute approximately 9 percent of the Arab population in Israel, a proportion that has been falling continuously from a high of 21 percent in 1950.[6]

A considerable number of Christians relocated to Jordan, particularly Amman; others went to Europe and the Gulf states. Palestinian Christians formed large expatriate communities in Latin America, most notably in Chile and Honduras—where, however, they continued to face prejudice, sometimes enduring the pejorative label *turcos*.[7] They also went to the United States; in the 2000 Census, nearly three-quarters of the 1.2 million Arab Americans counted identified themselves as Christian.[8] Australia and Canada emerged as attractive options as well for Palestinian Christians seeking to emigrate. These diasporic networks further facilitated high levels of Arab Christian emigration out of both Israel and the occupied territories. In one 1991 study, 55 percent of Palestinian Christian interviewees in the West Bank reported that they had family members living abroad, and 44 percent of Palestinian Christians between the ages of twenty and twenty-nine expressed an intention to emigrate.[9] A separate survey conducted in Haifa in the same year reported that three times as many Arab Christians as Muslims planned to emigrate out of Israel.[10]

Partly as a result of this continuing loss of population, Palestine's visibility as a cultural and historical center for Christianity has diminished in the sixty-odd years since the founding of Israel. Restrictions on travel to the West Bank have limited tourist and pilgrimage access to the Christian sites of Bethlehem and Jericho as well as to traditionally Christian villages like Bayt Jala, Bayt Sahur, and Taybeh. In Israel proper, visitors to Christian sites in Jerusalem, Nazareth, the Galilee, and along the Jordan River are now unlikely to encounter Palestinian Arab Christian guides, who have largely been replaced with Israelis and foreigners. This has become increasingly true as evangelical Christian tourism in the region has grown in importance, now constituting as much as a third of the American tourist trade in Israel.[11] Israeli and American tour companies offer Christian pilgrimage tours of Israel that emphasize the return of the Jews to the "Holy Land" in biblical terms; many—perhaps most—of these travelers are unaware of the presence of an indigenous Palestinian Arab Christian population in the region. An eschatological Protestant theological approach now dominates much Christian tourism in the area, replacing an older model focused around the Eastern Christian guardianship of Christianity's "Holy Places." The Arab Christian presence in Palestine/Israel is now of minimal prominence.

As Ussama Makdisi has written, sectarianism has often "been depicted as a monolithic force, unchanging in the face of history. . . . The truth of the matter, however, is quite the reverse: sectarianism was produced. Therefore it can be changed."[12] This is indisputable. But it must also be recognized that the making of sectarian identities in Palestine had serious and lasting consequences. The acknowledgment of sectarianism as a constructed phenomenon, owing much to the machinations of British colonial rule, cannot now reverse one of its major effects: the almost total marginalization of the Palestinian Arab Christian communities in their homeland.

NOTES

INTRODUCTION

1. The astonishing longevity of this notion became once again evident in 2007 with the appointment of former British Prime Minister Tony Blair to the position of special envoy of the "Quartet on the Middle East."

2. The *sanjak* (district) of Maʿan, primarily in what is now Jordan, included part of Palestine's Negev Desert; this sanjak reported to the *vilayet* (province) of Syria. For details on the provincial Ottoman administration of Palestine see Carter Findley, "The Evolution of the System of Provincial Administration as Viewed from the Center," in *Palestine in the Late Ottoman Period*, ed. David Kushner (Jerusalem: Yad Izhak Ben-Zvi Press, 1986), 3–30.

3. Justin McCarthy puts the figures for Palestine's Arab Christian population in 1914 at 79,734, out of a total population of about 722,143. The Jewish population, including noncitizens, was about 60,000, putting Jews at approximately 8 percent of the population, with the remainder Muslim Arabs. *The Population of Palestine: Population History and Statistics of the Late Ottoman Period and the Mandate* (New York: Columbia University Press, 1990), 10.

4. This is of course a much-simplified summary of the nature of the millet system. It has been written about extensively; for more detailed discussions see Benjamin Braude and Bernard Lewis, eds., *Christians and Jews in the Ottoman Empire: The Functioning of a Plural Society*, 2 vols. (New York: Holmes and Meier, 1982); Bruce Masters, *Christians and Jews in the Ottoman Arab World: The Roots of Sectarianism* (Cambridge: Cambridge University Press, 2001); Youssef Courbage and Phillipe Fargues, *Chrétiens et juifs dans l'Islam arabe et turc* (Paris: Fayard, 1992); and Xavier de Planhol, *Minorités en Islam: Géographie politique et sociale* (Paris: Flammarion, 1997). Also see descriptions in broader histories of the empire like Donald Quataert, *The Ottoman Empire, 1700–1922* (New York: Cambridge University Press, 2000); Halil Inalcik, Donald Quataert, and Suraiya Faroqhi, eds., *An Economic and Social History of the Ottoman Empire, 1300–1914*, 2 vols. (Cambridge: Cambridge University Press, 2004); Fadil Bayat, *Al-dawla al-ʿuthmaniyya fi al-majal al-ʿarabi: Dirasa tarikhiyya fi al-awdaʾ al-idariyya fi dawʾ al-wathaʾiq wa-al-masadir al-ʿuthmaniyya hasran* (Beirut: Markaz dirasat al-wahdah al-ʿarabiyya, 2007); and Caroline Finkel, *Osman's Dream: The Story of the Ottoman Empire 1300–1923* (New York: Perseus, 2005). Halil Inalcik, "The Status of the Greek Orthodox Patriarch under the Ottomans,"

Turcica 21–23 (1991): 407–436, offers a periodization of the history of the millet system with regard to the relationship between the Ottoman state and the Greek Orthodox Patriarchate.

5. It fell under special administrative arrangements by which it was allowed an agent to the Ottoman government and particular rights to internal self-government. This position resulted primarily from the claims of France to be an international protector of Roman Catholics and from formal agreements to this effect between the French and the Ottoman sultan.

6. In 1850, responding to pressure from the British ambassador Sir Stratford Canning, Sultan Abdulmecid proclaimed the Protestants a "separate community" with the legal rights attaching to that status. They were not a millet in the fullest sense, however, as the Protestant "agent" to the sultan was a lay Armenian without the religious authority that his Orthodox, Armenian, and Catholic counterparts had. Chapter 5 of the present volume presents the ramifications of this status in detail. For a useful exposition on this process see Vartan Artinian, "The Formation of Catholic and Protestant Millets in the Ottoman Empire," *Armenian Review* 28, 1 (Spring 1975): 3–15, and H.G.O. Dwight, "Translation of the Ferman Granted by Sultan Abd-ul-Mejeed to His Protestant Subjects," *Journal of the American Oriental Society* 4 (1854): 443–444.

7. For discussions of the various effects of the tanzimat on the Arab provinces see Ussama Makdisi, *The Culture of Sectarianism: Community, History, and Violence in Nineteenth-Century Ottoman Lebanon* (Berkeley: University of California Press, 2000); Itzchak Weismann and Fruma Zachs, eds., *Ottoman Reform and Muslim Regeneration* (London: Tauris, 2005); Donna Robinson Divine, *Politics and Society in Ottoman Palestine: The Arab Struggle for Survival and Power* (Boulder, CO: Lynne Rienner, 1994); Benjamin Fortna, *Imperial Classroom: Islam, the State, and Education in the Late Ottoman Empire* (Oxford: Oxford University Press, 2002); Moshe Ma'oz, *Ottoman Reform in Syria and Palestine, 1840–1861: The Impact of the Tanzimat on Politics and Society* (Oxford: Clarendon Press, 1968); B. Abu-Manneh, "Jerusalem in the Tanzimat Period: The New Ottoman Administration and the Notables," *Die Welt des Islams* 30, 1/4 (1990): 1–44; Elizabeth Thompson, "Ottoman Political Reform in the Provinces: The Damascus Advisory Council in 1844–45," *International Journal of Middle East Studies* 25, 3 (1993): 457–475; Mahmoud Yazbak, *Haifa in the Late Ottoman Period, 1864–1914: A Muslim Town in Transition* (Leiden, Netherlands: Brill, 1998); and Thomas Philipp and Birgit Schaebler, *The Syrian Land: Processes of Integration and Fragmentation: Bilad al-Sham from the 18th to the 20th Century* (Stuttgart: Steiner, 1998).

8. See Makdisi, *Culture of Sectarianism*, for an in-depth look at the *tanzimat* and sectarian violence in Lebanon during the mid-nineteenth century.

9. It is important, however, not to make too sharp a distinction between these middle classes and the Palestinian urban notable families who continued to dominate politics throughout the mandate period; the degree of social, political, and economic contact between this middle class and urban notable families like the Husaynis remained high throughout the mandate period. On the question of urban notables see especially Albert Hourani, "Ottoman Reform and the Politics of Notables," in *The Beginnings of Modernization in the Middle East*, ed. William Polk and Richard Chambers (Chicago: University of Chicago Press, 1968), 41–68; Philip Khoury, *Urban Notables and Arab Nationalism: The Politics of Damascus 1860–1920* (Cambridge: Cambridge University Press, 2003); Edhem Eldem, Daniel Goffman, and Bruce Masters, *The Ottoman City between East and West: Aleppo, Izmir, and Istanbul* (London: Cambridge University Press, 1999); and James

Gelvin, *Divided Loyalties: Nationalism and Mass Politics in Syria at the Close of Empire* (Berkeley: University of California Press, 1998). For some uses of the "urban notables" paradigm in the Palestinian context see especially Beshara Doumani, *Rediscovering Palestine: Merchants and Peasants in Jabal Nablus 1770–1900* (Berkeley: University of California Press, 1995); Issa Khalaf, *Politics in Palestine: Arab Factionalism and Social Disintegration, 1939–1948* (Albany: SUNY Press, 1991); and Gudrun Krämer, *A History of Palestine: From the Ottoman Conquest to the Founding of the State of Israel* (Princeton: Princeton University Press, 2008).

10. The definition of the term "middle class" has of course been debated endlessly in both Western and non-Western contexts; it may be useful to remember Eric Hobsbawn's note on the subject that "a middle-class lifestyle and culture was one such criterion, leisure activity, and especially the new invention of sport, was another; but the chief indicator of actual membership increasingly became, and has remained, formal education." *The Age of Empire: 1875–1914* (New York: Vintage, 1989), 174. Keith Watenpaugh offers an excellent examination of the nature of the middle class in the Arab provinces of the Ottoman Empire during this period in his *Being Modern in the Middle East: Revolution, Nationalism, Colonialism, and the Arab Middle Class* (Princeton: Princeton University Press, 2006). In this work I have used the terms "middle class" and "elite" to refer to the same group of people, as distinct from the "notables" class.

11. Gluck, "Top Ten Things to Know about Japan in the Early Twenty-First Century," *Education about Asia* 13, 3 (Winter 2008): 6. As Gluck points outs and as these global non-Western elites were proclaiming, this definition means there is "no single way to be modern—no Western way, no Asian way."

12. Of course, this is not to suggest that all colonies and mandates were run exactly alike. For a useful comparative look at the administration of the mandate states see D. K. Fieldhouse, *Western Imperialism in the Middle East 1914–1958* (Oxford: Oxford University Press, 2008).

13. The letter continues, "it being clearly understood that nothing shall be done which may prejudice the civil and religious rights of existing non-Jewish communities in Palestine, or the rights and political status enjoyed by Jews in any other country." For a useful reprinting of the many drafts of the Balfour Declaration see Charles Smith, *Palestine and the Arab-Israeli Conflict*, 6th edition (Boston: Bedford/St. Martin's, 2007), 102–103.

14. This happened in other parts of the Middle East, especially Iraq, where the British thought the Arab Christian community might represent a potential collaborator for the colonial state.

15. Benedict Anderson, *Imagined Communities: Reflections on the Origin and Spread of Nationalism*, revised edition (London: Verso, 1991), 184.

16. This interpretation has received unexpected support from some religious Muslim observers. Sami Zubaida has observed, "For religious and political Muslims, it is held with pride, as a steadfast attachment to God and his revelations, valid for all times. For Western commentators, it is part of Muslim (and Arab) exceptionalism—impervious to the march of modernity and progress." "Islam and Secularization," *Asian Journal of Social Science* 33, 3 (2005): 438.

17. Bernand Lewis coined the term "clash of civilizations" in his much-read article "The Roots of Muslim Rage," *Atlantic Monthly*, September 1990, 47–60. He expands on this premise in some of his other work, including *What Went Wrong? The Clash between Islam and Modernity in the Middle East* (New York: Oxford University Press, 2002). See

also Samuel Huntington's famous exposition on the theme in "The Clash of Civilizations?" *Foreign Affairs* 72, 3 (1993): 22–49, and *The Clash of Civilizations and the Remaking of World Order* (New York: Simon and Schuster, 1996).

18. "The ethnoconfessional model's most basic assumption," Eric Davis notes, "is that Middle Eastern society, especially its Muslim component, is comprised first and foremost of ethnic and confessional groups whose loyalties are subnational (ethnic) or supranational (Islamist) in character. Hence particularistic identities trump nationalist commitments. From this assumption, it is only a short conceptual leap to the theoretical conclusion that the region's political instability and violence are a function of a defective political culture. . . . This unidimensional analysis fits the thinking of many Western policymakers who find that the ethnoconfessional model allows them to more easily 'digest' Middle East politics and normatively avoid accepting responsibility for the West's complicity in impeding solutions to the Middle East's problems." "A Sectarian Middle East?" *International Journal of Middle East Studies* 40, 4 (2008): 555.

19. A number of scholars have offered critiques of this interpretation of sectarianism; see especially Ussama Makdisi, "Moving Beyond Orientalist Fantasy, Sectarian Polemic, and Nationalist Denial," *International Journal of Middle East Studies* 40, 4 (2008).

20. My thinking here owes much to the theoretical model proposed by Makdisi in his *Culture of Sectarianism*, in which he defines sectarianism as "the deployment of religious heritage as a primary marker of modern political identity" (7).

21. There are only a very few volumes that could be named as examples of this kind of case study, among them Makdisi's *Culture of Sectarianism* on the construction of Druze and Maronite identities in nineteenth-century Lebanon. Barbara Carter's *The Copts in Egyptian Politics* (London: Croom Helm, 1986) offers a similar look at Coptic political participation in modern Egypt, challenging the Egyptian nationalist historiography of peaceful coexistence between Muslims and Copts, but is weakened by its assumption of the permanent inferiority of Christians in a Muslim-majority state. For a useful critique of this work see the review by Joel Beinin, *International Journal of Middle East Studies* 20, 1 (1988): 123–126. Some shorter studies of religious communities in the Middle East appear in Maya Shatzmiller, ed., *Nationalism and Minority Identities in Islamic Societies* (Montreal: McGill-Queen's University Press, 2005).

22. For a useful look at this phenomenon with particular reference to Iraq see Sami Zubaida, "Communalism and Thwarted Aspects of Iraqi Citizenship," *Middle East Report* 237 (Winter 2005): 9.

23. This was especially true in Egypt, where important conversations about Islamist and Arabist ideologies emerged as early as the mid-nineteenth century, in the context of a reaction against the imposition of European economic intervention and then direct colonial rule.

24. My narrative focuses primarily on elites, who were the primary actors in the drive to reconstitute Palestine's Christian communities as politically meaningful entities. The question of non-elite groups, for whom the implications of an increasingly sectarian political system were naturally rather different, is unfortunately beyond the scope of this book. I hope that other scholars will be encouraged to explore the question of constructing sectarian identities in non-elite circles; it is a project that will be an important addition to the historiography of modern Palestine.

25. See the epilogue for further discussion of this point.

The Hajjar quote in the epigraph is found in Juni Mansur, *Ru'iya jadida li hayat wa 'amal al-mutran Grigorios Hajjar* (Haifa: J. I. Mansur, 1985), 101.

1. In this chapter I draw on some of the historiography of civil society in Europe to understand the nature of this self-consciously Western social and political space Palestinian elites tried to construct during these years. For two recent overviews of this European scholarship see Nancy Bermeo and Philip Nord, eds., *Civil Society Before Democracy: Lessons from Nineteenth-Century Europe* (Lanham, MD: Rowman and Littlefield, 2000), and Frank Trentmann, ed., *Paradoxes of Civil Society: New Perspectives on Modern German and British History* (New York: Berghahn Books, 2000). In the European historiography, Trentmann asserts, civil society is understood as "a realm of associations—the layer of supposedly non-coercive organizations located between the family and the state or the state party . . . [as well as] an aspiration, a target for political education" (ix). Although civil society in the European context has been explicitly contrasted with the "totalizing" ideologies of nationalism—see, for instance, Michael Walzer, "The Concept of Civil Society," in *Toward a Global Civil Society*, ed. Michael Walzer, 7–28 (Providence, RI: Berghahn Books, 1995)—the kind of civil society that emerged in Palestine and many other colonized places made anti-imperial political nationalism central to its ethos and operation.

2. S. N. Spyridon, "Annals of Palestine, 1821–1841, written by Neophitos," *Journal of the Palestine Oriental Society* 18, 1–2 (1938): 123–129. See also Ruth Kark and Michal Oren-Nordheim, eds., *Jerusalem and Its Environs: Quarters, Neighborhoods, Villages, 1800–1948* (Detroit: Wayne State University Press, 2001), 27.

3. For details on the Damascus councils see Thompson, "Ottoman Political Reform," 457–475. In this case the Ottoman government met with local resistance when it tried to promote the idea of minority representation on the council, and the furor led to the resignation of the council's only Christian member.

4. Masters, *Christians and Jews*, 137.

5. This clause was intended to suggest a challenge to clerical authority, and it aroused particular opposition among members of the religious leadership of the non-Muslim communities. Ibid., 139.

6. Alexander Scholch, *Palestine in Transformation, 1856–1882: Studies in Social, Economic, and Political Development* (Washington, DC: Institute for Palestine Studies, 1993), 272.

7. Ibid., 273.

8. Ibid., 270.

9. Ibid., 276–277.

10. Another scholar has noted in his history of Ottoman Palestine that "the patronizing and often antagonistic behavior which the representatives of the Christian powers displayed toward the indigenous Muslim population in general and toward the local Muslim elite in particular was becoming a major contributing factor" in the deterioration of communal relations by the 1860s. Yazbak, *Haifa in the Late Ottoman Period*, 202.

11. Quoted in Raymond Cohen, *Saving the Holy Sepulchre: How Rival Christians Came Together to Rescue Their Holiest Shrine* (Oxford: Oxford University Press, 2008), 8. Cohen notes that the Ottoman government's purpose in enforcing the "status quo" rules over the "Holy Places" was "not even to prevent local conflict between Latins and Greeks, [but] simply to defuse the situation between the great powers by removing the question of the holy places from the realm of international politics." Ibid.

12. See Jamil Toubbeh, *Day of the Long Night: A Palestinian Refugee Remembers the Nakba* (Jefferson, NC: McFarland, 1998), 36.

13. Rochelle Davis, "Ottoman Jerusalem: The Growth of the New City," in *Jerusalem 1948: The Arab Neighbourhoods and Their Fate in the War*, ed. Salim Tamari (Jerusalem: Institute of Jerusalem Studies, 1999), 21.

14. Ibid., 24.

15. 'Issam Nassar and Salim Tamari, eds., *Al-Quds al-'uthmaniyya fi al-mudhakkirat al-Jawhariyya: Al-kitab al-awwal min mudhakkirat al-musiqi Wasid Jawhariyya, 1904–1917* (Beirut: Mu'assasat al-dirasat al-filastiniyya, 2003), 19–20.

16. Toubbeh, *Day of the Long Night*, 35. Salim Tamari, in "Al-mudhakkirat al-Jawhariyya ka-marra li-hadatha al-Quds al-'uthmaniyya," his editorial introduction to *Al-Quds al-'uthmaniyya fi al-mudhakkirat al-Jawhariyya*, which he co-edited with 'Issam Nassar, notes that Jawhariyya's account suggests that the European division of Jerusalem into neighborhoods strictly segregated by creed is radically mistaken—a view reinforced by scholars investigating the later mandate period. Especially in these new neighborhoods, a new elite was emerging that included Muslims, Christians, and sometimes Jews.

17. May Seikaly, *Haifa: The Transformation of a Palestinian Arab Society 1918–1939* (London: Tauris, 1995), 21. In Aliks Karmil's *Tarikh Haifa fi 'ahd al-itrak al-'uthmaniyyin* (Haifa: Sharikat al-dirasat al-'ilmiyya al-'amaliyya, 1979, 262), a census is quoted from 1886 putting the number of Muslim families at 605, Greek Catholic at 393, Greek Orthodox at 129, Maronite at 80, and Latin at 46.

18. Seikaly, *Haifa*, 30. The Jewish community, which had historically represented only a tiny percentage of Haifa's population, grew substantially in the early part of the twentieth century.

19. Ruth Kark, *Jaffa: A City in Evolution, 1799–1917* (Jerusalem: Ben-Zvi Press, 1990), 169–170.

20. Ibid., 171.

21. Quoted in Salim Tamari, "The Vagabond Café and Jerusalem's Prince of Idleness," *Jerusalem Quarterly* 19 (2003).

22. Ami Ayalon, *Reading Palestine: Printing and Literacy, 1900–1948* (Austin: University of Texas Press, 2004), 141.

23. Ibid., 21.

24. A. L. Tibawi, *Arab Education in Mandatory Palestine: A Study of Three Decades of British Administration* (London: Luzac, 1956), 61. Tibawi's work still represents the most comprehensive examination of the educational system serving Arabs in mandate-era Palestine. See also his *British Interests in Palestine, 1800–1901: A Study of Religious and Educational Enterprise* (London: Oxford University Press, 1961); *Islamic Education: Its Traditions and Modernization into the Arab National Systems* (London: Luzac, 1972); and *Dirasat 'arabiyya wa-islamiyya* (Damascus: Dar al-fikr, 1983) for a further look at the types of education available to Palestinians during this period. Ela Greenberg, *Preparing the Mothers of Tomorrow: Education and Islam in Mandate Palestine* (Austin: University of Texas Press, 2010), adds to this picture by examining the education available to Muslim women during the mandate period.

25. Numbers vary widely on this. Katz states that 90 percent of Christian men and 80 percent of Christian women were literate in 1914, compared to 10 percent of Muslim men and 5 percent of Muslim women. Sheila Katz, *Women and Gender in Early Jewish and Palestinian Nationalism* (Gainesville: University Press of Florida, 2005), 122. Ayalon, by contrast, cites a 1931 census that put literacy among Christians at 72 percent for men

and 44 percent for women and among Muslims at 25 percent for men and 3 percent for women, noting that this came "after a decade of enhanced educational endeavor." *Reading Palestine*, 16–17. It is certain, however, that the gap between Christian and Muslim literacy rates was substantial and can in large part be attributed to the availability of mission education for Arab Christians.

26. 'Adil Manna' suggests that these schools were part of a general elite "cultural awakening" that resulted from the influx of foreign education in the late nineteenth century. *A'lam Filastin fi awakhir al-ahd al-'uthmani, 1800–1918* (Beirut: Mu'assasat al-dirasat al-filastiniyya, 1995).

27. Khalil Sakakini, *Kadha ana ya dunya* (Beirut: al-Ittihad al-'amm lil-kuttab wa-al-suhufiyyin al-filastiniyyin, 1982), 189, entry for November 21, 1919; translated quote in Rochelle Davis, "Commemorating Education: Recollections of the Arab College in Jerusalem, 1918–1948," *Comparative Studies of South Asia, Africa, and the Middle East*, 23: 1–2 (2003): 193.

28. Hala Sakakini, *Jerusalem and I: A Personal Record* (Amman: Economic Press, 1990), 18.

29. Mousa Kaleel, *When I Was a Boy in Palestine* (London: Harrap, 1920), 36.

30. This situation, in which a commitment to Western-style civil society was accompanied by an absolute rejection of Western political overlordship, is a common theme in a number of geographical contexts during this period. See particularly Watenpaugh, *Being Modern in the Middle East*; he notes that the "acceptance of the underlying logos of Western civilization while asserting the ability of non-Westerners to resist the political and cultural hegemony of the West is the quintessential ambivalence at the center of the historical experience of modernity in the colonial and postcolonial non-West" (5).

31. The choice of these five figures was naturally also driven by the availability of sources. The rich lives and works of these people suggest that the many other elite Palestinians for whom we have no documentary records likewise had complex and fascinating intellectual, social, and political histories. These five are, of course, all male. A woman whose life suggests the type of activity in which elite Arab Christian women participated is Adele 'Azar of Jaffa, who in 1910 helped to found the Jaffa Orthodox Ladies Society, an organization intended to assist orphaned or otherwise disadvantaged girls to receive an education. She acted as the president of the Orthodox Ladies' Society and the principal of the Orthodox girls school. Her political and religious activities, then, were inextricably intertwined, a coexistence of religious and political consciousness that was equally apparent among Muslim women of similar elite backgrounds during this period and that reached across communal lines. Even though 'Azar's public activities were primarily through church organizations, her consciousness was elite, modern, and urban rather than specifically Christian. For a valuable analysis of 'Azar's life and work in the context of the Palestinian women's movement, using her unpublished memoirs, see Ellen Fleischmann, *The Nation and Its "New" Women: The Palestinian Women's Movement, 1920–1948* (Berkeley: University of California Press, 2003).

32. Muhammad Muslih, in *The Origins of Palestinian Nationalism* (New York: Columbia University Press, 1988, 233), cites 'Azuri's birthplace as Jaffa. Stefan Wild, "Negib Azoury and His Book *Le Reveil de la Nation Arabe*," in *Intellectual Life in the Arab East*, ed. Marwan Buheiry (Beirut: Center for Arab and Middle East Studies, 1981, 93), puts it in 'Azur.

33. Negib Azoury [Najib 'Azuri], *Le réveil de la nation arabe dans l'Asie turque* (Paris: Plon-Nourrit, 1905), 249; Wild, "Negib Azoury and His Book," 93–94.

———

34. This book is referenced in nearly every English-language discussion of Arab nationalism as proof of the early existence of Arab nationalist sentiment, and discussions of it are primarily devoted either to validating it as a demonstration of the age and legitimacy of Arab nationalism (see, for instance, Rashid Khalidi, *Palestinian Identity: The Construction of Modern National Consciousness* [New York: Columbia University Press, 1997], 152) or invalidating it as the work of a scheming opportunist (see Elie Kedourie, *Arabic Political Memoirs and Other Studies* [London: Cass, 1974], 116–117).

35. For Palestinian Arab opposition to Zionism in the late Ottoman period see Khalidi, *Palestinian Identity*, and Neville Mandel, *The Arabs and Zionism Before World War I* (Berkeley: University of California Press, 1976).

36. Azoury, *Le réveil de la nation arabe*, v.

37. Wild suggests that the league "probably never had any members other than Azoury himself." "Negib Azoury and His Book," 94.

38. Azoury, *Le réveil de la nation arabe*, 246. He describes Egyptians as being African Berber in racial origin and claims that their language before the advent of Islam bore no relation to Arabic.

39. Ibid., 247.

40. Ibid., 165.

41. Ibid., 178.

42. On the relationship between nationalism and these independent church movements see Pedro Ramet, ed., *Religion and Nationalism in Soviet and East European Politics* (Durham: Duke University Press, 1989); Theodore H. Papadopoullos, *Studies and Documents Relating to the History of the Greek Church and People under Turkish Domination* (Aldershot, England: Gower, 1990); Olivier Gillet, *Balkans: Religions et nationalisme* (Brussels: Éditions OUSIA, 2001); and Celia Hawkesworth, Muriel Heppell, and Harry Norris, eds., *Religious Quest and National Identity in the Balkans* (Houndmills, England: Palgrave, 2001).

43. For this section I am much indebted to Salim Tamari's perceptive writing on al-Sakakini; his articles draw a convincing picture of the social milieu in which al-Sakakini became such a recognizable figure and provide a sharp portrait of the man himself. See Salim Tamari, "A Miserable Year in Brooklyn: Khalil Sakakini in America, 1907–1908," *Jerusalem Quarterly* 17 (2003): 19–40; "Lepers, Lunatics, and Saints: The Nativist Ethnography of Tawfiq Canaan and His Jerusalem Circle," *Jerusalem Quarterly* 20 (2004): 24–43; "Vagabond Café"; and *Jabal didda al-bahr: Dirasat fi ishkaliyat al-hadatha al-filastiniyya* (Ramallah: Al-mu'assasa al-filastiniyya li-dirasat al-dimuqratiyya, 2005).

44. From the nineteenth century forward it appears that Palestinian Christians emigrated at higher rates than their Muslim compatriots, and large numbers could be found not only in the United States but also in Lebanon and Latin America. During the early years of the mandate, the Bethehemite Christian expatriate community in South America was large enough to provide material for a newsletter published by 'Isa Bandak, *Bayt lahm*.

45. This is evident from his letters to Sultana describing his perambulations around New York, where he reports only on his Arab neighborhood and his Arab friends and acquaintances. See, for instance, Akram Musallam, ed., *Yawmiyat Khalil al-Sakakini: Yawmiyat, rasa'il wa-ta'ammulat*, vol. 1 (Ramallah: Markaz Khalil al-Sakakini al-thaqafi, Mu'assasat al-dirasat al-muqaddasiyya, 2003), 57. His companions seem to have been more enthusiastic about the city than he was; he quotes Hanna Farraj as urging him to "get out and go tour the streets on the great holiday of America," New Year's Day 1908 (83).

46. Al-Sakakini published a series called *al-Jadid* (The New) in which he explored pedagogical topics and explained his theories on language.

47. Issa Boullata, "Books and I," *Banipal* 29 (Spring 2007).

48. Wasif Jawhariyya described the shock of moving from the old system of schooling to al-Sakakini's Dusturiyya school in his memoirs. See Nassar and Tamari, *Al-Quds al-'uthmaniyya fi al-mudhakkirat al-Jawhariyya* (xxviii, 81) for discussions of Jawhariyya's relationship with al-Sakakini.

49. See Tamari, "Miserable Year," 22.

50. See Hala Sakakini, *Jerusalem and I.*

51. Quoted in Tamari, "Vagabond Café."

52. Salim Tamari makes this point very effectively in "Vagabond Café": "This mixture of populist egalitarianism and sardonic moralism in the party's manifesto camouflaged what was essentially a narcissistic streak in Sakakini's character, and one that was eminently suited to the emerging café culture of the new class of literati and salariat flaneurs in Mediterranean cultures. The culture of the public café suited Sakakini's like a glove."

53. Al-Sakakini, *Kadha ana ya dunya*, 153–154 (entry for June 20, 1918). This quote is also discussed in Tamari, "Vagabond Café."

54. Ishaq Musa al-Husayni, "Khalil al-Sakakini," in Abdul Hamid Yasin, ed., *Dhikra al-Sakakini* (Jerusalem: Modern Library, 1957), 60–63.

55. Hala Sakakini, *Jerusalem and I*, 22–23. "Neither at home nor at school did religion play an important role in our lives . . . Our parents never went to church except to attend funerals," she reported. Salim Tamari notes that Sakakini even flirted with an antinatalist philosophy, using a visiting card that read, "Khalil Sakakini, Ta'alu li Nanqarid" (Let us extinguish ourselves); "Miserable Year," 21.

56. Anthony O'Mahony, introduction to *Palestinian Christians: Religion, Politics, and Society*, ed. O'Mahony (London: Melisende, 1999), 50–51n101.

57. Quoted in Abd al-Wahhab Kayyali, *Palestine: A Modern History* (London: Croom Helm, 1978), 37.

58. Introduction by Yusef Ayyub Haddad to Musallam, *Yawmiyat Khalil al-Sakakini*, 3:10.

59. Ibid.

60. This date is according to Muhammad Muslih, *Origins of Palestinian Nationalism*, 80. Qustandi Shomali puts it at 1873, adding that he was educated at a primary school in the Shuf, received his secondary school education at Suq al-Gharb, and went on to study pharmaceuticals and political science at the American University of Beirut (AUB). Shomali, "Nagib Nassar l'intransigeant, 1873–1948," *Revue d'études palestiniennes* 54, 2 (1995): 80–90.

61. Muslih, *Origins of Palestinian Nationalism*, 80.

62. Shomali, "Nagib Nassar l'intransigeant," 83.

63. Ibid., 84.

64. *Al-Karmil*, October 8, 1911.

65. *Al-Karmil* June 7, 1911.

66. This was, Shomali notes, one of his main points of disagreement with 'Isa al-'Isa, who was convinced of the perfidy of the British from a very early date and expressed anti-British sentiments in *Filastin* from the beginning of the mandate; "Nagib Nassar l'intransigeant," 81–82.

67. This theme has been explored extensively in the field of comparative literature.

See, for instance, Ian Watt, *The Rise of the Novel: Studies in Defoe, Richardson, and Fielding* (Berkeley: University of California Press, 1957); Nancy Armstrong, *Desire and Domestic Fiction: A Political History of the Novel* (New York: Oxford University Press, 1987); Edward Said, *Culture and Imperialism* (New York: Knopf, 1993). These authors have pointed to the many ways the Western novel was intimately linked to the rise of industrial capitalism and the rise of the concept of the individual, and Said discusses how the history of the English novel is inextricably linked to Britain's imperial history. For early Arab contributions to the novel form see Stephen Sheehi, *The Foundations of Modern Arab Identity* (Gainesville: University Press of Florida, 2004), and Sabry Hafez, *The Genesis of Arabic Narrative Discourse: A Study in the Sociology of Modern Arabic Literature* (London: Saqi Books, 1993).

68. Shomali, "Nagib Nassar l'intransigeant," 82.

69. See quote from Habib Boulos in Shomali, "Nagib Nassar l'intransigeant," 83.

70. For further biographical information on 'Isa al-'Isa see Rashid Khalidi, *The Iron Cage: The Story of the Palestinian Struggle for Statehood* (Boston: Beacon Press, 2006), 94.

71. Tamari, "Vagabond Café."

72. Yehoshua Porath, *The Palestinian Arab National Movement: From Riots to Rebellion, 1929–1939* (London: F. Cass), 1977, 128.

73. For further discussion of this point see chapter 3.

74. 'Ajaj Nuwayhid, *Rijal min Filastin ma bayna bidayat al-qarm hatta 'am 1948* (Amman: Filastin al-muhtalla, 1981), 30.

75. J. Mansur, *Ru'iya jadida*, 17. This biography is somewhat hagiographical, but it represents the only comprehensive source on Hajjar's life and includes appendices that reproduce some of Hajjar's letters and poems.

76. Ibid., 52.

77. Ibid., 55–56. Mansur views the war years as a period of "crystallization of Hajjar's political convictions."

78. In ibid., 101.

79. Kamal Boullata, "The World, the Self, and the Body: Pioneering Women in Palestinian Art," in *Self-Portrait: Palestinian Women's Art*, ed. Tal Ben Azvi and Yael Lehrer (Tel Aviv: Andalus, 2001), 177.

80. See Porath, *Palestinian Arab National Movement*, 29. The idea of a Christian political bloc also appears in Muslih, *Origins of Palestinian Nationalism*; Anthony O'Mahony, ed., *Palestinian Christians: Religion, Politics, and Society* (London: Melisende, 1999); Daphne Tsimhoni, "The Arab Christians and the Palestinian Arab National Movement during the Formative Stage," in *The Palestinians and the Middle East Conflict*, ed. Gabriel Ben-Dor (Ramat Gan, Israel: Turtledove, 1978), "The Status of the Arab Christians under the British Mandate in Palestine," *Middle Eastern Studies* 20, 4 (1984): 166–192, and "The Greek Orthodox Patriarchate of Jerusalem during the Formative Years of the British Mandate in Palestine," *Asian and African Studies* 12 (1978): 77–122; and others.

81. For an examination of "third-world" engagement with the new conception of self-determination see Eres Manela, *The Wilsonian Moment: Self-Determination and the International Origins of Anticolonial Nationalism* (Oxford: Oxford University Press, 2007).

82. The Arab Revolt against the Ottomans during World War I was led by Sharif Husayn of Mecca in return for an unfulfilled British agreement to support an independent Arab state under his rule after the war.

83. See especially Khalidi, *Palestinian Identity*, for an analysis of how the Southern Syria movement fit into an emerging sense of Palestinian national identity during these years. The question of the origins and development of a sense of Palestinian national iden-

tity has been hotly debated, as much for its contemporary political ramifications as for its historical importance. Khalidi argues convincingly that a sense of Palestinian identity represented one among many strands in the loyalties of Arabs in Palestine during the late Ottoman period but that it crystallized quickly in the early years of the mandate as Ottomanism, Greater Syria, and Arabism fell away as viable political options and the Zionist threat became clearer.

84. The history of the MCAs has been discussed extensively in such works as Porath, *Palestinian Arab National Movement*; Muslih, *Origins of Palestinian Nationalism*; Khalidi, *Palestinian Identity*; and Seikaly, *Haifa*, among others. This discussion is not intended to provide a comprehensive history of the MCAs but to examine the nature of Christian participation in the associations and to explore the extent to which there was a Christian political approach to the nationalist politics in the MCAs and their main rivals during the first few years of the mandate period.

85. Statutes of the MCA Jerusalem, 1918, Israel State Archives (hereafter ISA), record group (hereafter RG) 2/m/28/20.

86. Ibid.

87. Muslih, *Origins of Palestinian Nationalism*, 160.

88. Quoted in Porath, *Palestinian Arab National Movement*, 33. Porath contends that there is some evidence that the MCA was formed under the encouragement of a British intelligence officer named Captain Brunton. This assertion, which Porath traces to Zionist Commission intelligence reports, is not corroborated in the British records, although there is evidence that the MCA was provided with a certain degree of British support after its founding during the first few years of British occupation.

89. Storrs to Occupied Enemy Territories Administration (hereafter OETA) headquarters, November 21, 1918, Foreign Office (hereafter FO) 371/3386; see also Porath, *Palestinian Arab National Movement*, 33–34.

90. Postlethwaite (military governor of Jaffa) to OETA Jerusalem, May 20, 1919, ISA 28/20/m. He asserted that Yusef al-'Isa and Ragib al-Dajani were the primary instigators of "dissatisfaction among the people" by "their Sherifian Propoganda [*sic*]."

91. Muslih, *Origins of Palestinian Nationalism*, 165.

92. Ibid., 168.

93. Muslih, *Origins of Palestinian Nationalism*, 158. "In addition," he writes, "the MCA leaders had a traditional outlook, taking a rather paternalistic view of their responsibilities for guiding the Palestinian Arab community. . . . [It was] merely a loose alliance of notables with no political structures designed to penetrate society and incorporate new social forces." Muslih, *Origins of Palestinian Nationalism*, 162–163.

94. Ibid., 159.

95. Intelligence Report on the Palestine Conference by Captain J. N. Camp, February 15, 1919, ISA RG2/m/28/20. These labels reflected the common imperial approach of categorizing people according to whether they might be useful to the colonial state. In *The Origins of Palestinian Nationalism* (180), Muslih renames these colonial categories as "Palestinian independence" (for "pro-British") and "Unity with Syria" (for pro-Arab), leaving "pro-French" the same. This reflects a common assumption among scholars of this period that colonial categories easily overlapped local ones.

96. The other three who did not sign were two delegates from Hebron who had left the conference early and 'Abd al-Hamid Abu Ghosh of the Jerusalem district, who was at this stage working as an intelligence officer for both the French and the Zionist Commission. It is unclear why Farraj did not sign the resolution, as he was as anti-Zionist as any

of the other delegates and felt free to express this on a number of other occasions. He did, however, tend to be quite pro-British and may have refrained from signing as an expression of loyalty to Britain. See Porath, *Palestinian Arab National Movement*, 81.

97. Quoted in ibid., 82.

98. Ibid.

99. Farraj and al-Dajani to Military Governor of Jerusalem, February 5, 1919, ISA RG2/m/28/20. It seems that these two delegates, under pressure, submitted a request in writing that their votes be declared void.

100. List, Intelligence Report on the Palestine Conference by Captain J. N. Camp, February 15, 1919, ISA RG2/m/28/20.

101. Public notice from president of Jerusalem Catholics Society, February 4, 1919, ISA RG2/m/7/12.

102. Political report, February 1921, FO 371/6375. Examples also are found in Military Governor of Tul Karm to OETA Jerusalem, February 16, 1919, ISA RG2/m/7/12, and Crew to OETA Jerusalem, September 1, 1919, ISA RG2/m/7/12.

103. Porath, *Palestinian Arab National Movement*, 108.

104. The cities represented were Jerusalem, Lydda, Ramleh, Jaffa, Safad, Nazareth, Acre, Jenin, Tul Karm, Tiberias, and Nablus; a total of forty-six delegates attended the congress. See Muslih, *Origins of Palestinian Nationalism*, 205.

105. Public announcement signed by Omar Bitar of the Jaffa MCA, n.d. (probably 1919), ISA RG2/m/28/20.

106. Musa Kazim al-Husayni to High Commissioner, December 18, 1920, FO 371/6374.

107. Quoted in Khalidi, *Palestinian Identity*, 169.

108. Political report, April 1921, FO 371/6375.

109. Lamington's address, June 15, 1921, FO 371/6375.

CHAPTER 2

The epigraph is from Harry Charles Luke, *Prophets, Priests, and Patriarchs: Sketches of the Sects of Palestine and Syria* (London: Faith Press, 1927), 6.

1. Although British policy toward Palestinian Muslims has been explored in detail, there has been no effort to contextualize this policy by examining it as part of a broader imperial approach. Some older scholarship, particularly Porath's in *The Emergence of the Palestinian-Arab National Movement, 1918–1929* (London: F. Cass, 1974), interprets this decision as a way to allow for the easy incorporation of relatively independent European Jewish institutions into the Palestinian political fabric, making possible the implementation of the Balfour Declaration with a minimum of trouble and expense. More recent efforts to explore the topic have focused primarily on internal Palestinian Arab and Jewish politics, treating Palestine as *sui generis*; see, for example, Uri Kupferschmidt, *The Supreme Muslim Council: Islam under the British Mandate for Palestine* (Leiden, Netherlands: Brill, 1987). My analysis is not intended to dispute either of these approaches but to point out the previously underestimated importance of the broader imperial context for understanding Britain's approach to the millet system in Palestine.

2. Colonial land policy derived from very similar imperial influences and justifications, a point made effectively in Martin Bunton, *Colonial Land Policies in Palestine, 1917–1936* (Oxford: Oxford University Press, 2007).

3. Adamantia Pollis, "Intergroup Conflict and British Colonial Policy: The Case of Cyprus," *Comparative Politics* 5, 4 (1973): 578. Pollis points out that this approach is in contrast to the French policy of "assimilation," whereby colonial subjects were expected to assume French forms and participate in French institutions as they "progressed" through the civilizing process of colonial rule.

4. See especially Adu Boahen, *African Perspectives on Colonialism* (Baltimore: Johns Hopkins University Press, 1987); Terence Ranger, "The Invention of Tradition in Colonial Africa," in *The Invention of Tradition*, ed. Eric Hobsbawn and Terence Ranger (Cambridge, England: Cambridge University Press, 1992), 211–262, and his *Missionaries, Migrants, and the Manyika: The Invention of Ethnicity in Zimbabwe* (Johannesburg: African Studies Institute, University of the Witwatersrand, 1984).

5. Nicholas Dirks, *Castes of Mind: Colonialism and the Making of Modern India* (Princeton, NJ: Princeton University Press, 2001).

6. On this process in India see Partha Chatterjee, *The Nation and Its Fragments: Colonial and Postcolonial Histories* (Princeton: Princeton University Press, 1993), and *Nationalist Thought and the Colonial World: A Derivative Discourse?* (London: Zed Books, 1986); Gyan Pandey, *The Construction of Communalism in Colonial North India* (Delhi: Oxford University Press, 1990); Ayesha Jalal, "Exploding Communalism: The Politics of Muslim Identity," in *Nationalism, Democracy, and Development: State and Politics in India*, ed. Ayesha Jalal and Sugata Bose (Delhi: Oxford University Press, 1998); Thomas Metcalf, *Ideologies of the Raj* (Cambridge: Cambridge University Press, 1997); Bernard Cohn, *Colonialism and Its Forms of Knowledge: The British in India* (Princeton, NJ: Princeton University Press, 1996); and C. A. Bayly, *Indian Society and the Making of the British Empire* (Cambridge, England: Cambridge University Press, 1988). The colonial construction of communalism in India has been a major theme in the historiography of the Raj, but this literature has made remarkably little impact on the historical study of the Middle East despite some striking parallels with British colonial strategies in Palestine, Egypt, and Iraq.

7. A few scholars have begun to investigate the parallels between British strategies in India and in the Middle East. See, for instance, C. A. Bayly's exploration of parallels between Egypt and India with regard to religious minorities in his "Representing Copts and Muhammadans: Empire, Nation, and Community in Egypt and India, 1880–1914," in *Modernity and Culture: From the Mediterranean to the Indian Ocean*, ed. Leila Fawaz and C. A. Bayly (New York: Columbia University Press, 2002), 158–203; Roger Owen's investigation of Cromer's deployment of Indian colonial strategies in Egypt in *Lord Cromer: Victorian Imperialist, Edwardian Proconsul* (Oxford: Oxford University Press, 2004); and Rashid Khalidi's brief investigation of Indian influences on the mandate government in Palestine in *The Iron Cage*.

8. See the introduction for sources on the Ottoman millet system.

9. The question of the nature and extent of the millet system prior to its institutionalization through the intervention of Western powers, particularly the British, in the nineteenth century remains disputed among Ottomanists, who have generally been somewhat reluctant to analyze Ottoman communities through a sectarian lens. However, the recent work that has been done on this question has tended to emphasize the codification of the millet system, the hardening of sectarian categories, and the legal, political, and cultural entrenchment of sectarian differences after the introduction of strong British influence in the Ottoman empire from the early nineteenth century onward. See, for instance, Masters, *Christians and Jews*; Makdisi, *Culture of Sectarianism*; and Jack Fairey, "The Great Game of Improvements: European Diplomacy and the Reform of the Ortho-

dox Church" (Ph.D. diss., University of Toronto, 2004). This approach had its beginnings with Benjamin Braude's article "Foundation Myths of the Millet System" in *Christians and Jews in the Ottoman Empire*, ed. Braude and Lewis, 1:69–88, in which he argues that there was no coherent Ottoman policy toward non-Muslims and no consistent use of the term "millet" to refer to non-Muslim populations until the European-influenced reforms of the early nineteenth century.

10. Masters, *Christians and Jews*, 147.

11. For an examination of these Christian communities and nationalist efforts in the Balkans see Hawkesworth, Heppell, and Norris, *Religious Quest and National Identity*; Peter Sugar, *Nationalism and Religion in the Balkans since the 19th Century* (Seattle: University of Washington Press, 1996); and Misha Glenny, *The Balkans, 1804–1999: Nationalism, War, and the Great Powers* (London: Granta, 1999).

12. The rich historiographical literature on this topic for India and Africa has been central to my thinking on this point. In the Indian and the African contexts, the colonial strategy of maintaining a "status quo" through the promotion of so-called customary law and the reinforcement of "traditional" ethnic, cultural, or religious divides has been the subject of massive historiographical and theoretical literatures. It should also be noted that this policy was carried out not only in the other British colonies in the Middle East (Iraq and Egypt) but also in the French-mandated territories of Syria and Lebanon. Elizabeth Thompson explains the French maintenance of legal autonomy for religious communities in Lebanon as a mode of "divide and rule." See her *Colonial Citizens: Republican Rights, Paternal Privilege, and Gender in French Syria and Lebanon* (New York: Columbia University Press, 2000), 114–116.

13. George Rankin, "Custom and the Muslim Law in British India," *Transactions of the Grotius Society* 25 (1939): 95.

14. Ibid., 96. The order comes in Regulation II of 1772, s. 27.

15. Robert Travers, *Ideology and Empire in Eighteenth Century India: The British in Bengal* (New York: Cambridge University Press, 2007), 105.

16. Jones to Governor-General, March 19, 1788, quoted in Rankin, "Custom and the Muslim Law in British India," 97. Rankin points out that the "sincerity of this belief is shown by the action of Warren Hastings in having the Hedaya translated into Persian . . . Also by the elaborate proposals of Jones for a digest of Hindu and Mahomedan law and by his own work on the *Sirajiyyah* and *Sharifiyyah*." Ibid.

17. Travers, *Ideology and Empire*, 107. This parallels Braude's proposal that the term "millet" did not acquire its meaning until the interventions of the British in Ottoman affairs during the nineteenth century.

18. Roger Owen, "Defining Traditional: Some Implications of the Use of Ottoman Law in Mandatory Palestine," *Harvard Middle Eastern and Islamic Review* 1, 2 (1994): 119.

19. Norman Bentwich, "The Legislation of Palestine, 1918–1925," *Journal of Comparative Legislation and International Law* 8, 1 (1926): 10.

20. For a recent investigation of the international effects of this rhetoric see Manela, *Wilsonian Moment*.

21. Sykes, "Our Position in Mesopotamia in Relation to the Spirit of the Age," FO 800/22. The full document is reprinted in Helmut Mejcher, *The Imperial Quest for Oil: Iraq 1910–1928* (London: Middle East Centre, St. Antony's College, 1976), appendix 2.

22. For further exploration of this point with regard to Iraq see Toby Dodge, *Inventing Iraq: The Failure of Nation-Building and a History Denied* (New York: Columbia University Press, 2003).

23. Tsimhoni, "Status of the Arab Christians," 168.

24. P. M. Brown, "British Justice in Palestine," *American Journal of International Law* 12, 4 (October 1918): 831.

25. F. M. Goadby, "Religious Communities and Courts in Palestine," *Tulane Law Review* 8, 2 (1934): 220.

26. Toby Dodge offers a useful comparison with Palestine in his *Inventing Iraq*. In a chapter on "British Visions of Ottoman Iraq" he argues that the British staffing the mandate government and civil service in Iraq after the imposition of the mandate had very little empirical understanding of how Ottoman institutions had functioned there and that this ignorance "allowed a collective understanding of the nature and effect of Ottoman rule in Iraq to become dominant" (43). This understanding, according to Dodge, was dominated by a view of Ottoman rule as despotic, corrupt, and irrational, by a conception of Iraq as fundamentally divided, and by an understanding of the rural Iraqi peasantry as oppressed and politically immature. The mandate government, operating under these assumptions, tried to codify and reform Ottoman law in such a way as to reject the "corrupt" influences of the educated, urban, politicized middle and upper classes of Iraqi society. Dodge quite correctly points out that this British conception of the Ottomans was a projection of deep anxiety about political and social developments in the metropole in the postwar era: "The pathologies of the Ottoman state—the corruption of its sprawling administration, the contamination of the countryside, by its presence and propensity to absolutism—were projections in a bitter ongoing dispute about the imagined social trajectory of post-war Britain" (60–61). In Palestine, because of its status as a multi-religious "Holy Land" and its prominence in British thought about both Islam and Christianity, the perceived divisions were religious rather than tribal, and the continuance and reform of the millet system represented a continuation of British policy toward Ottoman Palestine.

27. For background on Samuel see his own *Memoirs* (London: Cresset Press, 1945) and Bernard Wasserstein, *Herbert Samuel: A Political Life* (Oxford: Clarendon Press, 1992). Two works in particular focus on Samuel's years as high commissioner: Sahar Huneidi, *Broken Trust: Herbert Samuel, Zionism, and the Palestinians, 1920–1925* (London: Tauris, 2001), and M. Mossek, *Palestine Immigration Policy under Sir Herbert Samuel: British, Zionist, and Arab Attitudes* (London: F. Cass, 1978).

28. For further biographical information on Bentwich see his own numerous works: *My 77 Years: An Account of My Life and Times, 1883–1960* (Philadelphia, Jewish Publication Society of America, 1961); *A Wanderer in the Promised Land* (New York: Scribner, 1933); *Palestine* (London, 1934); and with Helen Bentwich, *Mandate Memories, 1918–1948* (London: Hogarth Press, 1965), among others. Bentwich's biography is also briefly covered in Likhovski, *Law and Identity in Mandate Palestine*.

29. F. M. Goadby, *An Introduction to the Study of Law: A Handbook for the Use of Law Students in Egypt and Palestine* (London: Butterworths, 1921).

30. Martin Bunton, "Inventing the Status Quo: Ottoman Land-Law during the Palestine Mandate, 1917–1936," *International History Review* 21, 1 (1999): 49. Bunton quotes J. B. Barron's preface to his 1922 report on "Mohammadan Wakfs" in which he apologized that he "was unable to obtain any modern work in English dealing with this subject."

31. Ibid.

32. Ibid.

33. Brown, "British Justice in Palestine," 832.

34. Owen, "Defining Traditional," 124.

35. Samuel, *Memoirs*, 161.

36. Bentwich, "Legislation of Palestine," 11–12, and *Palestine*, 120.

37. Bentwich, "Legislation of Palestine," 11–12.

38. Ibid., 13.

39. Samuel, *Memoirs*, 164. This particular form of retraditionalization was one Samuel undertook in Britain as well; he writes in a footnote that he "had always felt strongly about this vulgarization of modern life everywhere, and was glad to be able, when I was Under-Secretary at the Home Office, to help the passage of the first statute in Great Britain for checking the abuses of public advertising." This approach to architecture and public space in Palestine is explored in detail in Daniel Bertrand Monk, *An Aesthetic Occupation: The Immediacy of Architecture and the Palestine Conflict* (Durham, NC: Duke University Press, 2002). Monk describes his work as "a history of figures/monuments, which in their inadequacy to the norm of adequacy they are asked to sustain, immanently reconvene the abstract actuality of a conflict . . . a history of apotropaic response upon apotropaic response to a dialectical image" (12); Monk focuses in particular on the archaeological and architectural ideas of Palestine's director of antiquities E. T. Richmond.

40. Samuel, *Memoirs*, 164. He notes in particular returning the name of "Dome of the Rock" to what had come to be called the "Mosque of Omar" and that "the lake which the Romans named after the Emperor Tiberius, who had no claim as a ruler to such special honour, recovered the name more consonant with its charm, the Sea of Galilee."

41. The presence of the Jewish community gave a new urgency to questions of communal organization in Palestine. In 1924 a number of Jewish leaders requested that the British government pass a statute allowing for the political organization of a national Jewish religious community. This request met with some opposition in London, and after a discussion that stretched over two more years, the two factions compromised by creating the Religious Community Ordinance of 1926, which allowed each Palestinian religious community to set itself up as an autonomous political entity upon application. The only community actually to do this was the Jewish, which was recognized in 1927. See Goadby, "Religious Communities and Courts in Palestine," 218–219; also Tsimhoni, "Status of the Arab Christians," 170.

42. Bentwich, "Legislation of Palestine," 18–19.

43. Samuel's speech in House of Lords, December 8, 1938, FO 371/21871. Elie Kedourie approved of these comments as a "shrewd and judicious appreciation" in *The Chatham House Version and Other Middle Eastern Studies* (New York: Praeger, 1970), 69.

44. Herbert Samuel, *Report of the High Commissioner on the Administration of Palestine, 1920–1925* (London: HMSO, 1925), 50.

45. In Bentwich, *Palestine*, 139. Also see Owen, "Defining Traditional," 120–121. This point is reinforced with regard to land law in Bunton, *Colonial Land Policies in Palestine*, whose central argument is that colonial land policies were "ad hoc and makeshift, multidirectional and inconsistent, even contradictory" (27).

46. Robert Eisenman, *Islamic Law in Palestine and Israel: A History of the Survival of Tanzimat and Shar'ia in the British Mandate and the Jewish State* (Leiden, Netherlands: Brill, 1978), 75; Bernard Joseph, "Palestine Legislation under the British," *Annals of the American Academy of Political and Social Science* 164 (November 1932): 40.

47. The British lawyer Bernard Joseph, practicing in Jerusalem, suggested that not only were the British "averse to interfering unduly with existing customs and laws" but also that it was "not in keeping with British legal tradition and constitutional practice to

codify the law" and that this principle was extended to the Indian and Palestinian contexts. Joseph, "Palestine Legislation under the British," 40.

48. Sir Ernest Dowson, memo on "Preliminary Study of Land Tenure in Palestine," 1930, Colonial Office (hereafter CO) 733/109.

49. For biographical information on Keith-Roach see his memoirs, *Pasha of Jerusalem: Memoirs of a District Commissioner under the British Mandate*, ed. Paul Eedle (London: Radcliffe Press, 1994). He is also discussed in A. J. Sherman, *Mandate Days: British Lives in Palestine, 1918–1948* (London: Thames and Hudson, 1997).

50. Ronald Storrs served in various offices in Egypt before and during the war, becoming military governor of Jerusalem in 1917 and then civil governor of Jerusalem a from 1920 to 1926; he subsequently continued his colonial career in Cyprus and Rhodesia. Harry Charles Luke served as a colonial officer in Sierra Leone, Barbados, Cyprus, Armenia, and Azerbaijan before becoming the assistant governor of Jerusalem in 1924 and chief secretary in 1928 (after a period away in Sierra Leone from 1924 to 1928). After leaving Palestine in 1930, he served in Malta, Fiji, and the Caribbean. These men represented an imperial sensibility developed in the field, against Samuel's and Bentwich's metropole-derived imperial philosophies.

51. Keith-Roach, *Pasha of Jerusalem*, 74.

52. Quoted in Bunton, "Inventing the Status Quo," 50.

53. Ibid. Bunton points out that Bentwich's legal abilities were universally criticized to the extent that the term "Bentwichian" was coined to describe legislation needing radical revision. "His drafting is notoriously bad," wrote one critic, "his conduct of cases upon the rare occasion when he appears in Court borders on the ridiculous, and his knowledge and sympathy of English and Colonial law and institutions are lacking" (52). This appears to have been a point of near-general consensus, and the only reason he was not removed from his post earlier was a fear on the part of colonial officials of appearing to knuckle under to the Arab Executive, who had been demanding his dismissal for some time. See Bunton, "Inventing the Status Quo," for a more extensive discussion of opposition to Bentwich within the mandate government.

54. Ronald Storrs, *Orientations* (London: Ivor, Nicholson, and Watson, 1937).

55. Quoted in Monk, *Aesthetic Occupation*, 164n36.

56. Keith-Roach, *Pasha of Jerusalem*, 78.

57. Luke, *Prophets, Priests, and Patriarchs*, 6.

58. Storrs, *Orientations*, 341.

59. Tsimhoni, "Status of the Arab Christians," 169.

60. It should be noted that the idea of defining the Muslim community as a millet was not totally new; the upheavals of the nineteenth century saw Muslims in the Ottoman Arab provinces who felt economically and politically threatened by the rise in prominence and economic power of the Christian millets and began to consider the possibility of constituting themselves as a millet to reclaim some of their lost superiority. The phrase *milel-i erbaa*, "the four millets," referred to Orthodox Christians, Armenian Christians, Jews, and Muslims and was sometimes deployed by Ottoman bureaucrats in the late nineteenth century. See Masters, *Christians and Jews*, 134. However, the promulgation of a formal legal and political structure for a Muslim millet was a British innovation and had no precedent anywhere in the Ottoman world.

61. British political agent George Broadfoot, for instance, had argued in the nineteenth century that Britain needed a buffer zone between India and what he called "that great mass of unmixed Mahomedanism" from India to the eastern Mediterranean. M. E.

Yapp, "'That Great Mass of Unmixed Mahomedanism': Reflections on the Historical Links between the Middle East and Asia," *British Journal of Middle Eastern Studies* 19, 1 (1992): 9. Yapp argues that this feeling derived primarily from a British sense of the precariousness of their holdings in India, a view that Muslims necessarily regarded British rule as illegitimate, and the prevalence of British sentiments about the inherence of violence and fanaticism in Islam (12). He also points out, correctly, that although there were pan-Islamic and pro-caliphate movements in India during the late nineteenth and early twentieth centuries, they were proven feeble in the years immediately following World War I.

62. London's fear of an anticolonial pan-Islamism encompassing India continued unabated through the interwar years. A proposal from Herbert Samuel to raise money by subscription to restore the Dome of the Rock and al-Aqsa mosque, for instance, intended to have "a favourable effect upon Muslim opinion, not only in Palestine, but throughout the Muslim world," aroused intense India Office opposition on the grounds that "we cannot but anticipate exploitation for purpose of exciting Moslem sentiments throughout the world, if proposal that Mosque in Jerusalem should be restored according to plan of Christian Englishman mere fact of preparation of plans by him implying that he had had access to all parts of the building." Kupferschmidt, *Supreme Muslim Council*, 18, quoting Viceroy of India to Secretary of State, November 2, 1920, FO 141/513/9.

63. Bentwich, *Palestine*, 186.

64. For further discussion of this episode see Weldon Matthews, *Confronting an Empire, Constructing a Nation: Arab Nationalists and Popular Politics in Mandate Palestine* (London: Tauris, 2006), 224.

65. Smart to Bamford (Intelligence Bureau, Simla), October 28, 1938, CO 733/369/7.

66. Ibid.

67. For a comprehensive look at the relations and political ties between Indian and Palestinian Muslims during the mandate period see Taysir Jabara, *Al-Muslimun al-hunud wa-qadiyat filastin* (Amman: Dar al-Shuruq, 1998).

68. The clearest accounts of these legal changes come from Frederick Goadby, who worked under Bentwich and recorded the British alterations to the millet system in his articles and textbooks.

69. Goadby, "Religious Communities and Courts in Palestine," 217.

70. Ibid., 221.

71. Ibid., 225.

72. The election of Hajj Amin al-Husayni and the foundation of the Supreme Muslim Council (SMC) have been discussed extensively by scholars, many of whom have accepted Yehoshua Porath's argument that British policy on the creation of the SMC resulted primarily from Samuel's desire to recognize an assembly elected by the Yishuv (the Jewish community in Palestine) assembly as representative of the Jewish community in Palestine, which could not be done without some kind of Arab equivalent. Since a representative Arab body would never consent to work within the mandate framework as the Jewish assembly had done, the only other option was to appoint an institution like the SMC to act as a Muslim representative body. See Porath, *Emergence of the Palestinian-Arab National Movement*. This was certainly one aspect of the decision and one Samuel himself discussed in his memoirs. However, it represents an incomplete analysis of British motives.

73. Quoted in Porath, *Emergence of the Palestinian-Arab National Movement*, 188.

74. Kupferschmidt, *Supreme Muslim Council*, 21. That communal identifications were

not wholly a result of imperial policies is a point made in other historical contexts as well; Bose and Jalal write in reference to British India, "Not all of the social stirrings, of course, are reducible to colonial stimulus, even if they occurred within a broad colonial context of British rule." Sugata Bose and Ayesha Jalal, *Modern South Asia: History, Culture, and Political Economy* (London: Routledge, 1998), 87.

75. Quoted in Porath, *Emergence of the Palestinian-Arab National Movement*, 195–196.

76. Bayan al-Hut, *Qiyadat wa-al-mu'assasat al-siyasiyya fi Filastin, 1917–1948* (Beirut: Mu'assasat al-dirasat al-filastiniyya, 1981), 206.

77. Quoted in Yitzhak Reiter, *Islamic Endowments in Jerusalem under British Mandate* (London: F. Cass, 1996), 27.

78. This was explicitly noted by Samuel in a letter to Curzon in which he described the SMC as a provisional measure intended to replace the Ottoman Ministry of *awqaf* and the *sheikh al-islam*; Samuel to Curzon, January 7, 1921, FO 141/442/4. See also al-Hut, *Qiyadat wa-al-mu'assasat al-siyasiyya fi Filastin*, 205–206, and Kupferschmidt, *Supreme Muslim Council*, 25.

79. See Kupferschmidt, *Supreme Muslim Council*, 27.

80. Samuel to Curzon, January 7, 1921, FO 141/442/4.

81. Reiter, *Islamic Endowments*, 24, and al-Hut, *Qiyadat wa-al-mu'assasat al-siyasiyya fi Filastin*, 205.

82. Not all British officials supported al-Husayni's appointment; Keith-Roach, for instance, recorded that Husayni's "sole qualifications for the post were the pretensions of his family plus shrewd opportunism," and he noted scornfully that Husayni had not completed the requisite seven years study at al-Azhar but claimed his religious qualifications anyway. *Pasha of Jerusalem*, 94–95. For details on Husayni's educational background and his studies in Egypt see al-Hut, *Qiyadat wa-al-mu'assasat al-siyasiyya fi Filastin*, 201–205.

83. Quoted in Porath, *Emergence of the Palestinian-Arab National Movement*, 198.

84. Bentwich, *Palestine*, 181.

85. Samuel to Curzon, November 29, 1920, FO 141/442/4.

86. Shuckburgh to Wilson, March 11, 1926, CO 733/13. See also Kupferschmidt, *Supreme Muslim Council*, 18.

87. Malami to Attorney General, August 20, 1935, ISA RG2/m/736/20.

88. Zeina Ghandour, "Religious Law in a Secular State: The Jurisdiction of the Shari'a Courts of Palestine and Israel," *Arab Law Quarterly* 5, 1 (February 1990): 27.

89. For more details on this point see chapter 1.

90. The historiography on Hajj Amin al-Husayni and the SMC, while extensive, is plagued with a surfeit of polemical accounts. Uri Kupferschmidt's *Supreme Muslim Council* remains the most useful investigation of Husayni's role during the mandate period. Two other biographies, Philip Mattar's *The Mufti of Jerusalem: Al-Hajj Amin al-Husayni and the Palestinian National Movement* (New York: Columbia University Press, 1988), and Zvi Elpeleg, *The Grand Mufti: Haj Amin al-Hussaini, Founder of the Palestinian National Movement* (London: F. Cass, 1993), offer more modest narrative accounts of Husayni's life. Bayan al-Hut deals extensively with Husayni in her *Qiyadat wa-al-mu'assasat al-siyasiyya fi Filastin, 1917–1948* (Beirut: Mu'assasat al-dirasat al-filastiniyya, 1981), as does Majid Khadduri, *Arab Contemporaries* (Baltimore: Johns Hopkins University Press, 1973). A number of other accounts are either hagiographical or vilify al-Husayni for his anti-Zionism and his contacts with the Nazis; see, for instance, Joseph Schechtman, *The Mufti and the Fuehrer: The Rise and Fall of Haj Amin el-Husseini* (New York: T. Yoseloff, 1965). Hajj Amin al-Husayni also wrote a memoir, *Mudhakkirat al-Hajj Muhammad Amin al-Husayni*, ed.

'Abd al-Karim al-'Umar (Damascus: al-Ahali, 1999), which, however, focuses on the years following his escape from Palestine in 1937 and is therefore of limited usefulness for this earlier period.

91. For an overview of Husayni's early life and family background see his memoirs, *Mudhakkirat al-Hajj Muhammad Amin al-Husayni*, and al-Hut, *Qiyadat wa-al-mu'assasat al-siyasiyya fi Filastin*, 201–205. Mattar also discusses the ramifications of Husayni's early life, family background, and education in *Mufti of Jerusalem*.

92. Kupferschmidt, *Supreme Muslim Council*, 227.

93. Al-Hut, *Qiyadat wa-al-mu'assasat al-siyasiyya fi Filastin*. Al-Hut suggests that this repositioning was partly in response to the European portrayal of Jerusalem as central to Christianity and the international interest this had sparked. She also notes that Husayni was interested in engaging the Indian Muslim world in Palestinian affairs from an early date.

94. Wauchope to Cunliffe-Lister, November 20, 1931, and November 25, 1931, FO 371/15283. Also see the analysis of al-Husayni's actions and motives before and during the congress in Matthews, *Confronting an Empire*, 102–134. Kupferschmidt suggests that the SMC's establishment of the Islamic orphanage in Jerusalem was another manifestation of Husayni's political-Islamic approach; *Supreme Muslim Council*, 227.

95. Al-Hut elucidates this process clearly, emphasizing Husayni's multiple roles and his interest in taking on a position as a leader of world Islam as well as of Palestine and the Arab world. See *Qiyadat wa-al-mu'assasat al-siyasiyya fi Filastin*.

96. Criminal Investigation Department (CID) report, January 30, 1935, FO 371/18957.

97. Matthews, *Confronting an Empire*, 127.

98. Porath, *Palestinian Arab National Movement*, 57–58.

99. Such articles appeared in *al-Sirat* of October 26 and 29, 1931. Pro-Gandhi articles also appeared in the Istiqlalist paper *al-Yarmuk* throughout the summer of 1930. See also Matthews, *Confronting an Empire*, 133.

100. Confusion arose over the appropriate British response to the Mufti's actions at the Islamic Congress of 1931. The Foreign Office had suggested that the mufti be threatened with removal from the presidency of the SMC "if he did not exercise proper control of discussions at the forthcoming Moslem Congress," a suggestion to which High Commissioner Wauchope was opposed. The British uncertainty about the path Hajj Amin al-Husayni and the SMC were taking was expressed by O.G.R. Williams: "At one time it was thought, as is shown by the previous minutes on this file, that a curtailing of the powers enjoyed by Haj Amin as President of the Supreme Moslem Council would weaken his political influence . . . It may well be, however, that [in that event the Nashashibi party] would develop as hostile an attitude to the British Government as that of which the Mufti is suspected. There is also the risk of Communist influence amongst the Arabs." See minute by Williams, December 4, 1931, CO 733/193/9.

101. Report by His Majesty's Government in the United Kingdom of Great Britain and Northern Ireland to the Council of the League of Nations on the Administration of Palestine and Trans-Jordan 1936 (London: HMSO, 1937), 39–40.

102. Of course, ties between Europe and Christian communities in the Middle East predated the eighteenth century; the connections wrought by the Maronite Church (which, uniquely among Eastern Christians, is in communion with the bishop of Rome) in what would eventually become Lebanon from the seventh century onward, the contact brought by the Crusades, and the continuing spread of Eastern European influence through the growth of the Eastern Rite churches all contributed to a long-standing and

ongoing awareness of Europe (and vice versa) among Middle Eastern Christians. The eighteenth century, however, marked the beginning of a new period of deliberate European use of ties with Ottoman Christian subjects and institutions to make political claims over the Ottoman Empire.

103. After the Bolshevik Revolution, Russian influence on the Greek Orthodox Church dwindled to almost nothing. See chapter 3 for more detail on this point.

104. Cunningham to Hall, January 31, 1945, CO 733/471/14.

105. "Arab Who's Who," compiled by C. Eastwood, December 1933, CO 733/248/22.

106. Rendel to Undersecretary of State for Colonies, March 13, 1930, CO 733/187/5.

107. However, the French themselves were suspicious of Vatican influence on Catholic communities in Syria; de Charbonniere of the French embassy came to the British government in Palestine to complain of a draft statute received by the French government from the Vatican granting Rome extensive powers over the Syrian Catholic communities and to ask if anything similar had been received in Palestine. (It had not.) Memo by Baggalay, August 23, 1938, FO 371/21879.

108. Memo by H. F. Downie, December 5, 1931, FO 371/15333.

109. Political report, July 1921, FO 371/6376.

110. Luke, *Cities and Men*, 2:208. Luke notes that Barlassina refused to attend Chancellor's inauguration as high commissioner and that the Vatican eventually appointed an apostolic delegate for Palestine to prevent Barlassina from coming into such frequent contact with the mandate government.

111. Luke to Amery, September 20, 1928, reporting on increased interest in Palestine from fascist Italy, CO 733/153/5; correspondence from the British Legation to the Holy See to Cushendun, CO 733/152/5. On the Vatican's approach to Palestine and Zionism see Sergio Minerbi, *The Vatican and Zionism: Conflict in the Holy Land, 1895–1925*, trans. Arnold Schwarz (New York: Oxford University Press, 1990); Wahdat al-Tahlil al-Siyasi, *Al-Fatican wa-al-sira' al-'arabi al-sihyuni* (Gaza: Markaz Filastin lil-dirasat wa-al-buhuth, 2000); Livia Rokach, *The Catholic Church and the Question of Palestine* (London: Saqi Books, 1987); and Kail Ellis, *The Vatican, Islam, and the Middle East* (Syracuse: Syracuse University Press, 1987).

112. Count de Salis to Balfour, March 30, 1919, FO 608/1919.

113. Deedes to Tilley, January 14, 1921, FO 371/6374.

114. "Report on the Status Quo in the Holy Places" by L.G.A. Cust, December 1928, CO 733/152/6.

115. MacInnes to FO, May 2, 1917, and Graves to Deedes, December 4, 1917, FO 141/773. This argument was repeated in 1919 when the Anglo-Ottoman Society proposed restoring the Hagia Sophia as a Christian church, an idea received with delight by various church and archeological societies in Britain. Edwin Montagu, secretary of state for India, responded to the idea with horror: "After all it has been a Mohammedan Mosque for a very long time and its conversion will inflame religious feeling, as Mr. Toynbee has said, in a way which I think we have absolutely no right to contemplate; more especially as we used Moslem troops in the conquest of Turkey." Montagu's memo, April 4 1919, FO 609/111.

116. Executive Council minutes, April 18 1934, ISA RG1/m/4754/2.

117. The Vatican did indeed frequently appeal to the Ottoman status quo in its castigations of the British government. Its protests against immigration restrictions for Catholic clergy into Palestine in 1938 are found in FO 371/21875, among other sources.

118. T. Hachey, "The Archbishop of Canterbury's Visit to Palestine: An Issue in

---

Anglo-Vatican Relations," *Church History* 41, 2 (1972): 198–207. The concerns were that the Vatican might believe the visit to represent an Anglican claim to part of the Church of the Holy Sepulcher and that the visit might be interpreted by the Greeks as "implying that the Orthodox faith had acquired a privileged position within the Mandatory Power" (200). Neither of these concerns was deemed adequate to ask the archbishop to postpone the trip, but irritation with the Vatican's interference was counterbalanced with irritation over the timing of the visit and the Church's failure to consult with the government about the proposed plans.

119. Brown, "British Justice in Palestine," 831: "A foreign subject will not be left unprotected in the hands of native judicial officials . . . There is therefore no need for consular tribunals which, as a matter of fact, no longer exist and which it would be difficult to re-establish under actual conditions of military occupation."

120. See Alexander Scholch, "Britain in Palestine, 1838–1882: The Roots of the Balfour Policy," *Journal of Palestine Studies* 22, 1 (1992): 39–56, on this point and on the many ties between British Christianity and Zionism during the late nineteenth and early twentieth centuries. On these connections see also Regina Sharif, "Christians for Zion, 1600–1919," *Journal of Palestine Studies* 5, 3/4 (1976), 123–141; Dan Cohn-Sherbok, *The Politics of Apocalypse: The History and Influence of Christian Zionism* (Oxford, England: Oneworld, 2008); Douglas J. Culver, *Albion and Ariel: British Puritanism and the Birth of Political Zionism* (New York: P. Lang, 1995); Michael Polowetzky, *Jerusalem Recovered: Victorian Intellectuals and the Birth of Modern Zionism* (Westport: Praeger, 1995); and Paul Charles Merkley, *The Politics of Christian Zionism, 1891–1948* (London: F. Cass, 1998).

121. Government of Palestine report for October 1940, ISA RG65/p/3056/2.

122. MacKereth to FO, Nov 5 1938, CO 733/369/7.

123. Havard to Foreign Secretary, Mar 30 1938, FO 371/21875.

124. Record of Palestinian Arab Delegation meeting at Colonial Office, Aug 22 1921, ISA RG65/p/984/10.

125. Report on "The Status Quo in the Holy Places," by L.G.A. Cust, July 1927, CO 733/132/2.

126. Wauchope to Cunliffe-Lister, March 23 1933, CO 733/242/4.

127. Bentwich, *Palestine*, 112.

128. Keith-Roach, *Pasha of Jerusalem*, 156–157. "But out of evil came good," he added, "for I took the opportunity to have the grotto thoroughly washed, the first time within living memory" (157).

129. Luke, *Prophets, Priests, and Patriarchs*, 6–7, and *Cities and Men*, 3:30.

130. Storrs, *Orientations*, 478.

131. For a detailed treatment of the intercommunal disputes over the Holy Places see Cohen, *Saving the Holy Sepulchre*. Storrs noted this aspect of the arguments in his memoirs, saying that the religious communities were "outposts of world communities always on the watch for injustice against their representatives; so that a decision perfectly fair . . . may and often does arouse comment and even action in Cairo, Rome, London and New York." *Orientations*, 469.

132. This is a commonly discussed European trope with regard to Islam but has been less frequently explored in the context of European views of Eastern Christianity. On European views of Islam see Albert Hourani, *Islam in European Thought* (Cambridge: Cambridge University Press, 1991); Maxime Rodinson, *Europe and the Mystique of Islam*, trans. Roger Veinus (Seattle: University of Washington Press, 1987); Marshall Hodgson,

Rethinking World History: Essays on Europe, Islam, and World History (Cambridge: Cambridge University Press, 1993); Edward Said, *Orientalism* (New York: Vintage, 1978); Norman Daniel, *Islam and the West: The Making of an Image* (New York: Oneworld, 1960); Bernard Lewis, *Islam and the West* (New York: Oxford University Press, 1993); and Frederick Quinn, *Sum of All Heresies: The Image of Islam in Western Thought* (Oxford: Oxford University Press, 2008), to name only a few examples of an extensive literature on the topic. Scholarly discussion of Western views of Eastern Christianity has nearly always been in the context of mission studies; see, for instance, Ussama Makdisi, "Reclaiming the Land of the Bible: Missionaries, Secularism, and Evangelical Modernity," *American Historical Review* 102, 3 (June 1997): 680–713, and *Artillery of Heaven: American Missionaries and the Failed Conversion of the Middle East* (Ithaca, NY: Cornell University Press, 2007); Heather Sharkey, "American Presbyterian Missionaries and the Egyptian Evangelical Church: The Colonial and Postcolonial History of a Christian Community," *Chronos: Revue d'histoire de l'université Balamand* 15 (2007): 31–63, and *American Evangelicals in Egypt: Missionary Encounters in an Age of Empire* (Princeton, NJ: Princeton University Press, 2008).

133. Report on the Jaffa MCA by Postlethwaite, May 20 1919, ISA RG2/m/28/20. These kinds of representations were common in the mandate government.

134. Tsimhoni, "Status of the Arab Christians," 168.

135. Article 56 of the Palestine Order in Council, 1922.

136. Goadby, "Religious Communities and Courts in Palestine," 219.

137. When the Coptic Church applied for recognition in Palestine in 1947, claiming that its members had suffered from not having a religious court, the attorney general responded that he had been unable to uncover any record of the Copts having been recognized as a privileged community in Ottoman law and that therefore the Copts could only be given a separate court by ordinance, which was not granted. Enclosure in Chief Secretary to District Commissioner Jerusalem, December 29, 1947, ISA RG2/m/4312/25. In this particular case, the chief secretary noted, "Apart from other considerations, pressure of urgent matters would preclude the enactment of such an ordinance before the withdrawal." However, the refusal was consistent with previous British policy on such questions.

138. The Arab Episcopalian community applied to be recognized as a religious community numerous times, claiming (correctly) that it had in practice enjoyed this status under the Ottomans. The Episcopalians argued that the British refusal to countenance their application stemmed from pressure from the bishop of Jerusalem and the Church Missionary Society in Palestine rather than from Ottoman precedent; correspondence between the mandate government and the bishop of Jerusalem, ISA RG 2/m/24/17. Indeed, a number of prominent members of the CMS did not want the Arab Episcopalian community to become a separately organized denomination without English administrative and theological oversight. See chapter 5 for more details on this episode and on the position of the Arab Episcopalian community.

139. Tsimhoni, "Status of the Arab Christians," 172.

140. Khawwam and the Greek Catholics of Acre to District Commissioner Acre, November 19, 1942, ISA RG2/m/30/17.

141. Solicitor General to Chief Secretary, December 29, 1942, ISA RG2/m/30/17.

142. See correspondence with various church leaders on this point, ISA RG2/m/27/18.

143. Chief Secretary to Naifa Salem el-Khouri, January 12, 1944, ISA RG2/m/30/17.

144. Many of these protests came from secular Jews. In England civil marriages became a legal alternative to church ceremonies with the Marriage Act of 1836.

145. Palestine Royal Commission. *Report of the Palestine Royal Commission* (Peel Commission Report) (London: HMSO, 1937), 242.

CHAPTER 3

The epigraph is from Nicolas Khouri, Ya'qub Ghumi, and 'Isa Baghdad (delegates of the Executive Orthodox Committee) to 'Abd al-Rahman 'Azzam (secretary of the Arab League), January 24, 1946, CO 733/471/14.

1. Orthodox Arabs represented 45.7 percent of the Christian population of Palestine in 1922 (33,369 people), dropping marginally to 43.5 percent in 1931 (although its numbers grew to 39,727). O'Mahony, introduction to *Palestinian Christians*, 37–38. See also J. B. Barron, *Palestine: Report and General Abstracts of the Census of 1922* (Jerusalem: Greek Convent Press, 1923), and E. Mills, *The Census of Palestine, 1931* (Alexandria: Whitehead Morrison, 1933).

2. O'Mahony, introduction to *Palestinian Christians*, 38. This was out of eighteen total subdistricts in Palestine.

3. Sati' al-Husri (1869–1967) was a writer and educational reformer who worked in Syria, Iraq, and Egypt and is widely considered to have been a seminal figure in the development of Arab nationalism. Quoted in Derek Hopwood, *The Russian Presence in Syria and Palestine, 1843–1914: Church and Politics in the Near East* (Oxford, England: Clarendon Press, 1969), 175.

4. Quoted in Saul Colbi, *Christianity in the Holy Land* (Tel Aviv: Am Hassefer, 1969), 118.

5. Shehadi Khuri and Niqola Khuri, *Khulasat tarikh kanisat Urushalim al-urthudhuksiyya* (Jerusalem: Matba'at bayt al-maqdis, 1925), 301.

6. Anton Bertram and Harry Charles Luke, *Report of the Commission Appointed by the Government of Palestine to Inquire into the Affairs of the Orthodox Patriarchate of Jerusalem* (London: HMSO, 1921), 29.

7. Bertram and Luke, *Report of the Commission*, 29.

8. Ibid., 30.

9. Ibid., 225.

10. Ibid., 226.

11. Ibid., 228–234.

12. Itamar Katz and Ruth Kark, "The Greek Orthodox Patriarchate of Jerusalem and Its Congregation: Dissent over Real Estate," *International Journal of Middle East Studies* 37, 4 (2005): 509–534. Sales of land to the Palestine Land Development Company (PLDC) were being discussed as early as 1921; see agreement between PLDC and Orthodox Financial Commission, July 16, 1928, CZA L18/861.

13. Minutes of the Sixth Palestinian Arab Congress, July 1923, CO 733/46.

14. Orthodox Arab memorandum to Palestine Government, December 11, 1923, CO 733/66.

15. Luke's report on the Arab Orthodox Congress, CO 733/48. See also Anthony O'Mahony, "Religion and Politics and Church-State Relations in Jerusalem," *Chronos* 3 (2000): 74.

16. Luke's report on the Arab Orthodox Congress, CO 733/48.

17. See Katz and Kark, "Greek Orthodox Patriarchate," for a historical overview of the issue of land sales. This remains a serious point of contention between the Greek Orthodox patriarchate in Jerusalem and its Arab laity today.

18. The pamphlet was translated and printed in an appendix to the Bertram-Young report, Anton Bertram and J.W.A. Young, *The Orthodox Patriarchate of Jerusalem; Report of the Commission Appointed by the Government of Palestine to Inquire and Report upon Certain Controversies between the Orthodox Patriarchate of Jerusalem and the Arab Orthodox Community* (London, H. Milford, Oxford University Press, 1926), 279–283. See Tsimhoni, "Greek Orthodox Patriarchate of Jerusalem," for the British reaction.

19. Orthodox Youth Club of Jerusalem to High Commissioner, April 22, 1929, ISA RG2/m/25/5.

20. Ibid.

21. Michel Azar and Shihadeh Dalal (president and secretary of the Youth Orthodox Club Jaffa) to High Commissioner, March 24, 1933, ISA RG2/m/25/5.

22. Odeh Habash (secretary of Young Men's Orthodox Club of Lydda) to High Commissioner, August 26, 1937, ISA RG2/m/28/20.

23. Bertram and Young, *Orthodox Patriarchate of Jerusalem*, 107.

24. Ibid., 107–108.

25. Confidential Supplement to the Report of the Commission, January 26, 1925, ISA RG65/p/3049/3.

26. Ibid.

27. Ibid.

28. Ibid.

29. O'Mahony, "Religion and Politics," 77.

30. See notes of O.G.R. Williams' interview with Canon Noel A. Marshall, Chaplain to the English Church in Malta, November 16, 1934, CO 733/258/11. For more on this issue see chapter 5.

31. Qustandi Shomali, "Politics, Press, and Religious Identity, 1900–1948," in *The Christian Heritage in the Holy Land*, ed. Anthony O'Mahony, Göran Gunner, and Kevork Hintlian. (London: Scorpion Cavendish, 1995), 228.

32. Khalidi, *Palestinian Identity*, 154.

33. Ibid., 229; *Filastin*, January 1911.

34. Khalidi, *Palestinian Identity*, 156.

35. Nuwayhid, *Rijal min Filastin*, 30.

36. Shomali, "Politics, Press, and Religious Identity," 232.

37. *Filastin*, June 22, 1921.

38. *Filastin*, August 7, 1923.

39. *Filastin*, October 16, 1931.

40. Memorandum to the High Commissioner by the National Orthodox Body in Jerusalem, September 14, 1931, ISA RG65/p/3049/3.

41. *Filastin*, October 2, 1931.

42. *Filastin*, October 21, 1931.

43. Excerpt from Palestine Police Summary, 1931, CO 733/221/5.

44. Palestine Press Summary, December 24 1931, CO 733/221/5. It is worth noting that at this same Islamic congress, al-Husayni bitterly denounced the European missionary presence in Palestine and especially in Jerusalem, making a definite distinction be-

tween the European Christians, whom he associated with colonial oppression, and the indigenous Arab Orthodox Christian population, whom he praised for their efforts to free themselves and their religious institutions from foreign domination.

45. The Scottish Liberal Sir Arthur Grenfell Wauchope had a military background that had taken him all over the empire before his appointment in Palestine. Wauchope began his career with the Black Watch in South Africa, where he was severely wounded. From 1903 until 1914 he served in the army in India, returning to Europe for service in France when war broke out. In 1916 he was sent to Mesopotamia and was again wounded. After the war ended he directed the British section of the Berlin Control Commission; during the late 1920s he was sent to Northern Ireland in the campaign to quell insurrection there. In 1931 he took up the appointment of high commissioner of Palestine and Transjordan.

46. Antonius to Bertram, February 10, 1932, ISA RG65/p/3049/3.

47. *Filastin*, December 24, 1931.

48. Press summary, CO 733/221/5. This was a matter of discussion within the church; the archbishop of Canterbury told the secretary of state in 1934 that he was worried that a schism between the Arab laity and the Greek hierarchy would be deeply embarrassing for the Church of England, which had long since pledged not to proselytize to Orthodox communities. The archbishop suggested that any schismatic communities would be best off joining the Latin church; the secretary of state "indicated in general terms that he would personally prefer, if there was a secession, that the Arabophones should join the Church of England." See minute by O.G.R. Williams, March 27, 1934, CO 733/258/12.

49. Anticipating Damianos' death, Farraj told the high commissioner in 1930 that the main object of the laity was to guarantee "adequate representation" in the patriarchal election process. Chancellor to Passfield, May 3, 1930, CO 733/187/5.

50. Memo from National Orthodox Body in Jerusalem to High Commissioner, September 15, 1931, ISA RG65/p/3049/3.

51. Officers of the National Orthodox Community of Jerusalem (Kattan, Deib, Freij, Khouri and Jouzi) to the District Commissioner of Jerusalem, October 1931, ISA RG65/p/3049/3.

52. The team of three lawyers consisted of a Muslim, a Jew, and an Orthodox Christian.

53. The full finding of the court was printed in the *Palestine Bulletin*, January 28, 1932.

54. Michael McDonnell and F. H. Baker, report on the court case of Executive Committee of the Second Arab Orthodox Congress v. Archbishop Keladion of the Orthodox Patriarchate, January 1932, FO 371/16053.

55. McDonnell and Baker, January 1932, FO 371/16053.

56. Ibid.

57. *Filastin*, February 25, 1932.

58. Notes on interview between Orthodox Arab Executive and Wauchope, June 7, 1932, CO 733/221/7.

59. Ibid.

60. Wauchope to Secretary of State for Colonies, January 28, 1932, FO 371/16053.

61. Ibid.

62. Hopwood, *Russian Presence in Syria and Palestine*, 205.

63. Record of conversation between Wauchope and Hall, October 9, 1934, ISA RG65/p/3049/3.

64. *Arab Federation*, April 25, 1934; copy in CO 733/258/12.

---

65. Memo by ʿUda al-Qusus and Yusef al-ʿIsa on meetings in Jerusalem, September 10, 1935, ISA RG65/p/3055/28.

66. Wauchope to Cunliffe-Lister, June 1932, CO 733/221/7.

67. Wauchope to Antonius, August 6, 1935, ISA RG65/p/3049/3.

68. Wauchope to Cunliffe-Lister, June 1932, CO 733/221/7.

69. In the aftermath of the election the high commissioner received twenty-nine telegrams and letters refusing to recognize Timotheos, mainly from Orthodox societies in Palestinian towns. Interestingly, there does seem to have been a major split between Palestinian Orthodox communities and Jordanian ones; the high commissioner also received fourteen telegrams supporting the patriarch-elect and opposing the executive committee's actions, nearly all from towns in Jordan (Kerak, Amman, Madaba, Irbid, al-Hisn, al-Salt, and Ajlun). ISA RG2/m/27/29.

70. Members of the administration had serious doubts about his competency as well as lingering sympathies for the Orthodox Arabs. S. Gaselee of the Eastern Department noted in a report that Timotheos was "a genial creature, with a sly humour, but not of the best character, and his election would damage the prestige of the Patriarchate." Memo by Gaselee, August 28 1931, CO 733/204/9. Wauchope promised Farraj that the Berat would not be issued until there had been further negotiations with the laity and "an opportunity to reach an agreement within a reasonable limit of time"; there was, of course, no agreement, and London finally decided to take action in 1939 to confirm Timotheos. CO 733/400/5.

71. The Peel Commission was a Royal Commission of Inquiry appointed in the aftermath of the strike to investigate the causes of violence in Palestine and advise the British government on a course of action. Headed by Lord Robert Peel, it was the first body to recommend the partition of Palestine into an Arab state and a Jewish state.

72. Farraj to Peel Commission, February 16, 1937, CO 733/346/7.

73. Antonius to Bertram, February 10, 1932, ISA RG2/p/3049/3.

74. Ibid.

75. Ibid.

76. Ibid.

77. In Musallam, *Yawmiyat Khalil al-Sakakini*, 2:47 (entry for January 12, 1914); also in al-Sakakini, *Kadha ana ya dunya*, 57–58.

78. Musallam, *Yawmiyat Khalil al-Sakakini*, 2:157–158 (entry for March 26 1915); also in al-Sakakini, *Kadha ana ya dunya*, 89. Abigail Jacobson has commented on this quote, pointing out that this rejection of religious identifications came at a time when al-Sakakini was expressing an increased level of concern about intercommunal tensions resulting from the Ottoman state's declaration of *jihad* against the Allies. Jacobson, "Negotiating Ottomanism in Times of War: Jerusalem during World War I through the Eyes of a Local Muslim Resident," *International Journal of Middle East Studies* 40 (2008): 82.

79. Khalil al-Sakakini to Sari al-Sakakini, December 12, 1932, (letters translated by Sari al-Sakakini) ISA RG65/p/65/2646.

80. Ghori worked closely with the Husaynis and the Supreme Muslim Council for many years; Farraj, the ʿIsas, and Bandak were all associated with the Nashashibi opposition. Religious historians and anthropologists have pointed out that there was less of a religious divide between observant Orthodox Christians and Muslims than is often assumed. Among others, Anthony O'Mahony's introduction to *Palestinian Christians* and his article "Religion and Politics" and Glenn Bowman's "Christian, Muslim Palestinians Confront Sectarianism: Religion and Political Identity in Beit Sahour," *Middle East Re-*

port 164/165 (2000): 50–53, and "Nationalizing the Sacred: Shrines and Shifting Identities in the Israeli-Occupied Territories," *Man* 28, 3 (1993): 431–460, examine shared rituals, shrines, and festivals. Recent scholarship by Salim Tamari and Rochelle Davis has demonstrated that Muslims and Christians of the upper middle classes mixed freely in social settings, particularly in Jerusalem, during the late Ottoman period and the mandate. See Tamari's editorial introduction to *Al-Quds al-'uthmaniyya fi al-mudhakkirat al-Jawhariyya* and Davis' "Ottoman Jerusalem" (10–31) and "The Growth of the Western Communities: 1917–1948" (32–73) in *Jerusalem 1948*, ed. Tamari.

81. This is an especially important point in the case of al-Sakakini, whose writings some older scholarship has cited as demonstrating the essential dilemma of Christians in a majority-Muslim Palestine. The most famous exposition of this point of view is Elie Kedourie, *Chatham House Version*, but it is also represented in Yehoshua Porath's *Emergence of the Palestinian-Arab National Movement*, in Tsimhoni's work, and in O'Mahony's introduction to *Palestinian Christians* and his "Religion and Politics."

82. 'Isa al-Sifri, *Filastin al-'arabiyya bayn al-intidab wa al-Sahyuniyya* (Jaffa: Maktabat Filastin al-jadida, 1937), 192. See also Hopwood, *Russian Presence in Syria and Palestine*, 207.

83. Michael Tuma and George Khoury (vice-president and secretary of Haifa Orthodox Society), March 18 1943, ISA RG2/m/30/21. One of the chief complaints in this letter was that the community had finally found an appropriately educated priest, but the patriarchate was refusing him the appointment because he was Lebanese.

84. S. Daoud (secretary of executive committee) to Chief Secretary, October 3, 1944, CO 733/457/21.

85. Ibid.

86. Al-Husayni to High Commissioner, September 29, 1944, CO 733/457/21.

87. The last Arab patriarch in Jerusalem was in the sixteenth century, after which all the patriarchs were ethnically Greek.

88. Nicolas Khouri, Ya'qub Ghumi, and 'Isa Baghdad (delegates of the Executive Orthodox Committee) to 'Abd al-Rahman 'Azzam (secretary of the Arab League), January 24, 1946, CO 733/471/14.

89. Ibid.

90. Ibid.

91. 'Abd al-Rahman 'Azzam to Lord Killearn, January 1946, CO 733/471/14.

92. MacMichael to Stanley (Secretary of State for Colonies), October 18, 1944, CO 733/457/21.

93. Extract from P.P.R., November 6, 1947, ISA RG2/m/400/27.

94. Ibid.

CHAPTER 4

The epigraph is from Mughannam to Wauchope, September 28, 1934, ISA RG2/m/207/40.

1. For a description of this episode see especially Malcolm Yapp, *The Near East since the First World War* (London: Longmans, 1991), and Porath, *Emergence of the Palestinian-Arab National Movement*.

2. This diversity of political affiliation among Arab Christians has not been sufficiently acknowledged by scholars, who have tended to report, incorrectly, that Christians as a bloc belonged to the marginally more pro-British *mu'arida*.

3. Attachment to Chancellor's despatch, June 17, 1928, CO 733/167.

4. Memo by H. C. Luke, June 12, 1929, CO 733/167.

5. Chancellor to Colonial Secretary, June 12, 1929, CO 733/167.

6. *Filastin*, October 23, 1930.

7. *Filastin*, October 25, 1930.

8. *Sawt al-sha'b*, October 25, 1930.

9. *Sawt al-sha'b*, October 19, 1930.

10. *Al-jami'a al-'arabiyya*, October 29, 1930.

11. Chancellor to Colonial Secretary, February 13, 1931, CO. 733/197, and minute by O.G.R. Williams, May 27, 1931, CO 733/202. See also Porath, *Palestinian Arab National Movement*, 144–145.

12. On these protests and the upheavals of the early 1930s see especially Matthews, *Confronting an Empire*.

13. Ibid., 224.

14. Notes on Palestine Constitution by A. C. Parkinson, November 21, 1932, CO 733/235/5.

15. The racial approach, although it had the support of London, did not garner universal approval; Wauchope opposed it vehemently, as recorded in a memo stating in 1933 that he "would much rather that representation was on a territorial bases and not on a communal basis, that is to say, that there should be a common roll for all races. If that proved impossible he would rather keep the representation of Christian and Moslem apart." Memo on discussion between Wauchope and the Secretary of State, April 4, 1933, CO 733/235/5.

16. It is worth noting that the Druze were considered wholly different and often retained separate representation in these sorts of lists even after racial categorization had taken hold. On the legal status of the Druze during the mandate period see Laila Parsons, *The Druze between Palestine and Israel, 1947–49* (Houndmills, England: Macmillan, 2000).

17. McCarthy, *Population of Palestine*, 37. Nomads, as McCarthy points out, were assumed to be Arabs.

18. Mills, *Census of Palestine, 1931.*

19. Porath, *Palestinian Arab National Movement*, 145–146.

20. Sir Arthur Wauchope to Secretary of State, December 23, 1933, CO 733/320/5. Charles Crane was one of the leaders of the King-Crane Commission in 1919 and had a lasting interest in Palestine.

21. Memo on discussion between Wauchope and the Secretary of State, April 4, 1933, CO 733/235/5.

22. Wauchope to Cunliffe-Lister, August 25, 1934, CO 733/265/1.

23. Farraj to Wauchope, February 27, 1934, ISA RG2/m/207/40.

24. Ibid.

25. Ibid.

26. Ibid.

27. For his activities in the Arab Episcopalian community see chapter 5.

28. On Matiel Mughannam see Fleischmann, *The Nation and Its "New" Women*. On Mughannam Mughannam see Nuwayhid, *Rijal min Filastin*, 43; "Arab Who's Who," 1933, CO 733/248/22.

29. Mughannam to Wauchope, September 28, 1934, ISA RG2/m/207/40.

30. Ibid.

31. Barlassina to Wauchope, February 18, 1935, ISA RG2/m/207/40.

---

32. Members of the Catholic Community of Jerusalem to Wauchope, January 30 1935, ISA RG2/m/207/40.

33. Campbell to Chief Secretary, March 12, 1934, ISA RG2/m/207/40.

34. Kattan to Wauchope, March 20, 1934, ISA RG2/m/206/9.

35. Ibid.

36. Farraj to Wauchope, February 27, 1934, ISA RG2/m/207/40.

37. Campbell to Chief Secretary, March 12, 1934, ISA RG2/m/207/40.

38. See figures "corrected" from the 1931 census by McCarthy, *Population of Palestine*, 31.

39. Mughannam to Wauchope, September 28, 1934, ISA RG2/m/207/40.

40. Ibid.

41. Ibid.

42. Memo on conversation between Cunliffe-Lister and Wauchope, April 22, 1933, CO 733/235.

43. Wauchope to MacDonald, August 5, 1935, CO 733/275/1.

44. T. L. Hodgkin, Antonius Lecture at St. Antony's College, 1981, Middle East Centre Archive, St. Antony's College, Oxford.

45. Ibid.

46. CID report, August 5, 1935, FO 371/18957.

47. Memo of interview between Wauchope and Farraj, July 26, 1935, CO 733/275/1.

48. Ibid.

49. Memo of interview between Wauchope and Khayat, July 27, 1935, CO 733/275/1.

50. Ibid.

51. Ibid.

52. Wauchope to Thomas (Colonial Secretary) and enclosures from District Commissioners, March 9, 1936, CO 733/293/4.

53. Farraj and Rok to Wauchope, March 3, 1936, CO 733/293/4.

54. Porath, *Palestinian Arab National Movement*, 153.

55. Wauchope to MacDonald, July 11, 1935, CO 733/275/1.

56. Lugard to Thomas, May 4, 1936, CO 733/293/5.

57. Porath, *Palestinian Arab National Movement*, 156.

58. Wauchope to Colonial Secretary, March 28, 1936, CO 733/307/10.

59. *Filastin*, April 9, 1936.

60. Rather unexpectedly, his letter included a brief panegyric to Sir Herbert Samuel, "an English gentleman in the full sense of the word" with "a true heart and sincere conscience" with whom the Arabs should have cooperated during the first legislative council debate. Ibid.

61. Minutes of interview between Wauchope and Arab party leaders, April 21, 1936, CO 733/307/10.

62. CID reports, April 11 and May 6, 1936, FO 371/20018.

63. Seikaly, *Haifa*; see also Porath, *Palestinian Arab National Movement*, 157, and Zachary Lockman, *Comrades and Enemies: Arab and Jewish Workers in Palestine, 1906–1948* (Berkeley: University of California Press, 1996), 219.

64. Wauchope to Colonial Secretary, April 23, 1936, CO 733/307/1.

65. R. Nashashibi, J. al-Husayni, 'Abdul Latif Salah, Shibli Jamal, and Y. al-Ghusayn to Wauchope, April 22, 1936, CO 733/307/10.

66. Izzat Tannous ['Izzat Tannus], *The Palestinians: A Detailed Documented Eyewitness History of Palestine under British Mandate* (New York: I.G.T., 1988), 179.

67. Ghori to Ormsby-Gore, June 6, 1936, CO 733/312/1.

68. Ibid.

69. Minutes on interviews between Tannus and Macdonald, November 24 and August 19, 1938, CO 733/385/21.

70. Tannous, *The Palestinians*, 179.

71. Ibid., 180.

72. Ibid., 183.

73. Ibid., 182.

74. Minutes on interview between Tannous and MacDonald, November 24 1938, CO 733/385/21. The center published pamphlets covering all aspects of the Palestinian political argument, including a reprint of the MacMahon correspondence of 1915–1916 introduced by Chief Justice Sir Michael McDonnell (the same man who had presided over the decision in favor of Yaʿqub Farraj and the Arab Orthodox movement in 1932), pamphlets discussing the contradictions in the resolutions of the League of Nations, and even a statement by the All-India Muslim League Palestine Delegation submitted to the British in 1939. See "The Arab Case," "The MacMahon Correspondence," "Palestine: The Way to Peace," and "Statement of Indian Muslim Views on Palestine," all published in London by the Arab Centre in 1939.

75. In Mackereth to Colonial Office, October 20, 1938, CO 733/385/21.

76. Mansur to Linfield, September 29 1938, CMS G2/P/1.

77. Tannous, *The Palestinians*, 206. He records that this trip was suggested to him by Hajj Amin al-Husayni.

78. Ibid., 208.

79. Ibid., 210.

80. Rihani was a writer and intellectual who played a major role in the development of an Arab-American literary tradition in North America. The British official meeting the delegation reported that he was "brought up as a Maronite, but at present follows no religion in particular." Lindsay to Colonial Office, February 2, 1937, CO 733/344/1.

81. Arab National League to Baldwin, February 2, 1937, CO 733/344/1.

82. Indeed, Kenneth Stein notes that the Palestinian Arab leadership was "somewhat surprised by the outbreak of the uprisings . . . The absence of a fully accurate assessment by the leadership of the depth of disillusionment among the fellahin [peasantry] in the 1930s . . . explain[s] to some degree why [the leaders] were caught off guard when local violence turned into a prolonged general uprising." Stein, "The Intifada and the 1936–39 Uprising: A Comparison," *Journal of Palestine Studies* 19, 4 (1990), 66–67. For further discussions of this shift see especially Swedenburg, *Memories of Revolt: The 1936–1939 Rebellion and the Palestinian National Past* (Fayetteville: University of Arkansas Press, 2003), but also Matthews, *Confronting an Empire*; Ylana Miller, *Government and Society in Rural Palestine, 1920–1948* (Austin: University of Texas Press, 1985); Fleischmann, *The Nation and Its "New" Women*; al-Hut, *Qiyadat wa-al-muʾassasat al-siyasiyya fi Filastin, 1917–1948* (Beirut: Muʾassasat al-dirasat al-filastiniyya), 1981; Issa Khalaf, *Politics in Palestine*; W. F. Abboushi, "The Road to Rebellion: Arab Palestine in the 1930's," *Journal of Palestine Studies* 6, 3 (Spring, 1977), 23–46; Ann Mosely Lesch, *Arab Politics in Palestine, 1917–1939: The Frustration of a Nationalism Movement* (Ithaca: Cornell University Press, 1979); Gershom Shafir, *Land, Labor, and the Origins of the Israeli-Palestinian Conflict* (Berkeley: University of California Press, 1996); and Kamil, *Filastin wa-al-intidab al-baritani, 1922–1939* (Beirut: Munazzamat al-tahrir al-filastiniyya, 1974).

The epigraph is from Najwa Kawar Farah, *A Continent Called Palestine: One Woman's Story* (London: SPCK, 1996), 20.

1. Throughout this chapter I refer to Arab members of the Anglican church in Palestine as Arab Episcopalians. The community members frequently expressed opposition to the term "Anglicans" and did not view themselves as members of the Church of England, instead styling their church al-Kanisa al-injiliyya al-usqufiyya al-ʿarabiyya, the Arab Episcopal Evangelical Church, or sometimes simply al-Kanisa al-injiliyya, the Evangelical Church.

2. For some recent examinations of the missionary impact on various parts of the Middle East during the nineteenth and twentieth centuries see Ussama Makdisi, *Artillery of Heaven*; Heather Sharkey, *American Evangelicals in Egypt*; Ellen Fleischmann, "The Impact of American Protestant Missions in Lebanon on the Construction of Female Identity, c. 1860–1950," *Islam and Christian-Muslim Relations* 13, 4 (2002), 411–426; Michael Marten, *Attempting to Bring the Gospel Home: Scottish Missions to Palestine, 1839–1917* (London: Tauris, 2006); Michael Oren, *Power, Faith, and Fantasy: America in the Middle East, 1776 to the Present* (New York: W. W. Norton, 2007); and Eleanor Tejirian and Reeva Spector Simon, eds., *Altruism and Imperialism: Western Cultural and Religious Missions in the Middle East* (New York: Middle East Institute, 2002).

3. Proselytizing to Muslims was a punishable offense under Ottoman law, and when Jewish communities were unresponsive to the idea of conversion, European missionaries often turned their attention to the local Christian populations. This was a common pattern for European missionaries throughout the Middle East. See, for instance, Joseph Grabill, *Protestant Diplomacy and the Near East: Missionary Influence on American Policy, 1810–1927*, (Minneapolis: University of Minnesota Press, 1971); A. L. Tibawi, *American Interests in Syria, 1800–1901: A Study of Education, Literary and Religious Work* (Oxford: Clarendon Press, 1966) and *British Interests in Palestine*; and Sharkey, *American Evangelicals in Egypt*.

4. See C. Peter Williams, *The Ideal of the Self-Governing Church: A Study in Victorian Missionary Strategy* (Leiden, Netherlands: Brill, 1990). Williams offers a detailed analysis of Venn's approach and the changes in CMS policy during the nineteenth century, focusing particularly on the CMS in Africa.

5. Bishop Blyth supported this move, and when the council disbanded after only nine months—ostensibly for financial reasons—he blamed its failure on the unwillingness of the British missionaries to relinquish any power to the Arabs. See Tibawi, *British Interests in Palestine*, 241–242.

6. Pittman, "Missionaries and Emissaries: The Anglican Church in Palestine 1841–1948," Ph.D. diss., University of Virginia, 1998, 97.

7. Memo by F. S. Cragg on CMS Policy in Palestine, 1928, CMS G3/P/P7.

8. Minutes of Conference meeting, February 22, 1933, CMS G3/P/P7.

9. This was partially because of Ottoman laws outlawing proselytizing to Muslims, but the CMS and other Protestant missions viewed Eastern Christianity as nearly as foreign to Protestantism as Islam and wrote of their work among Orthodox Arabs as important. Some missionary societies like the London Jews Society had as their main purpose proselytizing to the Jews, which was almost totally unsuccessful. Arab Orthodox interest in Protestantism certainly had something to do with the internal difficulties of the Orthodox church.

10. Mitri Raheb, *I Am a Palestinian Christian* (Minneapolis: Fortress, 1995), 7. A very

similar conversion narrative can be found in Farah, *Continent Called Palestine*, describing the conversion of her mother and aunts after they were taken in by a Protestant orphanage following the death of their parents.

11. The official title of the Anglican bishop was the "bishop in Jerusalem" rather than "bishop of Jerusalem," in a careful display of sensitivity toward the other Christian denominations with a strong presence in the holy sites of Jerusalem.

12. MacInnes to Davidson, February 11, 1922, Lambeth Palace Library (hereafter LPL) Davidson Papers 398. MacInnes' refusal to convert willing Arabs to Anglicanism was in direct opposition to the earlier approach of the CMS and was by no means the only example of the kinds of tensions that characterized the relationship between the Jerusalem bishopric (appointed and run from Lambeth Palace) and the missionary societies that represented the first Protestant presence in Palestine. Lambeth Palace frequently found itself in conflict all over the globe with missionary societies like the CMS, which had been dominated by evangelicals for nearly a century and was vigorously opposed to any hints of Anglo-Catholicism in Anglican theology or ritual. See Andrew Porter, *Religion versus Empire? British Protestant Missionaries and Overseas Expansion, 1700–1914* (Manchester, England: Manchester University Press); Williams, *Ideal of the Self-Governing Church*; and Lamin Sanneh, *West African Christianity: The Religious Impact* (London: C. Hurst, 1983) and *Encountering the West: Christianity and the Global Cultural Process, The African Dimension* (Maryknoll, NY: Orbis Books, 1993), for valuable discussions of the early days of the CMS in various geographical contexts.

13. See, for instance, minutes of PNCC Jerusalem, October 20, 1936, CMS G2/P/3/1.

14. See Inger Marie Okkenhaug, *The Quality of Heroic Living, of High Endeavour and Adventure: Anglican Mission, Women, and Education in Palestine, 1888–1948* (Leiden, Netherlands: Brill, 2002), for a discussion of female employment in mission schools. Ellen Fleischmann offers an investigation of women's education in Palestine and its role in the development of the Palestinian women's movement in *The Nation and Its "New" Women*. See also Tibawi, *Arab Education in Mandatory Palestine*, for an overview of mandate education policy.

15. Stewart to Davidson, June 6, 1936, LPL Lang Papers 52.

16. Memo by Saba on "The Status and Aims of the PNCC," 1946, CMS G2/P3/1.

17. In the church context, the term "dissenting" refers to Protestants who separated from or protested the Church of England, preferring a more radically Protestant or evangelical theological and liturgical approach.

18. Makdisi, *Artillery of Heaven*, 13.

19. For an account of the earliest days of the PNCC see Estelle Blyth, *When We Lived in Jerusalem* (London: John Murray, 1927), 158.

20. CMS, Regulations for the PNCC, 1905; see also Pittman, "Missionaries and Emissaries," 102.

21. Eric Bishop, "Jerusalem Byways of Memory II," *Muslim World* 50, 3 (1960): 201. In an indication of the makeshift nature of the Anglican church in prewar Palestine, Bishop also reports that Baz was ordained by one Bishop Hannington, who happened to pass through Jerusalem on his way to an assignment in Uganda.

22. Farah, *Continent Called Palestine*, 3

23. Cash, preliminary report of CMS work in Palestine 1914–1917, January 1, 1918, CMS G3/P/P6.

24. Ibid.

25. It may be instructive to think of this wartime experience as somewhat analogous

to the development of a sense of nationhood among what Benedict Anderson calls "creole pioneers." Anderson suggests that the administrative culture among creole colonial functionaries in the Americas led to the early emergence of a kind of protonationalist "imagined community" even before nationalisms began to emerge in the metropole. Here, the experience of acting as local functionaries for an international church may have solidified a specifically modern communal identity in some of the same ways. Anderson, *Imagined Communities*, 47–65. For an examination of the usefulness of this aspect of Anderson's analysis for Latin America see Michiel Baud, "Beyond Benedict Anderson: Nation-Building and Popular Democracy in Latin America," *International Review of Social History* 50 (2005): 485–498.

26. Minutes of PNCC meeting Jerusalem, April 5–9, 1921, CMS G3/P/P7.

27. Cash to CMS, "Report on a visit to Egypt, the Sudan and Palestine," 1933, CMS G3/P/P8.

28. Bandak to Lang, December 4 1938, and Graham Brown to Lang, December 18, 1938, LPL Council on Foreign Relations (hereafter CFR) Papers AC 18.

29. MacInnes to Manning, March 1, 1924, LPL Davidson Papers 399.

30. Graham Brown to Matthew, July 24, 1935, LPL CFR Papers, AC 18.

31. *Filastin*, July 24, 1935.

32. Bishop, "Jerusalem Byways of Memory II," 204.

33. Record of Palestine Sub-committee meeting, April 8, 1932, CMS G2/P/1.

34. Farah, *Continent Called Palestine*, 20.

35. "High Church" denotes ritualistic practices associated with an Anglo-Catholic liturgical approach, while "Low Church" is associated with Nonconformist practices.

36. This dress can be seen in the photos of various clergymen and congregations at St. George's Cathedral Church, Jerusalem; I would like to thank the Reverend Canon Hosam Naoum for generously showing me the photo collections there and discussing the history of the church with me. See also Pittman, "Missionaries and Emissaries," 193–194.

37. Carpenter, Hardman, and Webb, the CMS "visitors" to the PNCC meetings in 1924, reported that these desires had been "strengthened by seeing the Ceremonial adopted in some instances by the Anglo-Catholic pilgrims in this country." Carpenter, Webb, and Bardnam to CMS Africa Committee, September 5, 1924, CMS G3/P/P7.

38. PNCC Declaration for Bishop with proposed amendments, December 1924, CMS G3/P/P7.

39. Minutes of PNCC meeting Jerusalem, April 18, 1937, CMS G2/P3/1.

40. See Pittman, "Missionaries and Emissaries," 221.

41. Stewart to Lang, June 6, 1936, JEM 21/3.

42. Carpenter, Webb, and Bardnam to CMS Africa Committee, September 5, 1924, CMS G3/P/P7. "This point looms large in their eyes," the CMS visitors wrote, "as connected with Eastern Hospitality: however much they may be running against Ecclesiastical Law."

43. PNCC Minutes December 1924, CMS G3/P/P7.

44. MacInnes to CMS, June 2, 1931, CMS G3/P/P3.

45. Bishop, Jerusalem "Byways of Memory III," *Muslim World* 51, 4 (1961): 269.

46. Hardman comments on PNCC minutes, April 9, 1923, CMS G3/P/P7.

47. Memo of Group III Committee Meeting, June 11, 1924, CMS G3/P/P7.

48. Carpenter, Webb, and Bardnam to CMS Africa Committee, September 5, 1924, CMS G3/P/P7.

49. Ward and Bickersteth to Lang, Memo on the Jerusalem Bishopric, January 1932, LPL Lang Papers 44.

50. Ibid. This kind of language and thinking adversely affected many Palestinian Arab elites who were routinely refused jobs on racist grounds. George Antonius, for instance, was refused promotion in the British civil service in Palestine because he was an Arab.

51. Quoted in Charles Sennott, *The Body and the Blood: The Holy Land's Christians at the Turn of a New Millennium: A Reporter's Journey* (New York: Public Affairs, 2001), 100.

52. The standing committee of the CMS' missionary conference in 1922 passed a resolution "deprecating association of pastoral and political work, and urging paramount importance of whole time being given to spiritual work." Minutes of Standing Committee of Missionary Conference, November 14–15, 1922, CMS G3/P/P7.

53. MacIntyre to CMS, May 23, 1923, CMS G3/P/P6.

54. Report by Lang on meeting with MacInnes, October 9, 1931, LPL CFR Papers, OC 144.

55. Stefan Wild, "Judentum, Christentum und Islam in der palastinensischen Poesie," *Die Welt des Islams* 23, 1/4 (1984): 262n6.

56. As will be seen later in this chapter, many British missionaries were actually quite opposed to Zionism and came into conflict with the mandate government on a number of occasions over its policies on Jewish immigration into Palestine. On this point see Maria Smaberg, *Ambivalent Friendship: Anglican Conflict Handling and Education for Peace in Jerusalem 1920–1948* (Lund, Sweden: Lund University Press, 2005), 108; Daphne Tsimhoni, *Christian Communities in Jerusalem and the West Bank since 1948: An Historical, Social, and Political Study* (Westport, CT: Praeger, 1993), 139–140; and Okkenhaug, *Quality of Heroic Living*, 124.

57. Bishop, "Jerusalem Byways of Memory II," 204.

58. Barbara Parmenter, *Giving Voice to Stones: Place and Identity in Palestinian Literature* (Austin: University of Texas Press, 1994), 34.

59. Bishop, "Jerusalem Byways of Memory II," 204. Some heavily Anglicized versions of Palestinian carol melodies can be found in Rolla Foley, *Song of the Arab: The Religious Ceremonies, Shrines and Folk Music of the Holy Land Christian Arab* (New York: Macmillan, 1953). Although Foley was a missionary at the American Friends School in Ramallah from 1938 to 1946, he does not seem to have been aware of Marmura's contributions to the genre.

60. Bishop apparently saw this work but reports, "Alas, it disappeared in the tragic events of 1948 and yet remains to be found." Bishop, "Jerusalem Byways of Memory II," 204.

61. Ilyas Marmura, *Al-Samiriyyun* (Jerusalem: Maktabat Filastin al-'Ilmiyya, 1934). Many thanks to Tarif Khalidi for providing me with information about this work.

62. Farah, *Continent Called Palestine*, 33–37; Farah records that she submitted three tales. Marmura died in May 1947, and his house was destroyed in the fighting that followed the bombing of the King David Hotel.

63. As'ad Mansur, *Ta'rikh al-Nasira min aqdam azmaniha ila ayamina al-hadira* (Cairo: Matba'at al-hilal, 1924), 3.

64. Ibid.

65. Tarif Khalidi suggests that Mansur's history, along with 'Arif al-'Arif's history of Gaza and Ihsan al-Nimr's investigation of Nablus, constitute "a kind of land survey where the authors seek to repeople the terrain with the thick presence of ancestors, as if

in response to the continuing obliteration of Palestine by Zionist settlers." Beshara Doumani suggests something similar by categorizing Mansur's work as part of what he calls an "affirmation of identity" category of Palestinian historiography; he also classifies the work of Khalil Totah and 'Umar al-Barghuthi, among others, under this rubric. See Tarif Khalidi, "Palestinian Historiography: 1900–1948," *Journal of Palestine Studies* 10, 3 (1981): 68, and Beshara Doumani, "Rediscovering Ottoman Palestine: Writing Palestinians into History," *Journal of Palestine Studies* 21, 2 (1992): 13–14. Mansur's narrative and sense of urban topography is also discussed briefly in Chad Emmett, *Beyond the Basilica: Christians and Muslims in Nazareth* (Chicago: University of Chicago Press, 1995), 36.

66. Mansur was particularly interested in engaging the archaeologists and biblical historians who were involved with the American School of Archaeology. On European sources, Mansur cites in particular Gaston le Hardy, *Histoire de Nazareth et de ses sanctuaires: Étude chronologique des documents* (Paris: Lecoffre, 1905); Prosper Viaud, *Nazareth et ses deux églises de l'Annonciation et de Saint-Joseph, d'après les fouilles récentes pratiquées* (Paris: A. Picard, 1910); R.F. Athenase Prun, *Nazareth* (1908, no publishing data available); and F. J. Scrimgeour, *Nazareth of To-day* (Edinburgh: W. Green, 1913). Mansur owed a special debt to this last work, which is referenced multiple times; see in particular the discussion in 281.

67. Mansur, *Ta'rikh al-Nasira*.

68. Ibid., 33.

69. Mansur includes discussions of the Church of Mar Yusef, 132; Church of the Rock (Kanisa al-balata), 140; Jabal al-qafza, 141; Dayr al-banat, 142; the Church of the Annunciation; and many others. Ibid., 124.

70. Ibid., 131.

71. Ibid., 124.

72. Dwight, "Translation of the Ferman." See also Artinian, "Formation of Catholic and Protestant Millets." Many thanks to the anonymous reviewer who pointed out these sources to me.

73. Report on a visit to Egypt, the Sudan, and Palestine by W. W. Cash, February 1933, CMS G3/P/P8.

74. Minutes of PNCC meeting, Jaffa, April 3, 1938, CMS G2/P3.1.

75. Graham Brown to Chief Secretary, July 21, 1933, ISA RG2/m/24/17.

76. Saba to Warren, October 1946, CMS G2/P3.1.

77. Cragg to MacInnes, December 5, 1927, CMS G3/P/P7.

78. PC to Hardman, July 28, 1926, CMS G3/P/L16.

79. MacInnes to Cash, September 24, 1930, JEM 21/2.

80. Cash to MacInnes, March 24, 1931, JEM 21/2.

81. Quoted in Pittman, "Missionaries and Emissaries," 204.

82. Hooper to PNCC, August 1, 1935, JEM 21/3. This is a particularly interesting comment in light of the British decision, discussed in chapter 2, that the millet system was peculiarly appropriate for the governance of Palestine.

83. Marmura to Hooper, February 2, 1934, JEM 21/3.

84. Memo by Saba on "The Status and Aims of the PNCC," 1946, CMS G2/P3/1.

85. Minutes of PNCC meeting, May 7, 1933, CMS G/G3/P/P8. My italics.

86. It should be noted that this was not absolutely accurate; in fact, the Copts were also denied recognition by the British mandate government despite repeated protests.

87. Cubain [Quba'in] to Hooper, March 7, 1935, CMS G2/P3.1.

88. Minute of PNCC meeting Jerusalem. May 27, 1938, CMS G2/P3/1.

89. Minutes of PNCC meeting Nazareth, April 30, 1947, CMS G2/P3/1.

90. Ibid.

91. Bishop to Hooper, April 1945, CMS G2/Pd/1.

92. Marmura to MacMichael, April 16, 1943, JEM 21/3.

93. One seminal work on Palestinian nationalism suggests that the revolt sparked major hostility toward Christians, manifested in attacks on Christian villages as well as less serious incidents of forcing Christian women to wear the veil and making Christians observe their day of rest on Fridays; Porath, *Palestinian-Arab National Movement*, 269–271. But another study based on oral sources notes that no evidence of sectarian tensions emerged in interviews with participants in the revolt, suggesting that Muslim-Christian tensions were elided as a nationalist historiography of the revolt emerged among Palestinians; Swedenburg, *Memories of Revolt*, 89–90.

94. Graham Brown to Peel Commission, January 12, 1937, LPL Lang Papers, vol. 52.

95. PNCC to Lang, June 6, 1936, LPL Lang Papers 52.

96. Bishop to Hooper, June 6, 1936, CMS G2/P/1.

97. Cash to Marmura, June 30, 1936, CMS G2/Pd/1.

98. Graham Brown to JEM, October 15, 1936, JEM 61/1. See also Rafiq Farah, *In Troubled Waters: A History of the Anglican Diocese in Jerusalem 1841–1998* (Leicester: Christians Aware, 2002), 111.

99. Paton to Graham Brown, November 12, 1936, JEM 61/1.

100. Minutes of PNCC meeting Jerusalem, September 24, 1937, CMS G2/P/3.1.

101. Graham Brown to Lang, July 28, 1937, LPL Lang Papers 52.

102. *Filastin*, July 24, 1937; *Palestine Post*, July 22, 1937.

103. See, for instance, Taufik Canaan [Tawfiq Kana'an], *The Palestine Arab Cause* (Jerusalem: Modern Press, 1936) and *Conflict in the Land of Peace* (Jerusalem: Syrian Orphanage Press, 1936).

104. Canaan, *Palestine Arab Cause*, 16.

105. Wild, "Judentum, Christentum und Islam," 262n6.

106. Several sources discuss this theme, but it is not clear whether a significant number of Christians actually did convert to Islam. The discussion can, however, be taken as an indication of Palestinian Episcopalians' level of distress over the political situation in which they found themselves.

107. Marmura to Lang, August 12, 1937, LPL Lang Papers 52.

108. Ibid.

109. Ibid.

110. Ibid.

111. Graham Brown to Lang, July 28, 1937, JEM 60/1/2.

112. "Some Christian Considerations in regard to the partition problem," by Graham Brown, Warburton, Bridgeman, and Stewart, 1937, JEM 65/4.

113. Graham Brown to Lang, January 15, 1937, LPL Lang Papers 52.

114. Warburton to Hooper, August 19, 1936, CMS G2/P/1.

115. Hooper to Bishop, June 29, 1936, CMS G2/P/1. The implication of such letters is that there were a number of cases in which individual missionaries departed from their instructions due to private political convictions about the situation in Palestine.

116. Lang to Francis, September 9, 1937, LPL Lang Papers 52.

117. Saba to Warren, October 1946, CMS G2/P3.1.

118. El-Assal, *Caught in Between: The Story of an Arab Palestinian Christian Israeli* (London: SPCK, 1999), 52. El-Assal suggests that Saba did this at the instigation of the local

District Commissioner. In an interesting side note, Saba's daughter Charlotte, who had trained as a doctor in London, applied for a position as a Lady Medical Officer (LMO) in the Palestine Department of Health and started a furor when she demanded to be paid at the same rate as a British LMO. See Fleischmann, *The Nation and Its "New" Women*, 56, for an analysis of this episode.

119. CMS Palestine Mission Report on Moslem Evangelism, Conference 1936, CMS G2/P/2.

120. Minutes of PNCC Standing Committee meeting, August 10, 1938, JEM 21/3.

121. Minutes of PNCC meeting Nazareth, April 27, 1947, CMS G2/P3/1.

122. Minutes of PNCC meeting Jaffa, May 9, 1943, CMS G2/P/3.1.

123. Minutes of PNCC meeting Nazareth, April 28, 1947, CMS G2/P3/1.

124. Minutes of PNCC meeting Nazareth, April 30, 1947, CMS G2/P3/1.

125. Memo by Hooper on interview with Suleiman Tannus, London, December 31, 1946, CMS G2/P3/1.

126. See Graham Brown, "Notes of conversations with leading Arab Christians in Jerusalem," January 1937, LPL Lang Papers 52.

127. There were so many Christian immigrants just from the town of Bethlehem in Latin America that the nationalist leader and journalist 'Isa Bandak started a local newspaper devoted to following their doings. For discussions of Palestinian Christians in the diaspora see Bernard Sabella, "Palestinian Christian Emigration from the Holy Land," *Proche-Orient Chrètien* 41 (1991): 74–85, and "The Emigration of Christian Arabs: Dimensions and Causes of the Phenomenon," in *Christian Communities in the Arab Middle East: The Challenge of the Future*, ed. Andrea Pacini, 127–154 (Oxford: Clarendon Press, 1998); Helena Lindholm Schulz and Juliane Hammer, *The Palestinian Diaspora: Formation of Identities and Politics of Homeland* (London: Routledge, 2003); Mohammad Mustafa, *Palestinian Diaspora* (Ramallah: Arab Economists Association, 1996); Sari Hanafi, *Huna wa hunaka: Nahwa tahlil lil-'alaqah bayn al-shatat al-filastini wa-al-markaz* (Ramallah: Mutawin, 2001); and Bassma Kodmani-Darwish, *La diaspora palestinienne* (Paris: Presses universitaires de France, 1997).

EPILOGUE

1. For an overview of Palestinian Arab losses in the war see Sami Hadawi, *Palestinian Rights and Losses in 1948: A Comprehensive Study* (London: Saqi Books, 1988).

2. The high rates of Christian emigration out of the Palestinian territories has led some to the conclusion that Christians are persecuted by the Muslim majority and are therefore more anxious to leave than Muslim Palestinians. Sociological research on this question, however, has demonstrated that the impetus to leave Palestine is nearly always economic and that the high rate of Christian emigration is due more to greater opportunity than to a greater desire to leave. See Philippe Fargues, "Demographic Islamization: Non-Muslims in Muslim Countries," *SAIS Review* 21, 2 (2001): 103–116, and "The Arab Christians of the Middle East: A Demographic Perspective," in *Christian Communities in the Arab Middle East*, ed. Andrea Pacini (Oxford: Clarendon Press, 1998), 48–66.

3. Stavro Danilov, quoted in Bernard Sabella, "Socio-Economic Characteristics and the Challenges to Palestinian Christians in the Holy Land," in *Christians in the Holy Land*, ed. Michael Prior and William Taylor (London: World of Islam Trust, 1994), 41.

4. The Christian population in Jerusalem went from 29,350 to 10,982, according to Tsimhoni, *Christian Communities in Jerusalem and the West Bank*, 19.

5. See As'ad Ganim, *The Palestinian-Arab Minority in Israel, 1948–2000: A Political Study* (Albany: SUNY Press, 2001), 20. For an investigation of the many legal and political sectarian institutions carried over from the British into the Israeli state structures see Eisenman, *Islamic Law in Palestine and Israel*.

6. Nurit Yaffe, "The Arab Population of Israel 2003" (Jerusalem: Central Bureau of Statistics, Israel 2003). The Palestinian Arab population of Israel constitutes approximately 20 percent of the population (about 1.3 million people). Most of the Palestinian Christian population is now concentrated in the Galilee region.

7. Sabella, "Palestinian Christian Emigration," 74. See also one of the few case studies of the Palestinian diaspora in Latin America, Nancie L. Solien González' *Dollar, Dove, and Eagle: One Hundred Years of Palestinian Migration to Honduras* (Ann Arbor: University of Michigan Press, 1993), 10.

8. Bernard Sabella, "Palestinian and Arab Christians: The Challenges Ahead," Sami Hadawi Memorial Lecture, September 22, 2004. (Many thanks to the author for providing me with this text). Of course, this category includes other Middle Eastern Christians besides Palestinians.

9. Sabella, "Palestinian Christian Emigration," 79–80.

10. Ibid., 83.

11. "1/3 of US tourists Evangelicals," *Jerusalem Post*, October 9, 2006. For an examination of the rise of pro-Israeli American evangelical Christianity see Stephen Spector, *Evangelicals and Israel: The Story of American Christian Zionism* (New York: Oxford University Press, 2008).

12. Makdisi, *Culture of Sectarianism*, 166.

BIBLIOGRAPHY

ARCHIVES

Central Zionist Archives (CZA), Jerusalem
Church Missionary Society (CMS) Collections, University of Birmingham Library, Birmingham, England
Israel State Archives (ISA), Jerusalem
Lambeth Palace Library (LPL), London
Middle East Centre Archives, St. Antony's College, Oxford
    Jerusalem and the East Mission Collection (JEM)
National Archives, Kew
    Colonial Office (CO)
    Foreign Office (FO)
School of Oriental and African Studies Archives, London
St. George's College Library, Jerusalem

WORKS CITED

Abboushi, W. F. "The Road to Rebellion: Arab Palestine in the 1930's." *Journal of Palestine Studies* 6, 3 (Spring 1977): 23–46.

Abu El-Assal, Riah. *Caught in Between: The Story of an Arab Palestinian Christian Israeli.* London: SPCK, 1999.

Abu-Manneh, B. "Jerusalem in the Tanzimat Period: The New Ottoman Administration and the Notables." *Die Welt des Islams* 30, 1/4 (1990): 1–44.

Anderson, Benedict. *Imagined Communities: Reflections on the Origin and Spread of Nationalism.* Revised edition. London: Verso, 1991.

Anderson, Lisa. "The State in the Middle East and North Africa." *Comparative Politics* 20, 1 (1987): 1–18.

Antonius, George. *The Arab Awakening: The Story of the Arab National Movement.* London: H. Hamilton, 1938.

Arab Centre. *The Arab Case: The MacMahon Correspondence.* London: Arab Centre, 1939.

———. *Palestine: The Way to Peace.* London: Arab Centre, 1939.

———. *Statement of Indian Muslim Views on Palestine.* London: Arab Centre, 1939.

Armstrong, Nancy. *Desire and Domestic Fiction: A Political History of the Novel.* New York: Oxford University Press, 1987.

Artinian, Vartan. "The Formation of Catholic and Protestant Millets in the Ottoman Empire," *Armenian Review* 28, 1 (Spring 1975): 3–15.

Ateek, Naim. *Faith and the Intifada: Palestinian Christian Voices.* Maryknoll, NY: Orbis, 1992.

———. *Justice, and Only Justice: A Palestinian Theology of Liberation.* Maryknoll, NY: Orbis, 1989.

Ayalon, Ami. *Reading Palestine: Printing and Literacy, 1900–1948.* Austin: University of Texas Press, 2004.

Ayubi, Nazih. *Over-Stating the Arab State: Politics and Society in the Middle East.* London: Tauris, 1995.

Azoury, Negib [Najib ʿAzuri]. *Le réveil de la nation arabe dans l'Asie turque.* Paris: Plon-Nourrit, 1905.

Barron, J. B. *Palestine: Report and General Abstracts of the Census of 1922.* Jerusalem: Greek Convent Press, 1923.

Baud, Michiel. "Beyond Benedict Anderson: Nation-Building and Popular Democracy in Latin America." *International Review of Social History* 50 (2005): 485–498.

Baumgart, Winfried. *The Crimean War, 1853–56.* London: Oxford University Press, 1999.

Bayat, Fadil. *Al-dawla al-ʿuthmaniyya fi al-majal al-ʿarabi: Dirasa tarikhiyya fi al-awdaʾ al-idariyya fi dawʾ al-wathaʾiq wa-al-masadir al-ʿuthmaniyya hasran.* Beirut: Markaz dirasat al-wahdah al-ʿarabiyya, 2007.

Bayly, C. A. *Indian Society and the Making of the British Empire.* Cambridge: Cambridge University Press, 1988.

———. "Representing Copts and Muhammadans: Empire, Nation, and Community in Egypt and India, 1880–1914." In *Modernity and Culture: From the Mediterranean to the Indian Ocean,* ed. Leila Fawaz and C. A. Bayly, 158–203. New York: Columbia University Press, 2002.

Beinin, Joel. Review of *The Copts in Egyptian Politics,* by Barbara L. Carter. *International Journal of Middle East Studies* 20, 1 (1988): 123–126.

Beinin, Joel, and Zachary Lockman. *Workers on the Nile: Nationalism, Communism, Islam, and the Egyptian Working Class, 1882–1954.* Princeton: Princeton University Press, 1987.

Ben-Arieh, Yehoshua, and Moshe Davis, eds. *Jerusalem in the Mind of the Western World, 1800–1948.* Westport, CT: Praeger, 1997.

Benson, Kathleen, and Philip Kayal, eds. *A Community of Many Words: Arab Americans in New York City.* New York: Museum of the City of New York, 2002.

Bentwich, Norman. "The Legislation of Palestine, 1918–1925." *Journal of Comparative Legislation and International Law* 8, 1 (1926): 9–20.

———. *My 77 Years: An Account of My Life and Times, 1883–1960.* Philadelphia: Jewish Publication Society of America, 1961.

———. *Palestine.* London: Benn, 1934.

———. *A Wanderer in the Promised Land.* New York: Scribner, 1933.

Bentwich, Norman, and Helen Bentwich. *Mandate Memories, 1918–1948.* London: Hogarth Press, 1965.

Bermeo, Nancy, and Philip Nord, eds. *Civil Society before Democracy: Lessons from Nineteenth-Century Europe.* Lanham, MD: Rowman and Littlefield, 2000.

Bertram, Anton, and Harry Charles Luke. *Report of the Commission Appointed by the Gov-*

ernment of Palestine to Inquire into the Affairs of the Orthodox Patriarchate of Jerusalem. London: Oxford University Press, H. Milford, 1921.

Bertram, Anton, and J.W.A. Young. *The Orthodox Patriarchate of Jerusalem; Report of the Commission Appointed by the Government of Palestine to Inquire and Report upon Certain Controversies between the Orthodox Patriarchate of Jerusalem and the Arab Orthodox Community.* London: H. Milford, Oxford University Press, 1926.

Bishop, Eric. "Jerusalem Byways of Memory II." *Muslim World* 50, 3 (1960): 199–206.

———. "Jerusalem Byways of Memory III." *Muslim World* 51, 4 (1961): 265–273.

———. "Jerusalem Byways of Memory IV." *Muslim World* 52, 2 (1962): 97–109.

Blyth, Estelle. *When We Lived in Jerusalem.* London: John Murray, 1927.

Boahen, Adu. *African Perspectives on Colonialism.* Baltimore: Johns Hopkins University Press, 1987.

Bose, Sugata, and Ayesha Jalal. *Modern South Asia: History, Culture, and Political Economy.* London: Routledge, 1998.

Boullata, Issa. "Books and I." *Banipal* 29 (Spring 2007). http://www.banipal.co.uk/selections/56/79/issa_j_boullata.

Boullata, Kamal. "The World, the Self, and the Body: Pioneering Women in Palestinian Art." In *Self-Portrait: Palestinian Women's Art*, ed. Tal Ben Azvi and Yael Lehrer, 167–178. Tel Aviv: Andalus, 2001.

Bowman, Glenn. "Christian, Muslim Palestinians Confront Sectarianism: Religion and Political Identity in Beit Sahour." *Middle East Report* 164/165 (2000): 50–53.

———. "Nationalizing the Sacred: Shrines and Shifting Identities in the Israeli-Occupied Territories." *Man* 28, 3 (1993): 431–460.

Boyle, Susan Silsby. *Betrayal of Palestine: The Story of George Antonius.* Boulder, CO: Westview Press, 2001.

Braude, Benjamin. "Foundation Myths of the Millet System." In *Christians and Jews in the Ottoman Empire*, ed. Braude and Lewis, 1:69–88.

Braude, Benjamin, and Bernard Lewis, eds. *Christians and Jews in the Ottoman Empire: The Functioning of a Plural Society.* 2 vols. New York: Holmes and Meier, 1982.

Brown, P. M. "British Justice in Palestine." *American Journal of International Law* 12, 4 (October 1918): 828–832.

Bulliet, Richard. *The Case for Islamo-Christian Civilization.* New York: Columbia University Press, 2006.

Bunton, Martin. *Colonial Land Policies in Palestine, 1917–1936.* Oxford: Oxford University Press, 2007.

———. "Inventing the Status Quo: Ottoman Land-Law during the Palestine Mandate, 1917–1936." *International History Review* 21, 1 (1999): 28–56.

Canaan, Taufik [Tawfiq Kana'an]. *Conflict in the Land of Peace.* Jerusalem: Syrian Orphanage Press, 1936.

———. *Mohammedan Saints and Sanctuaries.* London: Luzac, 1927.

———. *The Palestine Arab Cause.* Jerusalem: Modern Press, 1936.

Carter, Barbara. *The Copts in Egyptian Politics.* London: Croom Helm, 1986.

Chatterjee, Partha. *The Nation and Its Fragments: Colonial and Postcolonial Histories.* Princeton: Princeton University Press, 1993.

———. *Nationalist Thought and the Colonial World: A Derivative Discourse?* London: Zed Books, 1986.

Cliffe, L., J. S. Coleman, and M. R. Doornbos, eds. *Government and Rural Development in East Africa: Essays on Political Penetration.* The Hague: Martinus Nijhoff, 1977.

Cohen, Raymond. *Saving the Holy Sepulchre: How Rival Christians Came Together to Rescue Their Holiest Shrine.* Oxford: Oxford University Press, 2008.

Cohn, Bernard. *Colonialism and Its Forms of Knowledge: The British in India.* Princeton: Princeton University Press, 1996.

Cohn-Sherbok, Dan. *The Politics of Apocalypse: The History and Influence of Christian Zionism.* Oxford: Oneworld, 2008.

Colbi, Saul. *Christianity in the Holy Land.* Tel Aviv: Am Hassefer, 1969.

Courbage, Youssef, and Phillipe Fargues. *Chrétiens et juifs dans l'Islam arabe et turc.* Paris: Fayard, 1992.

Cragg, Kenneth. *The Arab Christian: A History in the Middle East.* London: Mowbray, 1992.

Culver, Douglas J. *Albion and Ariel: British Puritanism and the Birth of Political Zionism.* New York: P. Lang, 1995.

Cunningham, Allan. *Eastern Questions in the Nineteenth Century.* Ed. E. Ingram. 2 vols. London: F. Cass, 1993.

Daniel, Norman. *Islam and the West: The Making of an Image.* New York: Oneworld, 1960.

Davis, Eric. "A Sectarian Middle East?" *International Journal of Middle East Studies* 40, 4 (2008): 555–558.

Davis, Rochelle. "Commemorating Education: Recollections of the Arab College in Jerusalem, 1918–1948." *Comparative Studies of South Asia, Africa, and the Middle East* 23, 1–2 (2003): 190–204.

———. "The Growth of the Western Communities: 1917–1948." In *Jerusalem 1948: The Arab Neighbourhoods and Their Fate in the War*, ed. Salim Tamari, 32–73. Jerusalem: Institute of Jerusalem Studies, 1999.

———."Ottoman Jerusalem: The Growth of the New City." In *Jerusalem 1948: The Arab Neighbourhoods and Their Fate in the War*, ed. Salim Tamari, 10–31. Jerusalem: Institute of Jerusalem Studies, 1999.

Dawn, C. Ernest. *From Ottomanism to Arabism: Essays on the Origins of Arab Nationalism.* Urbana-Champaign: University of Illinois Press, 1973.

Dirks, Nicholas. *Castes of Mind: Colonialism and the Making of Modern India.* Princeton: Princeton University Press, 2001.

Divine, Donna Robinson. *Politics and Society in Ottoman Palestine: The Arab Struggle for Survival and Power.* Boulder, CO: Lynne Rienner, 1994.

Dodge, Toby. *Inventing Iraq: The Failure of Nation-Building and a History Denied.* New York: Columbia University Press, 2003.

Doornbos, Martin. "The African State in Academic Debate: Retrospect and Prospect." *Journal of Modern African Studies* 28, 2 (1990): 179–198.

Doumani, Beshara. "Rediscovering Ottoman Palestine: Writing Palestinians into History." *Journal of Palestine Studies* 21, 2 (1992): 5–28.

———. *Rediscovering Palestine: Merchants and Peasants in Jabal Nablus 1770–1900.* Berkeley: University of California Press, 1995.

Dwight, H.G.O. "Translation of the Ferman Granted by Sultan Abd-ul-Mejeed to His Protestant Subjects," *Journal of the American Oriental Society* 4 (1854): 443–444.

Eisenman, Robert H. *Islamic Law in Palestine and Israel: A History of the Survival of Tanzimat and Shari'a in the British Mandate and the Jewish State.* Leiden, Netherlands: Brill, 1978.

Eldem, Edhem, Daniel Goffman, and Bruce Masters. *The Ottoman City between East and West: Aleppo, Izmir, and Istanbul.* London: Cambridge University Press, 1999.

Ellis, Kail. *The Vatican, Islam, and the Middle East.* Syracuse, NY: Syracuse University Press, 1987.

Elpeleg, Zvi. *The Grand Mufti: Haj Amin al-Hussaini, Founder of the Palestinian National Movement.* London: F. Cass, 1993.

Emmett, Chad. *Beyond the Basilica: Christians and Muslims in Nazareth.* Chicago: University of Chicago Press, 1995.

Fairey, Jack. "The Great Game of Improvements: European Diplomacy and the Reform of the Orthodox Church." Ph.D. diss., University of Toronto, 2004.

Farah, Najwa Kawar. *A Continent Called Palestine: One Woman's Story.* London: SPCK, 1996.

Farah, Rafiq. *In Troubled Waters: A History of the Anglican Diocese in Jerusalem 1841–1998.* Leicester, England: Christians Aware, 2002.

Fargues, Philippe. "The Arab Christians of the Middle East: A Demographic Perspective." In *Christian Communities in the Arab Middle East*, ed. Andrea Pacini, 48–66. Oxford: Clarendon Press, 1998.

———. "Demographic Islamization: Non-Muslims in Muslim Countries." *SAIS Review* 21, 2 (2001): 103–116.

Fawaz, Leila, and C. A. Bayly, eds. *Modernity and Culture: From the Mediterranean to the Indian Ocean.* New York: Columbia University Press, 2002.

Fieldhouse, D. K. *Western Imperialism in the Middle East 1914–1958.* Oxford: Oxford University Press, 2008.

Findley, Carter. "The Evolution of the System of Provincial Administration as Viewed from the Center." In *Palestine in the Late Ottoman Period*, ed. David Kushner, 3–30. Jerusalem: Yad Izhak Ben-Zvi Press, 1986.

Finkel, Caroline. *Osman's Dream: The Story of the Ottoman Empire 1300–1923.* New York: Perseus, 2005.

Fleischmann, Ellen. "The Impact of American Protestant Missions in Lebanon on the Construction of Female Identity, c. 1860–1950." *Islam and Christian-Muslim Relations* 13, 4 (2002): 411–426.

———. *The Nation and Its "New" Women: The Palestinian Women's Movement, 1920–1948.* Berkeley: University of California Press, 2003.

Foley, Rolla. *Song of the Arab: The Religious Ceremonies, Shrines, and Folk Music of the Holy Land Christian Arab.* New York: Macmillan, 1953.

Fortna, Benjamin. *Imperial Classroom: Islam, the State, and Education in the Late Ottoman Empire.* Oxford: Oxford University Press, 2002.

Ganim, As'ad. *The Palestinian-Arab Minority in Israel, 1948–2000: A Political Study.* Albany: SUNY Press, 2001.

Gelvin, James. *Divided Loyalties: Nationalism and Mass Politics in Syria at the Close of Empire.* Berkeley: University of California Press, 1998.

Ghandour, Zeina. "Religious Law in a Secular State: The Jurisdiction of the Shari'a Courts of Palestine and Israel." *Arab Law Quarterly* 5, 1 (February 1990): 25–48.

Ghori, Imil. *Filastin 'abr sittin 'aman.* 2 vols. Beirut: Dar al-nahar, 1972.

Gillet, Olivier. *Balkans: Religions et nationalisme.* Brussels: Éditions OUSIA, 2001.

Glenny, Misha. *The Balkans, 1804–1999: Nationalism, War, and the Great Powers.* London: Granta, 1999.

Gluck, Carol. "Top Ten Things to Know about Japan in the Early Twenty-First Century." *Education About Asia* 13, 3 (Winter 2008): 5–11.

Goadby, F. M. *An Introduction to the Study of Law: A Handbook for the Use of Law Students in Egypt and Palestine.* London: Butterworths, 1921.

————. "Religious Communities and Courts in Palestine." *Tulane Law Review* 8, 2 (1934): 215–235.

Goldfrank, David. *The Origins of the Crimean War*. London: Longman, 1994.

González, Nancie L. Solien. *Dollar, Dove, and Eagle: One Hundred Years of Palestinian Migration to Honduras*. Ann Arbor: University of Michigan Press, 1993.

Grabill, Joseph. *Protestant Diplomacy and the Near East: Missionary Influence on American Policy, 1810–1927*. Minneapolis: University of Minnesota Press, 1971.

Greenberg, Ela. *Preparing the Mothers of Tomorrow: Education and Islam in Mandate Palestine*. Austin: University of Texas Press, 2010.

Hachey, T. "The Archbishop of Canterbury's Visit to Palestine: An Issue in Anglo-Vatican Relations." *Church History* 41, 2 (1972): 198–207.

Hadawi, Sami. *Palestinian Rights and Losses in 1948: A Comprehensive Study*. London: Saqi Books, 1988.

Haddad, Yusuf Ayyub. Introduction to *Yawmiyat Khalil al-Sakakini: Yawmiyat, rasa'il wa-ta'ammulat*, ed. Akram Musallam, vol. 3. Ramallah: Markaz Khalil al-Sakakini al-thaqafi, Mu'assasat al-dirasat al-muqaddasiyya.

————. *Khalil al-Sakakini: Hayatuhu, mawqfuhu wa-atharuhu*. Beirut: Al-Ittihad al-'amm lil-kuttab wa-al-suhufiyyin al-filastiniyyin, 1981.

Hafez, Safry. *The Genesis of Arabic Narrative Discourse: A Study in the Sociology of Modern Arabic Literature*. London: Saqi Books, 1993.

Hajj, Badr al-. "Khalil Raad—Jerusalem Photographer." *Jerusalem Quarterly* 11–12 (2001): 34–39.

Hanafi, Sari. *Huna wa hunaka: Nahwa tahlil lil-'alaqah bayn al-shatat al-filastini wa-al-markaz*. Ramallah: Mutawin, 2001.

Hawkesworth, Celia, Muriel Heppell, and Harry Norris, eds. *Religious Quest and National Identity in the Balkans*. Houndsmill, England: Palgrave, 2001.

Hobsbawn, Eric. *The Age of Empire: 1875–1914*. New York: Vintage, 1989.

Hobsbawn, Eric, and Terence Ranger, eds. *The Invention of Tradition*. Cambridge: Cambridge University Press, 1992.

Hodgson, Marshall. *Rethinking World History: Essays on Europe, Islam, and World History*. Cambridge: Cambridge University Press, 1993.

Hopwood, Derek. *The Russian Presence in Syria and Palestine, 1843–1914: Church and Politics in the Near East*. Oxford: Clarendon Press, 1969.

Hourani, Albert. *Islam in European Thought*. Cambridge: Cambridge University Press, 1991.

————. "Ottoman Reform and the Politics of Notables." In *The Beginnings of Modernization in the Middle East*, ed. William Polk and Richard Chambers, 41–68. Chicago: University of Chicago Press, 1968.

Huneidi, Sahar. *Broken Trust: Herbert Samuel, Zionism, and the Palestinians, 1920–1925*. London: Tauris, 2001.

Huntington, Samuel. "The Clash of Civilizations?" *Foreign Affairs* 72, 3 (1993): 22–49.

————. *The Clash of Civilizations and the Remaking of World Order*. New York: Simon and Schuster, 1996.

Husayni, Hajj Amin al-. *Mudhakkirat al-Hajj Muhammad Amin al-Husayni*. Ed. 'Abd al-Karim al-'Umar. Damascus: Al-Ahali, 1999.

Husayni, Ishaq Musa al-. "Khalil al-Sakakini." In *Dhikra al-Sakakini*, ed. Abdul Hamid Yasin, 60–63. Jerusalem: Modern Library, 1957.

Hut, Bayan al-. *Qiyadat wa-al-mu'assasat al-siyasiyya fi Filastin, 1917–1948*. Beirut: Mu'assasat al-dirasat al-filastiniyya, 1981.

———

———, ed. *Sittun 'aman ma'a al-qafilah al-'arabiyya: Mudhakkirat 'Ajaj Nuwayhid*. Beirut: Dar al-istiqlal, 1993.

Inalcik, Halil. "The Status of the Greek Orthodox Patriarch under the Ottomans." *Turcica* 21–23 (1991): 407–436.

Inalcik, Halil, Donald Quataert, and Suraiya Faroqhi, eds. *An Economic and Social History of the Ottoman Empire, 1300–1914*. 2 vols. Cambridge: Cambridge University Press, 2004.

Jabara, Taysir. *Al-Muslimun al-hunud wa-qadiyat Filastin*. Amman: Dar al-shuruq, 1998.

Jacobson, Abigail. "Negotiating Ottomanism in Times of War: Jerusalem during World War I through the Eyes of a Local Muslim Resident." *International Journal of Middle East Studies* 40 (2008): 69–88.

Jad, Islah. "Tatawwur al-dawr al-siyassi lik-mar'a al-filastiniyya hatta al-intifada." *Shu'un al-mar'a*, part 1 (May 1991): 94–107 and part 2 (January 1992): 75–83.

Jalal, Ayesha. "Exploding Communalism: The Politics of Muslim Identity." In *Nationalism, Democracy, and Development: State and Politics in India*, ed. Ayesha Jalal and Sugata Bose, 76–193. Delhi: Oxford University Press, 1998.

Jalal, Ayesha, and Sugata Bose, eds. *Nationalism, Democracy, and Development: State and Politics in India*. Delhi: Oxford University Press, 1998.

Jankowski, James P., and Israel Gershoni, eds. *Rethinking Nationalism in the Arab Middle East*. New York: Columbia University Press, 1997.

Joseph, Bernard. "Palestine Legislation under the British." *Annals of the American Academy of Political and Social Science* 164 (November 1932): 39–46.

Kaleel, Mousa. *When I Was a Boy in Palestine*. London: Harrap, 1920.

Kark, Ruth. *Jaffa: A City in Evolution, 1799–1917*. Jerusalem: Ben-Zvi Press, 1990.

———, ed. *Land that Became Israel: Studies in Historical Geography*. New Haven: Yale University Press, 1990.

Kark, Ruth, and Michal Oren-Nordheim, eds. *Jerusalem and Its Environs: Quarters, Neighborhoods, Villages, 1800–1948*. Detroit: Wayne State University Press, 2001.

Karmil, Aliks. *Ta'rikh Haifa fi 'ahd al-itrak al-'uthmaniyyin*. Haifa: Sharikat al-dirasat al-'ilmiyya al-'amaliyya, 1979.

Katz, Sheila. *Women and Gender in Early Jewish and Palestinian Nationalism*. Gainesville: University Press of Florida, 2005.

Katz, Itamar, and Ruth Kark. "The Greek Orthodox Patriarchate of Jerusalem and Its Congregation: Dissent over Real Estate." *International Journal of Middle East Studies* 37, 4 (2005): 509–534.

Kayyali, Abd al-Wahhab. *Palestine: A Modern History*. London: Croom Helm, 1978.

Kedourie, Elie. *Arabic Political Memoirs and Other Studies*. London: F. Cass, 1974.

———. *The Chatham House Version and Other Middle Eastern Studies*. New York: Praeger, 1970.

Keith-Roach, Edward. *Pasha of Jerusalem: Memoirs of a District Commissioner under the British Mandate*. Ed. Paul Eedle. London: Radcliffe Press, 1994.

Khadduri, Majid. *Arab Contemporaries*. Baltimore: Johns Hopkins University Press, 1973.

Khalaf, Issa. *Politics in Palestine: Arab Factionalism and Social Disintegration, 1939–1948*. Albany: SUNY Press, 1991.

Khalidi, Rashid. "Arab Nationalism: Historical Problems in the Literature." *American Historical Review* 96, 5 (December 1991): 1363–1373.

———. *The Iron Cage: The Story of the Palestinian Struggle for Statehood*. Boston: Beacon Press, 2006.

———

————. *Palestinian Identity: The Construction of Modern National Consciousness*. New York: Columbia University Press, 1997.

Khalidi, Rashid, Lisa Anderson, Muhammad Muslih, and Reeva Simon, eds. *The Origins of Arab Nationalism*. New York: Columbia University Press, 1991.

Khalidi, Tarif. "Palestinian Historiography: 1900–1948," *Journal of Palestine Studies* 10, 3 (1981): 59–76.

Khalidi, Walid. *Before Their Diaspora: A Photographic History of the Palestinians*. Washington, DC: Institute of Palestine Studies, 1984.

Khillah, Kamil. *Filastin wa-al-intidab al-baritani, 1922–1939*. Beirut: Munazzamat al-tahrir al-filastiniyya, 1974.

Khoury, Philip. *Urban Notables and Arab Nationalism: The Politics of Damascus 1860–1920*. Cambridge: Cambridge University Press, 2003.

Khuri, Shehadi, and Niqola Khuri. *Khulasat tarikh kanisat Urushalim al-urthudhuksiyya*. Jerusalem: Matba'at bayt al-maqdis, 1925.

Kodmani-Darwish, Bassma. *La diaspora palestinienne*. Paris: Presses universitaires de France, 1997.

Krämer, Gudrun. *A History of Palestine: From the Ottoman Conquest to the Founding of the State of Israel*. Princeton: Princeton University Press, 2008.

Kramer, Martin. "Azoury: A Further Episode." *Middle Eastern Studies* 18 (1982): 351–358.

Kupferschmidt, Uri. *The Supreme Muslim Council: Islam under the British Mandate for Palestine*. Leiden, Netherlands: Brill, 1987.

Lambert, Andrew. *The Crimean War: British Grand Strategy, 1853–56*. Manchester: Manchester University Press, 1990.

League of Nations. Permanent Mandates Commission. *Minutes of Sessions Held at Geneva*. Geneva: League of Nations, 1922–1940.

Lesch, Ann Mosely. *Arab Politics in Palestine, 1917–1939: The Frustration of a Nationalist Movement*. Ithaca, NY: Cornell University Press, 1979.

Lewis, Bernard. *Islam and the West*. New York: Oxford University Press, 1993.

————. "The Roots of Muslim Rage." *Atlantic Monthly*, September 1990, 47–60.

————. *Semites and Anti-Semites: An Inquiry into Conflict and Prejudice*. New York: Norton, 1999.

————. *What Went Wrong? The Clash between Islam and Modernity in the Middle East*. New York: Oxford University Press, 2002.

Likhovski, Assaf. *Law and Identity in Mandate Palestine*. Chapel Hill: University of North Carolina Press, 2006.

Lockman, Zachary. *Comrades and Enemies: Arab and Jewish Workers in Palestine, 1906–1948*. Berkeley: University of California Press, 1996.

Luke, H. C. *Cities and Men: An Autobiography*. 3 vols. London: Bles, 1953–1956.

————. *Prophets, Priests, and Patriarchs; Sketches of the Sects of Palestine and Syria*. London: Faith Press [1927].

Ma'oz, Moshe. *Ottoman Reform in Syria and Palestine, 1840–1861: The Impact of the Tanzimat on Politics and Society*. Oxford: Clarendon Press, 1968.

Makdisi, Ussama. *Artillery of Heaven: American Missionaries and the Failed Conversion of the Middle East*. Ithaca, NY: Cornell University Press, 2007.

————. *The Culture of Sectarianism: Community, History, and Violence in Nineteenth-Century Ottoman Lebanon*. Berkeley: University of California Press, 2000.

————. "Moving Beyond Orientalist Fantasy, Sectarian Polemic, and Nationalist Denial." *International Journal of Middle East Studies* 40, 4 (2008): 559–560.

————. "Reclaiming the Land of the Bible: Missionaries, Secularism, and Evangelical Modernity." *American Historical Review* 102, 3 (June 1997): 680–713.

Mandel, Neville. *The Arabs and Zionism before World War I.* Berkeley: University of California Press, 1976.

Manela, Eres. *The Wilsonian Moment: Self-Determination and the International Origins of Anticolonial Nationalism.* Oxford: Oxford University Press, 2007.

Manna', 'Adil. *A'lam Filastin fi awakhir al-ahd al-'uthmani, 1800–1918.* Beirut: Mu'assasat al-dirasat al-filastiniyya, 1995.

Mansur, As'ad. *Ta'rikh al-Nasira min aqdam azmaniha ila ayamina al-hadira.* Cairo: Matba'at al-hilal, 1924.

Mansur, Juni. *Ru'iya jadida li hayat wa 'amal al-mutran Grigorios Hajjar.* Haifa: J. I. Mansur, 1985.

Marmura, Ilyas. *Al-Samiriyyun.* Jerusalem: Maktabat Filastin al-'ilmiyya, 1934.

Marten, Michael. *Attempting to Bring the Gospel Home: Scottish Missions to Palestine, 1839–1917.* London: Tauris, 2006.

Masters, Bruce. *Christians and Jews in the Ottoman Arab World: The Roots of Sectarianism.* Cambridge: Cambridge University Press, 2001.

Mattar, Philip. *The Mufti of Jerusalem: Al-Hajj Amin al-Husayni and the Palestinian National Movement.* New York: Columbia University Press, 1988.

Matthews, Weldon. *Confronting an Empire, Constructing a Nation: Arab Nationalists and Popular Politics in Mandate Palestine.* London: Tauris, 2006.

McCarthy, Justin. *The Population of Palestine: Population History and Statistics of the Late Ottoman Period and the Mandate.* New York: Columbia University Press, 1990.

Mejcher, Helmut. *The Imperial Quest for Oil: Iraq 1910–1928.* London: Middle East Centre, St. Antony's College, 1976.

Merkley, Paul Charles. *The Politics of Christian Zionism, 1891–1948.* London: F. Cass, 1998.

Metcalf, Thomas. *Ideologies of the Raj.* Cambridge: Cambridge University Press, 1997.

Miller, Ylana. *Government and Society in Rural Palestine, 1920–1948.* Austin: University of Texas Press, 1985.

Mills, E. *Census of Palestine, 1931: Population of Villages, Towns, and Administrative Areas.* Jerusalem: Greek Convent and Goldberg Presses, 1932.

Minerbi, Sergio. *The Vatican and Zionism: Conflict in the Holy Land, 1895–1925.* Trans. Arnold Schwarz. New York: Oxford University Press, 1990.

Mitchell, Timothy. *Colonising Egypt.* Cambridge: Cambridge University Press, 1988.

————. *Rule of Experts: Egypt, Techno-Politics, Modernity.* Berkeley: University of California Press, 2002.

Monk, Daniel Bertrand. *An Aesthetic Occupation: The Immediacy of Architecture and the Palestine Conflict.* Durham, NC: Duke University Press, 2002.

Mossek, M. *Palestine Immigration Policy under Sir Herbert Samuel: British, Zionist, and Arab Attitudes.* London: F. Cass, 1978.

Mousa, Matti. *The Origins of Modern Arabic Fiction,* 2nd edition. Boulder: Lynne Rienner, 1997.

Musallam, Akram, ed. *Yawmiyat Khalil al-Sakakini: Yawmiyat, rasa'il wa-ta'ammulat.* 8 vols. Ramallah: Markaz Khalil al-Sakakini al-thaqafi, Mu'assasat al-dirasat al-muqaddasiyya, 2003–2008.

Muslih, Muhammad. *The Origins of Palestinian Nationalism.* New York: Columbia University Press, 1988.

Mustafa, Mohammad. *Palestinian Diaspora*. Ramallah: Arab Economists Association, 1996.

Nassar, 'Issam. *Laqatatt mughayyira: Al-taswir al-mahalli fi Filastin, 1850–1948*. Beirut: Kutub, 2005.

Nassar, 'Issam, and Salim Tamari, eds. *Al-Quds al-'uthmaniyya fi al-mudhakkirat al-Jawhariyya: Al-kitab al-awwal min mudhakkirat al-musiqi Wasid Jawhariyya*. Beirut: Mu'assasat al-dirasat al-filastiniyya, 2003.

Nuwayhid, 'Ajaj. *Rijal min Filastin ma bayna bidayat al-qarm hatta 'am 1948*. Amman: Filastin al-muhtalla, 1981.

O'Mahony, Anthony, ed. *Christian Communities of Jerusalem and the Holy Land: Studies in History, Religion, and Politics*. Cardiff: University of Wales Press, 2003.

———, ed. *Eastern Christianity: Studies in Modern History, Religion, and Politics*. London: Melisende, 2004.

———. Introduction to *Palestinian Christians*, ed. O'Mahony, 9–55.

———, ed. *Palestinian Christians: Religion, Politics, and Society in the Holy Land*. London: Melisende, 1999.

———. "Religion and Politics and Church-State Relations in Jerusalem," *Chronos* 3 (2000): 61–87.

O'Mahony, Anthony, Goran Gunner, and Kevork Hintlian, eds. *Christian Heritage in the Holy Land*. London: Scorpion Cavendish, 1995.

Okkenhaug, Inger Marie. *The Quality of Heroic Living, of High Endeavour and Adventure: Anglican Mission, Women, and Education in Palestine, 1888–1948*. Leiden, Netherlands: Brill, 2002.

Oren, Michael. *Power, Faith, and Fantasy: America in the Middle East, 1776 to the Present*. New York: W. W. Norton, 2007.

Owen, Roger. "Defining Traditional: Some Implications of the Use of Ottoman Law in Mandatory Palestine." *Harvard Middle Eastern and Islamic Review* 1, 2 (1994): 115–131.

———. *Lord Cromer: Victorian Imperialist, Edwardian Proconsul*. Oxford: Oxford University Press, 2004.

Pacini, Andrea, ed. *Christian Communities in the Arab Middle East: The Challenge of the Future*. Oxford: Clarendon Press, 1998.

Palestine Arab Delegation. *The Holy Land: The Moslem-Christian Case against Zionist Aggression*. London: HMSO, 1921.

Palestine Royal Commission. Report of the Palestine Royal Commission (Peel Commission Report). London: HMSO, 1937.

Pandey, Gyan. *The Construction of Communalism in Colonial North India*. Delhi: Oxford University Press, 1990.

Papadopoullos, Theodore H. *Studies and Documents Relating to the History of the Greek Church and People under Turkish Domination*. Aldershot, England: Gower, 1990.

Pappe, Ilan. *A History of Modern Palestine: One Land, Two Peoples*. Cambridge: Cambridge University Press, 2004.

Parmenter, Barbara. *Giving Voice to Stones: Place and Identity in Palestinian Literature*. Austin: University of Texas Press, 1994.

Parsons, Laila. *The Druze between Palestine and Israel, 1947–49*. Houndmills, England: Macmillan, 2000.

Philipp, Thomas, and Birgit Schaebler. *The Syrian Land: Processes of Integration and Fragmentation: Bilad al-Sham from the 18th to the 20th Century*. Stuttgart: Steiner, 1998.

Pittman, Lester. "Missionaries and Emissaries: The Anglican Church in Palestine 1841–1948." Ph.D. diss., University of Virginia, 1998.

Planhol, Xavier de. *Minorités en Islam: Géographie politique et sociale.* Paris: Flammarion, 1997.

Pollis, Adamantia. "Intergroup Conflict and British Colonial Policy: The Case of Cyprus," *Comparative Politics* 5, 4 (1973): 575–599.

Polowetzky, Michael. *Jerusalem Recovered: Victorian Intellectuals and the Birth of Modern Zionism.* Westport, CT: Praeger, 1995.

Porath, Yehoshua. *The Emergence of the Palestinian-Arab National Movement, 1918–1929.* London: F. Cass, 1974.

———. *The Palestinian Arab National Movement: From Riots to Rebellion, 1929–1939.* London: F. Cass, 1977.

Porter, Andrew. *Religion versus Empire? British Protestant Missionaries and Overseas Expansion, 1700–1914.* Manchester, England: Manchester University Press.

Qatshan, 'Abdallah al-. *Al-ta'lim al-khass al-yahudi wa-al-masihi wa-al-islami, 1922–1948.* Amman: Manshurat al-karmal-samid, 1988.

Quataert, Donald. *The Ottoman Empire, 1700–1922.* New York: Cambridge University Press, 2000.

Quinn, Frederick. *Sum of All Heresies: The Image of Islam in Western Thought.* Oxford: Oxford University Press, 2008.

Raheb, Mitri. *I Am a Palestinian Christian.* Minneapolis: Fortress Press, 1995.

———. *Verwurzelt im Heiligen Land: Einführung in das palästinensische Christentum.* Frankfurt: J. Knecht, 1995.

Ramet, Pedro, ed. *Religion and Nationalism in Soviet and East European Politics.* Durham, NC: Duke University Press, 1989.

Ranger, Terence. "The Invention of Tradition in Colonial Africa." In *The Invention of Tradition,* ed. Eric Hobsbawn and Terence Ranger, 211–262. Cambridge: Cambridge University Press, 1992.

———. *Missionaries, Migrants, and the Manyika: The Invention of Ethnicity in Zimbabwe.* Johannesburg: African Studies Institute, University of the Witwatersrand, 1984.

Rankin, George. "Custom and the Muslim Law in British India." *Transactions of the Grotius Society* 25 (1939): 89–118.

Reiter, Yitzhak. *Islamic Endowments in Jerusalem under British Mandate.* London: F. Cass, 1996.

Report by His Majesty's Government in the United Kingdom of Great Britain and Northern Ireland to the Council of the League of Nations on the Administration of Palestine and Trans-Jordan 1936. London: HMSO, 1937.

Ricks, Thomas, ed. *Turbulent Times in Palestine: The Diaries of Khalil Totah, 1886–1955.* Jerusalem and Ramallah: Institute for Palestine Studies, 2009.

Robinson, Glenn. *Building a Palestinian State: The Incomplete Revolution.* Bloomington: Indiana University Press, 1997.

Robson, Laura. "American Missionaries in Lebanon and Syria, 1819–1850." Unpublished paper, 2005.

———. "Archeology and Mission: The British Presence in Nineteenth-Century Jerusalem." *Jerusalem Quarterly* 10, 1 (2010): 5–17.

———. "Palestinian Liberation Theology, Muslim-Christian Relations, and the Arab-Israeli Conflict." *Islam and Christian-Muslim Relations* 21, 1 (2010): 39–50.

Rodinson, Maxime. *Europe and the Mystique of Islam.* Trans. Roger Veinus. Seattle: University of Washington Press, 1987.

Rokach, Livia. *The Catholic Church and the Question of Palestine.* London: Saqi Books, 1987.

Roussos, Sotiris. "The Greek Orthodox Tradition: International Politics, Ethnicity, and Theological Development in the Middle East." *Bulletin of the Royal Institute for Inter-Faith Studies* 7, 2 (2005): 141–157.

———. "The Patriarchate of Jerusalem in the Greek, Palestinian, Israeli Triangle." *One in Christ* 39, 3 (2004): 15–25.

Sabella, Bernard. "The Emigration of Christian Arabs: Dimensions and Causes of the Phenomenon." In *Christian Communities in the Arab Middle East: The Challenge of the Future,* ed. Andrea Pacini, 127–154. Oxford: Clarendon Press, 1998.

———. "Palestinian and Arab Christians: The Challenges Ahead." Sami Hadawi Memorial Lecture, September 22, 2004. Text provided by Bernard Sabella.

———. "Palestinian Christian Emigration from the Holy Land." *Proche-Orient Chrètien* 41 (1991): 74–85.

———. "Socio-Economic Characteristics and the Challenges to Palestinian Christians in the Holy Land." In *Christians in the Holy Land,* ed. Michael Prior and William Taylor, 31–44. London: World of Islam Trust, 1994.

Said, Edward. *Culture and Imperialism.* New York: Knopf, 1993.

———. *Orientalism.* New York: Vintage, 1978.

Sakakini, Hala. *Jerusalem and I: A Personal Record.* Amman: Economic Press, 1990.

Sakakini, Khalil al-. *Kadha ana ya dunya.* Beirut: Al-Ittihad al-ʿamm lil-kuttab wa-al-suhufiyyin al-filastiniyyin, 1982.

Samuel, Herbert. *Memoirs.* London: Cresset Press, 1945.

———. *Report of the High Commissioner on the Administration of Palestine, 1920–1925.* London: HMSO, 1925.

Sanneh, Lamin. *Encountering the West: Christianity and the Global Cultural Process, The African Dimension.* Maryknoll, NY: Orbis Books, 1993.

———. *West African Christianity: The Religious Impact.* London: C. Hurst, 1983.

Schechtman, Joseph. *The Mufti and the Fuehrer: The Rise and Fall of Haj Amin el-Husseini.* New York: T. Yoseloff, 1965.

Scholch, Alexander. "Britain in Palestine, 1838–1882: The Roots of the Balfour Policy." *Journal of Palestine Studies* 22, 1 (1992): 39–56.

———. *Palestine in Transformation, 1856–1882: Studies in Social, Economic, and Political Development.* Washington, DC: Institute for Palestine Studies, 1993.

Schulz, Helena Lindholm, and Juliane Hammer. *The Palestinian Diaspora: Formation of Identities and Politics of Homeland.* London: Routledge, 2003.

Seikaly, May. *Haifa: The Transformation of a Palestinian Arab Society 1918–1939.* London: Tauris, 1995.

Sennott, Charles. *The Body and the Blood: The Holy Land's Christians at the Turn of a New Millennium: A Reporter's Journey.* New York: Public Affairs, 2001.

Shafir, Gershom. *Land, Labor, and the Origins of the Israeli-Palestinian Conflict.* Berkeley: University of California Press, 1996.

Sharif, Regina. "Christians for Zion, 1600–1919." *Journal of Palestine Studies* 5, 3/4 (1976): 123–141.

Sharkey, Heather. *American Evangelicals in Egypt: Missionary Encounters in an Age of Empire.* Princeton: Princeton University Press, 2008.

———. "American Presbyterian Missionaries and the Egyptian Evangelical Church: The Colonial and Postcolonial History of a Christian Community." *Chronos* 15 (2007): 31–63.

Shatzmiller, Maya, ed. *Nationalism and Minority Identities in Islamic Societies.* Montreal: McGill-Queen's University Press, 2005.

Sheehi, Stephen. *The Foundations of Modern Arab Identity.* Gainesville: University Press of Florida, 2004.

Sherman, A. J. *Mandate Days: British Lives in Palestine, 1918–1948.* London: Thames and Hudson, 1997.

Shomali, Qustandi. "Nagib Nassar l'intransigeant, 1873–1948." *Revue d'études palestiniennes* 54, 2 (1995): 80–90.

———. "Politics, Press, and Religious Identity, 1900–1948." In *The Christian Heritage in the Holy Land*, ed. Anthony O'Mahony, Göran Gunner, and Kevork Hintlian. London: Scorpion Cavendish, 1995.

Sifri, 'Isa al-. *Filastin al-'arabiyya bayn al-intidab wa al-Sahyuniyya.* Jaffa: Maktabat Filastin al-jadida, 1937.

Siyasi, Wahdat al-Tahlil al-. *Al-Fatikan wa-al-sira' al-'arabi al-sihyuni.* Gaza: Markaz Filastin lil-dirasat wa-al-buhuth, 2000.

Smaberg, Maria. *Ambivalent Friendship: Anglican Conflict Handling and Education for Peace in Jerusalem 1920–1948.* Lund, Sweden: Lund University Press, 2005.

Smith, Charles. *Palestine and the Arab-Israeli Conflict.* 6th edition. Boston: Bedford/ St. Martin's, 2007.

Spector, Stephen. *Evangelicals and Israel: The Story of American Christian Zionism.* New York: Oxford University Press, 2008.

Spyridon, S. N. "Annals of Palestine, 1821–1841, Written by Neophitos." *Journal of the Palestine Oriental Society* 18, 1–2 (1938): 123–129.

Stein, Kenneth. "The Intifada and the 1936–39 Uprising: A Comparison." *Journal of Palestine Studies* 19, 4 (1990): 64–85.

Storrs, Ronald. *Orientations.* London: Ivor, Nicholson, and Watson, 1937.

Sugar, Peter. *Nationalism and Religion in the Balkans since the 19th Century.* Seattle: University of Washington Press, 1996.

Swedenburg, Ted. *Memories of Revolt: The 1936–1939 Rebellion and the Palestinian National Past.* Fayetteville: University of Arkansas Press, 2003.

Tamari, Salim. "Al-mudhakkirat al-Jawhariyya ka-marra li-hadatha al-Quds al-'uthmaniyya." Introduction to *Al-Quds al-'uthmaniyya fi al-mudhakkirat al-Jawhariyya: Al-kitab al-awwal min mudhakkirat al-musiqi Wasid Jawhariyya, 1904–1917*, ed. 'Issam Nassar and Salim Tamari. Beirut: Mu'assasat al-dirasat al-filastiniyya, 2003.

———. *Jabal didda al-bahr: dirasat fi ishkaliyat al-hadatha al-filastiniyya.* Ramallah: Muwatin, al-mu'assasa al-filastiniyya li-dirasat al-dimuqratiyya, 2005.

———, ed. *Jerusalem 1948: The Arab Neighbourhoods and Their Fate in the War.* Jerusalem: Institute of Jerusalem Studies, 1999.

———. "Lepers, Lunatics, and Saints: The Nativist Ethnography of Tawfiq Canaan and his Jerusalem Circle." *Jerusalem Quarterly* 20 (2004): 24–43.

———. "A Miserable Year in Brooklyn: Khalil Sakakini in America, 1907–1908." *Jerusalem Quarterly* 17 (2003): 19–40.

———. "The Vagabond Café and Jerusalem's Prince of Idleness." *Jerusalem Quarterly* 19 (2003). http://www.palestinearchives.org/viewarticle.aspx?id=139.

Tamcke, Martin, and Michael Marten, eds. *Christian Witness between Continuity and New Beginnings: Modern Historical Missions in the Middle East.* Münster: Transaction, 2006.

Tannous, Izzat ['Izzat Tannus]. *The Palestinians: A Detailed Documented Eyewitness History of Palestine under British Mandate.* New York: IGT, 1988.

Tejirian, Eleanor, and Reeva Spector Simon, eds. *Altruism and Imperialism: Western Cultural and Religious Missions in the Middle East.* New York: Middle East Institute, 2002.

Thompson, Elizabeth. *Colonial Citizens: Republican Rights, Paternal Privilege, and Gender in French Syria and Lebanon.* New York: Columbia University Press, 2000.

———. "Ottoman Political Reform in the Provinces: The Damascus Advisory Council in 1844–45." *International Journal of Middle East Studies* 25, 3 (1993): 457–475.

Tibawi, A. L. *American Interests in Syria, 1800–1901: A Study of Education, Literary, and Religious Work.* Oxford: Clarendon Press, 1966.

———. *Arab Education in Mandatory Palestine: A Study of Three Decades of British Administration.* London: Luzac, 1956.

———. *British Interests in Palestine, 1800–1901: A Study of Religious and Educational Enterprise.* London: Oxford University Press, 1961.

———. *Dirasat 'arabiyya wa-islamiyya.* Damascus: Dar al-fikr, 1983.

———. *Islamic Education: Its Traditions and Modernization into the Arab National Systems.* London, Luzac, 1972.

Toubbeh, Jamil. *Day of the Long Night: A Palestinian Refugee Remembers the Nakba.* Jefferson, NC: McFarland, 1998.

Travers, Robert. *Ideology and Empire in Eighteenth Century India: The British in Bengal.* New York: Cambridge University Press, 2007.

Trentmann, Frank, ed. *Paradoxes of Civil Society: New Perspectives on Modern German and British History.* New York: Berghahn Books, 2000.

Tsimhoni, Daphne. "The Arab Christians and the Palestinian Arab National Movement during the Formative Stage." In *The Palestinians and the Middle East Conflict,* ed. Gabriel Ben-Dor, 73–98. Ramat Gan, Israel: Turtledove, 1978.

———. "The British Mandate and the Arab Christians in Palestine, 1920–1925." Ph.D. diss., School of Oriental and African Studies, University of London, 1967.

———. *Christian Communities in Jerusalem and the West Bank since 1948: An Historical, Social, and Political Study.* Westport, CT: Praeger, 1993.

———. "The Greek Orthodox Patriarchate of Jerusalem during the Formative Years of the British Mandate in Palestine." *Asian and African Studies* 12 (1978): 77–122.

———. "The Status of the Arab Christians under the British Mandate in Palestine." *Middle Eastern Studies* 20, 4 (1984): 166–192.

Walzer, Michael. "The Concept of Civil Society." In *Toward a Global Civil Society,* ed. Walzer.

———, ed. *Toward a Global Civil Society.* Providence, RI: Berghahn Books, 1995.

Wasserstein, Bernard. *Herbert Samuel: A Political Life.* Oxford: Clarendon Press, 1992.

Watenpaugh, Keith. *Being Modern in the Middle East: Revolution, Nationalism, Colonialism, and the Arab Middle Class.* Princeton: Princeton University Press, 2006.

Watt, Ian. *The Rise of the Novel: Studies in Defoe, Richardson, and Fielding.* Berkeley: University of California Press, 1957.

Weismann, Itzchak, and Fruma Zachs, eds. *Ottoman Reform and Muslim Regeneration.* London: Tauris, 2005.

Wild, Stefan. "Judentum, Christentum und Islam in der palastinensischen Poesie." *Die Welt des Islams* 23, 1/4 (1984): 259–297.

———. "Negib Azoury and His Book *Le Reveil de la Nation Arabe*." In *Intellectual Life in the Arab East*, ed. Marwan Buheiry, 93–95. Beirut: Center for Arab and Middle East Studies, 1981.

Wilken, Robert L. *The Land Called Holy: Palestine in Christian History and Thought*. New Haven, CT: Yale University Press, 1992.

Williams, C. Peter. *The Ideal of the Self-Governing Church: A Study in Victorian Missionary Strategy*. Leiden, Netherlands: Brill, 1990.

Yaffe, Nurit. "The Arab Population of Israel 2003." Jerusalem: Central Bureau of Statistics, Israel, 2003.

Yapp, M. E. "'That Great Mass of Unmixed Mahomedanism': Reflections on the Historical Links between the Middle East and Asia." *British Journal of Middle Eastern Studies* 19, 1 (1992): 3–15.

———. *The Near East since the First World War*. London: Longmans, 1991.

Yazbak, Mahmoud. *Haifa in the Late Ottoman Period, 1864–1914: A Muslim Town in Transition*. Leiden, Netherlands: Brill, 1998.

Zubaida, Sami. "Communalism and Thwarted Aspects of Iraqi Citizenship," *Middle East Report* 237 (Winter 2005): 8–11.

———. "Islam and Secularization," *Asian Journal of Social Science* 33, 3 (2005): 438–448.

INDEX

'Abd al-Hamid, 41, 175n96
'Abdu, Sultana, 29
Abdulmecid, 18, 166n6
Abu Ghosh, 'Abd al-Hamid, 41, 175n96
acre, 3, 18, 35, 73, 93, 146, 176n104, 197n140
ahl al-kitab, 5
Alexander, Michael Solomon, 129
'Ali, Muhammed, 17, 18
Allenby, Edmund, 6, 37, 47, 52, 79, 158
American University of Beirut (formerly Syrian Protestant College), 25, 31, 34, 131, 139, 173n60
Anglicanism, 86, 90, 127, 128, 130, 131, 132, 134–156. *See also* Episcopalianism; Protestant church
Anton, Farah, 29
Antonius, George, 76, 92, 94–96, 108, 190n46, 191n73, 199n50
Arab Bureau, 123
Arab Centre, 102, 123–124, 195n74
Arab Executive, 81, 109, 111, 181n53
Arab Federation, 92
Arab League, 98, 99, 125, 188
Arab National League, 124
Arab Orthodox Congresses, 81, 89, 97, 188n15, 189n16, 190n54. *See also* Arab Orthodox movement; Executive Orthodox Committee
Arab Orthodox movement, 35, 75–100, 102, 109, 113, 134. *See also* Arab Orthodox Congresses; Executive Orthodox Committee; Orthodox church
Arab Parliamentary Conference, 58

Arab Patriarch Party, 89
Arab Revolt, 37, 39, 174n82
Arab Workers Society, 103
Asquith, Herbert, 51
Assal, Riah Abu El-, 140
Atassi, Hashem al-, 122
Attala, Anton, 91, 97
'Ayn Tura College, 27
'Azar, Michel, 103, 189n21
Azhar, al-, 25, 63, 183n82
'Azur, 27, 171n32
'Azuri, Najib, 26, 27–29, 32, 33, 34, 171nn32–33. *See also* Le reveil de la nation arabe; ligue de la patrie arabe, La
'Azzam, 'Abd al-Rahman, 98, 99, 188, 192n88, 192n91

Baha'is, 23, 108
Balfour Declaration, 7, 32, 37, 51, 84, 105, 156, 167n13, 176n1, 186n120
Bandak, 'Isa, 63, 76, 81, 82, 96, 97, 100, 103, 105, 134, 172n44, 191n80, 198n28, 202n127
Baq'a, 22
Bardakash, Ya'qub, 81
Barlassina, Louis, 67, 112, 185n110, 193n31. *See also* Latin Catholic church
Bayt al-maqdis, 87
Bayt Jala, 93, 163
Bayt Lahm, 81, 87, 172n44
Bayt Sahur, 130, 163
Baz, Ibrahim, 133
Beisan, 43
Ben-Gurion, David, 116

90, 91, 92, 93, 95, 96, 100, 103, 104,
109, 110, 111, 113, 114, 116, 117, 118,
175n96, 176n99, 190n49, 191n70,
191n72, 191n80, 193n23, 194n36,
194n47, 194n53, 195n74
Fatat, al-, 39
Faysal, 34, 37, 39, 42, 71, 123
Fida'iyya, al-, 34
Filastin, 13, 23, 34, 76, 81, 87, 88, 89, 90,
91, 95, 104, 105, 106, 120, 134, 153,
173n66, 189n33, 189nn37–39, 189nn41–
42, 190n47, 190n57, 193nn6–7, 194n59,
198n31, 201n102
Finn, James, 19
firman, 19, 54
Free Church of Scotland, 32
Fundamental Law, 78, 80, 85, 92

George, Peter, 125
Ghori, Imil, 13, 92, 100, 103, 121, 122,
191n80, 195n67
Goadby, Frederic, 51
Gobat, Samuel, 129
Gottheil, Richard, 29
Graham Brown, Francis, 134, 137, 138, 146,
147, 151, 152, 154
Great Revolt (al-Thawra al-kubra), 93, 97,
99, 126, 150, 151, 201n93
Greater Syria (Bilad al-sham), 34, 37, 39,
42, 175n83. *See also* Southern Syria
movement
Greek Catholic church, 5, 16, 23, 72, 73,
117, 118, 170n17

Habib, Bishara, 27
Habibi, Jamil, 149
Hadi, Awni 'Abd al-, 104, 111
Haifa, 13, 16, 23, 24, 32, 35, 41, 43, 55, 81,
83, 93, 97, 111, 114, 120, 123, 133, 134,
137, 149, 156, 162
Hajjar, Grigorios, 16, 26, 27, 35, 169,
174n75, 174n77
Hanna, Reverend Ya'qub al-, 99
Hatt-i Humayun, 19
Hatt-i Sherif of Gülhane, 18
High Church, 135, 138, 198n35
Hijaz, 28
Hizb al-umma al-islamiyya, 64

Holy Sepulcher, 18, 20, 23, 77, 78, 186n118
Huntington, Samuel, 9, 167n17
Husayn, Sharif, 37, 123, 174n82
Husayni, al- (family), 39, 59, 63, 64, 103,
104, 105, 116, 118, 118, 119, 153, 166n9,
191n80. *See also* Husayni, Hajj Amin
al-; Husayni, Hamdi al-; Husayni,
Jamal al-; Husayni, Kamil al-; Hu-
sayni, Musa Kazim al-; Husayni, Taw-
fiq Saleh al-; majlisi
Husayni, Hajj Amin al-, 39, 46, 58, 59,
60, 61, 62, 63, 64, 75, 89, 99, 107, 116,
121, 153, 154, 182n72, 183n82, 183n90,
184nn91–95, 184n100, 189n44, 195n77
Husayni, Hamdi al-, 64, 65
Husayni, Jamal al-, 38, 103, 104, 111, 121,
194n65
Husayni, Kamil al-, 59
Husayni, Musa Kazim al-, 38, 176n106
Husayni, Tawfiq Saleh al-, 98, 192n86
Husri, Sati' al-, 77, 188n3

Ibrahim Pasha, 17, 18
India, 2, 8, 9, 14, 44, 45, 46, 48, 49, 50,
54, 55, 56, 57, 58, 61, 65, 107, 158, 160,
177n6, 177n7, 178n12, 181n47, 181n61,
182n62, 183n74, 184n93, 185n115,
190n45, 195n74
India Office, 58, 182n62
Iqbal, Muhammad, 57
Iqdam, al-, 32
Iraq, 6, 14, 50, 107, 122, 123, 160, 167n14,
177n6, 178n12, 179n26, 188n3
'Isa, 'Isa al-, 23, 26, 27, 34–35, 36, 63, 71,
76, 81, 87–88, 89, 95, 96, 100, 103,
104, 173n66, 174n70, 191n80. See also
Filastin
'Isa, Yusef al-, 23, 26, 36, 41, 63, 71, 76, 87,
92, 95, 96, 100, 175n90, 191n65, 191n80.
See also *Filastin*
Islamic Congress, 63, 64, 89, 184n100,
189n44
Istiqlal, 64, 65, 103, 107, 116, 120, 184n99

Jabiri, Sa'adallah al-, 122
Jaffa, 13, 23, 24, 27, 34, 37, 41, 42, 76, 81,
83, 87, 89, 93, 111, 114, 117, 118, 131, 133,
134

Jamal, Shibli, 69, 103, 121, 122, 127, 134, 194n65

Jam'iyyat al-shabiba al-islamiyya (Society of Muslim Youth), 42

Jam'iyyat al-shabiba al-masihiyya (Society of Christian Youth), 42

Jami'a, al-, 30

Jami'a al-'arabiyya, al-, 105, 193n10

Jawhariyya, Wasif, 22

Jerusalem, 1, 3, 5, 6, 13, 17, 18, 20–24, 26–31, 34, 35, 37–41, 44, 45, 47, 51, 52, 54–56, 59, 61, 63, 64, 66–68, 70, 76, 78, 79–83, 86, 89, 90, 93, 95, 97, 99, 104, 105, 109–112, 114, 117, 127–131, 133–139, 141, 142, 146–150, 152–155, 158, 160–163, 170n16, 181n50, 182n62, 184n93, 189n17, 189n44, 192n80, 197nn11–12, 203n4

Jerusalem and East Mission (JEM), 14, 129, 152. *See also* Anglicanism; missions; Protestant church

Jerusalem Catholics Society, 41, 176n101

Jewish Agency, 62

Jewish National Home, 7, 59, 67, 107, 152

Jews, 1–3, 5–7, 12, 14, 21, 22, 27, 32, 33, 37, 47, 51, 58, 59, 62, 63, 67–69, 71, 72, 80, 83, 92, 93, 97, 99, 101–104, 106–109, 111, 113–117, 119–122, 124–126, 129, 132, 137, 144, 149, 151–156, 158–163, 165n3, 167n13, 170n16, 170n18, 176n1, 180n41, 181n60, 182n72, 188n144, 196n3, 196n9. *See also* Zionism

Jmai'an, Ya'qub, 97

Jones, William, 49

Jung, Eugene, 27

Kaleel, Mousa, 26

Kana'an, Hafiz, 39

Kana'an, Tawfiq, 153, 201nn103–104

Karmi, Shukhri al-, 41

Karmil, al-, 13, 32, 33, 34, 86

Kassab, Iskandar, 81

Kattan, Nakhleh, 89, 113, 190n51, 193n34

Ka'war, Ilyas, 41

Kazma, Jubran Iskandar, 41, 43, 81

Keith-Roach, Edward, 55, 56, 71, 181n49, 183n82, 186n128

Keladion, 90, 91, 112, 190n54

Khalidi, Husayn, 118

Khattab, 'Umar ibn al-, 16, 35

Khayat, Francis, 117, 194n49

Khouri, Faris al-, 122

Khouri, Jiryes, 137, 156

Khouri, Michel George, 81

King-Crane Commission, 41, 193n20

Koussa, Ilyas, 120

kuttab, 25

Lambeth Palace, 14, 130, 137, 150, 197n12

Lamington (Lord), 123

Lang, Cosmo, 151, 152, 153, 154, 155, 156, 198n28, 198n41, 199n49, 199n54, 201n95, 201n101, 201nn107–110, 201n111, 201n116

Latin Catholic church, 5, 23, 40, 41, 67, 72, 77, 112, 146

League of Nations, 6, 116, 123, 151

Lebanon, 6, 8, 10, 19, 23, 32, 34, 35, 69, 107, 124, 128, 132, 138, 139, 157, 160, 172n44, 178n12, 184n102

Legislative representation, 12, 13, 48, 49, 53, 55, 90, 101–126, 160, 194n60

Le reveil de la nation arabe, 27–29. *See also* 'Azuri, Najib

Lewis, Bernard, 9, 167n17

ligue de la patrie arabe, La, 27. *See also* 'Azuri, Najib

L'independance arabe, 27

Liwa, al-, 119

London Jews Society, 129, 196n9

Lugard, Frederick, 119

Lydda, 84, 93, 176n104

MacDonald, Malcolm, 119

MacInnes, Rennie, 67, 130, 132, 134, 137, 138, 139, 140, 141, 146, 147, 197n12. *See also* Anglicanism

MacMichael, Harold, 99

madrasa, 25

majlisi, 64, 65, 103, 104, 105, 107, 116, 118, 121. *See also* Husayni, al- (family); Supreme Muslim Council

Majma' al-kanisa al-injiliyya al-usqufiyya (Council of the Episcopal Evangelical Church). *See* Palestine Native Church Council (PNCC)

Majmaʿ al-watani al-kanisi fi Filastin wa-al-Urdun, 141

Makdisi, Ussama, 10, 132, 163, 166n7, 166n8, 168nn19–21, 177n9, 187n132, 196n2

Manassa, Iskandar, 41

Mansur, Asʿad, 13, 134, 141, 142, 143–145, 151, 199nn65–66, 200n69

Mansur, George, 103, 124

Mansur, Shafiq, 149

Marmura, Ilyas, 13, 133, 134, 141, 142, 143, 144, 145, 148, 151, 152, 153, 199n59, 199n62

Maronite church, 5, 23, 27, 72, 168n21, 170n17, 184n102, 195n80

Meletios, 95

Milhis, Rashidi al-Salif, 38

millet system, 5, 6, 9, 12, 19, 44–74, 108, 128, 138, 145, 146, 147, 148, 150, 160, 165n4, 166n6, 176n1, 177n9, 178n17, 179n26, 181n60, 182n68, 200n82

Mirʾat al-sharq, 13, 86, 125

missions, 5, 14, 17, 18, 19, 21, 24, 25, 31, 32, 50, 66, 122, 123, 125, 127–132, 135, 138–141, 151–156, 160, 171n25, 187n132, 196nn2–5, 196n9, 197n12, 199n52, 199n56, 199n59, 201n115. *See also* Church Missionary Society; Jerusalem and East Mission; Anglicanism; Protestant church

muʿarida, 64, 103, 107, 192n2. *See also* Nashashibi family

mufti, 58–63, 184n100. *See also* Husayni, Kamil al-; Husayni, Hajj Amin al-

Mughals, 49

Mughannam, Matiel, 13, 111, 153

Mughannam, Mughannam Ilyas, 101, 104, 111, 114, 149

Mughrabi, Muhammed al-, 26

Municipal Corporations Ordinance, 109

Muntada al-adabi, al-, 38–42

mushaʿ, 52

Mushahwar, Bandali Ilyas, 86

Muslih, Muhammad, 39, 40, 175n93, 175n95

Muslim-Christian Associations (MCAs), 37–43, 175n84, 175n88, 175n93

mutasarrifs, 18

Nadi al-ʿarabi, al-, 38–42

Nahda College, Jerusalem, 31

Najah school, 26

Nashashibi (family), 38, 39, 64, 65, 103, 107, 118, 120, 184n100, 191n80. *See also* muʿarida; Nashashibi, ʿArif Hikmat al-; Nashashibi, ʿAzmi al-; Nashashibi, Fakhri al-; Nashashibi, Isʾaf al-; Nashashibi, Raghib al-

Nashashibi, ʿArif Hikmat al-, 38

Nashashibi, ʿAzmi al-, 143

Nashashibi, Fakhri al-, 104

Nashashibi, Isʾaf al-, 26

Nashashibi, Raghib al-, 64, 104, 111, 115, 194n65

Nasir, Butrus, 133, 134

Nassar, Najib, 26, 32–34, 36, 63, 71, 86

National Bloc, 118

National Defense Party, 111

Nazareth, 32, 33, 41, 81, 93, 131, 133, 134, 141, 142, 143, 144, 156, 163, 176n104

Nebi Musa festival, 63

New City, Jerusalem, 22, 161

Occupied Enemy Territories Administration (OETA), 37

Old City, Jerusalem, 1, 22, 23, 34, 161

Orthodox church, 3, 12, 29, 34, 66, 67, 75–100, 112, 130, 131, 134, 136, 152, 185n103, 196n9. *See also* Arab Orthodox movement; Brotherhood of the Holy Sepulcher; Patriarchate

Orthodox Renaissance Society in Jericho, 113

Orthodox Youth Club of Jerusalem, 83

Ottoman Empire, 3, 5, 18, 21, 29, 32, 34, 44, 46, 47, 50, 66, 130, 146, 167n10, 177n9, 185n102

Ottoman Grand Vizier, 91, 93

Ottomanism, 17, 32, 34, 87, 175n83

Palestine Arab Party, 98, 118, 119, 120, 121

Palestine Broadcasting Service, 143

Palestine Defense Committee in Damascus, 124

Palestine Land Development Company, 80, 82, 188n12

Palestine Native Church Council (PNCC), 127, 128, 131, 132–141, 145–152, 156, 157, 198n37. *See also* Episcopalianism; Protestant church

Palestine Orthodox Society, 66

Palestinian Arab Congresses, 42, 81, 103, 118

pan-Arabism, 34, 38, 39, 40, 64, 65, 103, 107

Parkinson, Cosmo, 107

Patriarchate (Greek Orthodox), 3, 5, 20, 21, 78–80, 82, 83, 84–86, 88–90, 92, 95, 97–99, 112, 113, 129, 166n4, 188n17, 189n17, 191n70, 192n83. *See also* Orthodox church; Brotherhood of the Holy Sepulcher

Peel Commission, 93, 121, 151, 191n71

Permanent Mandates Commission, 115, 119

Plymouth, Ivor (Lord), 121

Pro-Arab Parliamentary Committee, 123

Protestant church, 14, 134, 138–141. *See also* Anglicanism; Episcopalianism; missions; Palestine Native Church Council

qadis, 60, 64

Qatamon, 22

Quba'in, Najib, 148, 149, 151, 156. *See also* Episcopalianism; Palestine Native Church Council; Protestantism

Qusus, 'Uda, 92

Raheb, Mitri, 130, 138

ra'is al-'ulama, 60

Ramallah, 26, 93, 101, 104, 111, 131, 133, 138, 143, 199n59

Ramleh, 34, 93, 131, 176n104

Rankin, George, 49, 178n16

Rawdat al-Ma'arif school, 26

Reform party, 103, 118, 120

Religious Community Ordinance, 73, 180n41

Rendel, G. W., 66, 69

Richmond, E. T., 56, 180n39

Rihani, Amin al-, 125, 195n80

Rimawi, 'Ali al-, 26

Rok, Alfred, 103, 111, 118, 120

Rothschild, Walter, 7

Russian Compound, 22

Russian Ecclesiastical Mission, 66

Saba, Nicola, 131, 146, 148, 155, 156, 202n118

Saba, Salih, 134

Sahyuniyya, al-, 33. *See also* Nassar, Najib

Said, George, 113

Sakakini, Khalil al-, 13, 23, 26, 29–32, 33, 34, 76, 86, 94–96, 172n43, 173n46, 173n52, 173n55, 191n78, 192n81

Salah, 'Abd al-Latif, 118

Salama, Hanna, 97

Samuel, Herbert, 43, 45, 49, 51–54, 56, 57, 59–61, 150, 180n39–40, 182n62, 182n72, 183n78, 194n60

sanjaks, 18, 165n2

Sawt al-sha'b, 81, 87, 105

Schneller School (Syrian Orphanage), 22, 130, 138

Seyhulislam, 60

Shammas, Ibrahim, 81

Shanti, Muhammed al-, 32

shari'a, 19, 58, 59, 60, 62, 64, 68, 82

Shef 'Amru, 143

Shertok, Moshe, 119

Shihada, Bulus, 86, 103, 125

Shomali, Qustandi, 33

Shuckburgh, John, 61

Siddiqi, 'Abd al-Rahman al-, 58

Sidon, 18, 35

Sirat al-mustaqim, al-, 64, 184n99

Southern Syria movement, 37, 39, 40, 41, 42, 71, 174n83. *See also* Greater Syria

"status quo," 9, 20, 44, 48–51, 54, 56, 68, 70, 71, 83, 84, 88, 110, 111, 169n11, 178n12, 179n30, 185n117

St. George's Cathedral Church and College, 129, 131, 134, 138, 198n36

St. Paul's Church, 133, 138, 142

Storrs, Ronald, 38, 55, 56, 71, 181n50, 186n131

Sulh, Riad al-, 122

Supreme Muslim Council (SMC), 60–65, 103, 104, 107, 192n72, 183n78, 183n90, 184n94, 184n100. *See also* Husayni, Hajj Amin al-; majlisi

www.ingramcontent.com/pod-product-compliance
Ingram Content Group UK Ltd.
Pitfield, Milton Keynes, MK11 3LW, UK
UKHW032333060125
453254UK00004B/201